Six Tyco

The lives of

John Jacob Astor

Cornelius Vanderbilt

Andrew Carnegie

John D Rockefeller

Henry Ford

and

Joseph P Kennedy

Published by Spiramus Press Ltd,
102 Blandford Street, London, W1U 8AG.

This revised edition published March 2011

First published in hardback by Spiramus Press Ltd, September 2008

ISBN

978 1904905 84 4 Hardback

978 1904905 85 1 Paperback

9781907444 36 4 Digital

British Library Cataloguing-in-Publication Data.

A catalogue record for this book is available from the British Library.

Cover illustration: Standard Oil Building, Bowling Green, New York
c.1925

For Bill Neal

About the author

Wyn Derbyshire originally trained as a research chemist, gaining a PhD from the University of Cambridge before qualifying as a lawyer. Now a partner at City law firm SJ Berwin LLP, he has for many years been interested in the lives of the great tycoons and financial matters generally.

His other books for Spiramus Press include *Money and Work: An Essential Guide*, *Home Truths: A Guide to Buying and Selling Property* and *TUPE: Law and Practice*. He lives in St Albans, Hertfordshire with his wife and daughter.

Contents

List of illustrations

---

* Reproduced with the kind permission of The National Archives and Records Administration.

Introduction

John D Rockefeller. Cornelius Vanderbilt. Andrew Carnegie. John Jacob Astor. Henry Ford. Joseph P Kennedy. Even today, long after their deaths, their surnames continue to be synonymous with wealth and power. When they were alive, they dominated the worlds in which they lived in ways that few men had done before, and few have achieved since.

For most people, there is something inherently fascinating about extremely wealthy individuals, especially where that wealth is self-made, as was the case for all these men. And perhaps this is especially so when that wealth was made in a world that now has largely disappeared – the America of the past. The stories of these six men allow us windows into ways of life that most of us can only imagine, and times when laws, attitudes, prejudices and opportunities were very different from today. This book tells those stories.

This immediately raises the question: why select these six tycoons? Why not include J P Morgan, for instance, or Meyer Guggenheim, or Hetty Green – the Witch of Wall Street – or Frick or Gould or Flagler (all three of whom do in fact make appearances in this book, as does J P Morgan) or one or more of the many other famous tycoons of the nineteenth and twentieth centuries? There is no single or simple answer to this and certainly the lives of many other tycoons make intriguing reading.

But most people, when asked to name famous multi-millionaires of the past, would not immediately name Frick or Gould or Flagler or even Hetty Green but rather one or more of the tycoons whose stories are told here. Their names are now firmly part of America's – and the world's – financial folklore. And there is good reason for this.

Four of them at least – Astor, Vanderbilt, Rockefeller and Carnegie - could claim at some time in their lives to be considered the richest man in the United States. By some measures, Henry Ford too fell into this enviable class of individuals, and invariably when lists of the wealthiest men in American history are compiled (with due allowance being made for the effects of inflation) the names of all five appear, typically with Rockefeller, Vanderbilt and (frequently but not invariably) Astor being ranked in the first, second and third positions respectively. This was so, for instance, in a list of the richest ever Americans prepared and updated by Michael Klepper and Robert Gunther in which each person's wealth was measured by reference to the United States' GDP at the date of death, or 2006, if the person listed was then living. According to this measure, Andrew Carnegie ranked as the sixth richest ever American, behind Bill Gates, whose wealth at that time was estimated at $82 billion. Fourth place incidentally was occupied by Stephen Girard, a merchant and ship owner who had accumulated a fortune estimated at $7.5 million by the time of his death in 1831.

In one sense, Joe Kennedy is an outsider in this select group (which is perhaps only fitting, as he in many ways considered himself to be an outsider all of his life) – Joe Kennedy's fortune was estimated by *Fortune* magazine in 1957 to be in the range of $200 million to $400 million, which if accurate meant that he was "only" somewhere between the ninth and sixteenth richest American at the time. But Joe Kennedy was surely one of the most fascinating tycoons ever produced by America and for this reason alone, his name can justifiably be included on the list of those who feature in this book.

Then too, all six are famous for the ways in which they used their fortunes, for they did so in ways that had repercussions throughout America's subsequent history. Carnegie and Rockefeller, having dominated the steel and oil industries respectively, ultimately devoted much of the second halves of their lives to philanthropy and did so in ways that still benefit us today. Vanderbilt, having started his life as a sailboat owner plying his trade in New York harbour, expanded his interests into steamships (with the result that by the middle of the nineteenth century he was amongst the most powerful of America's steamship magnates, with shipping interests that stretched as far as Nicaragua and the Pacific, and across the Atlantic to Great Britain and Europe) and then switched his attention to America's burgeoning railroad industry. Over the last twenty or so years of his life, he worked to rationalise and expand the American railroad network, especially in the north east of the country, laying down important transport links which helped America to emerge into the twentieth century as the new industrial superpower.

Astor gained effective control over much of the fur trade in the early years following the United States' break from Great Britain before concentrating on real estate and becoming the dominant landlord in New York. Generations of immigrants lived (and frequently suffered) in Astor-owned slum tenements, creating in the process yet another of America's cultural legacies. Henry Ford helped to revolutionise America's industrial processes, and more than any man ensured America would become a nation of car owners, with profound effects on American society and indeed the American landscape. And Joe Kennedy, perhaps the first tycoon to recognise that one effect of the Great Depression was to transfer power from Wall Street to Washington, devoted his life and money to creating a political dynasty that would capture and then tragically lose the greatest prize of all.

Assembling the biographies of six of America's richest men into one volume allows us to compare different aspects of their lives and to ask whether there were any common factors. One trait that all these men had in common was that they all effectively built their fortunes out of nothing. That is not to say that they all suffered dire childhood poverty before becoming wealthy, although each of them, at various times in their lives, suggested as much. In fact, only Andrew Carnegie could truthfully claim to have spent his earliest years at or near the breadline, though none of the others (again, with the exception of Kennedy) could claim to have been raised in plenitude. Rockefeller and Ford were raised on small family farms, Vanderbilt's father was a boatman in New York harbour and Astor's a village butcher in Germany, and in each case their families' circumstances, whilst money was not overly abundant, nevertheless allowed each of them to attain sufficient education to enable them to make a start in their chosen professions when the time came for them to do so.

As for Joe Kennedy, his grandfather had unquestionably been a poor immigrant who had died when Joe's father "PJ" was less than a year old. But PJ, who grew up to become a successful bar owner and local politician, had sufficient money to send Joe to Harvard (Joe was the only one of the six tycoons featured in this book to attain a formal University education) and to gather all the accoutrements of late nineteenth century middle-class life. For Joe, therefore, his early years were not inexorably dominated by the necessity of making money simply in order to be able to survive (although money of course was always welcome) but rather by the search for social acceptability in face of real or perceived anti-Irish Catholic prejudice, during the course of which money could prove useful.

Ultimately however, none of the six tycoons who feature in this book received substantial parental financial aid in the creation of their fortunes.

To that extent, they may therefore all be considered to be "self-made multi-millionaires".

Another reason for the dominance of the names of these tycoons in American folklore is the fact that those names (with the exception of Carnegie) became attached to the financial dynasties which they effectively founded and which subsequently flourished for several generations (and indeed in some cases continue to flourish to this day). The Astors and Vanderbilts in particular dominated the social pages and social register of their day, and many of the palatial homes built by descendants of those families still stand as mute testament to the material excesses of America's Gilded Age. Rockefeller and Ford descendants too still benefit from the fortunes created by their famous ancestors whilst the Kennedys remain a wealthy and influential force in politics.

Carnegie alone failed to establish a dynasty. This was partly because of Carnegie's publicly voiced suspicions of the dangers posed by inherited wealth – when he died in 1919, his wife and daughter, although well provided for, inherited only a small fraction of the wealth that he had accumulated over his lifetime, much of which he had continued to hold until only a few years before his death despite nearly twenty years of charitable donations. However, one cannot help but wonder if Carnegie would have adopted exactly the same approach had he in fact had a son to act as an heir. After all, John D Rockefeller, who did have a son, John D Rockefeller Junior (as well as three surviving daughters) contrived to leave a fortune to Junior as well as donating hundreds of millions of dollars to charitable purposes.

It is also interesting to consider and compare the various ways in which each of these men were viewed by their contemporaries and in particular by the media of their day. In doing so, however, we must remember that the power of the press, and its approach to reporting the activities of the wealthy has varied over the years, as has society's perception of what are and what are not acceptable means of building a fortune. Consequently, for example, whilst many of Astor's contemporaries were certainly well aware that he was a rich man, there was relatively little public criticism of him or his fortune during his lifetime (although if there had been, one suspects that he probably would not have cared too much. We should also remember that throughout his life, Astor was always somewhat secretive about his business affairs, a trait that became more pronounced as he grew older). This lack of public criticism may well partly have been because investigative journalism as we know it today had yet to be fully developed – as indeed it was during the last decades of the nineteenth century. In addition, however, in Astor's time, being extremely rich was as likely to cause expressions of envy and admiration as it was of public criticism. To some extent, this was also true of Vanderbilt, although he did suffer his share of criticism in the press from time to time, particularly later in life at the time of the Erie Railroad wars.

In contrast, when Rockefeller first came to public prominence, he was widely demonised as the creator of the "Standard Oil monopoly", which was seen as threatening the livelihoods of independent oil refiners by the use of illegal and immoral business tactics. So bad did the publicity become that Rockefeller was castigated from church pulpits and in the newspapers and magazines of the day even after he had effectively retired from business and eventually he was forced to hire a public relations specialist in an attempt to reduce the levels of criticism. Gradually, as the years passed, and his philanthropic endeavours became better known (and as many of his louder critics literally died away – one of the advantages of a long lifespan) his public image softened, and he began to be hailed as one of the country's greatest philanthropists. In this, he was matched only by Andrew Carnegie, who had himself received some criticism for the way in which workers at his steel and iron plants were treated (especially at the time of the Homestead massacre), with contrasts being drawn between the semi-socialist pronouncements in some of Carnegie's writings and his accumulation of a great fortune, but who for the last eighteen years of his life basked in the warm glow of favourable reporting of his philanthropic generosity.

Henry Ford, who found business success relatively late in life, initially found himself hailed in the press as a "model industrialist", and as a man who spoke plainly and openly and whose dream was to ensure that the new technologies were applied for the benefit of all Americans. As such, he was generally seen as a welcome contrast to his fellow industrial magnates of the day. Over the years, however, a darker side to Ford's personality seemed to emerge (especially after his newspaper – the *Dearborn Independent* - began to publish articles that were widely seen as being anti-Semitic in tone and as his opposition to union representation at his factories hardened during the Great Depression) and he began increasingly to be depicted by the press as a crank.

Joe Kennedy began his career with the advantage of being exceptionally skilled at manipulating and in some cases even controlling the press. On at least one occasion, when a journalist prepared a story that cast him in less than a flattering light, he ensured that pressure was brought to bear which led to the story being rewritten in a manner that was much more to his liking. Having said that, there is little doubt that for much of his early life, Joe Kennedy enjoyed a particularly good relationship with the press. Even Kennedy's appointment as Chairman of the SEC – which was greeted with considerable scepticism in the press (not to mention howls of anguish from Wall Street itself) – was eventually hailed as a triumph when Kennedy stepped down from the post in 1935. For Joe Kennedy, his relationship with the press began to go sour towards the end of 1940 when, whilst US Ambassador to the Court of St James, he gave an interview (which he may well have considered to be largely off the record but which was nevertheless reported) in which he was seen as a defeatist and a Nazi appeaser. The resulting article, and others which swiftly followed, effectively killed off any hopes of a political career for himself that he may have harboured, and for the next twenty years, as he laboured to protect his fortune whilst encouraging and supporting the political career of his son Jack, he was forced as far as possible to stay out of the limelight. This he managed to do with considerable success, but even at the time of Jack's successful Presidential bid in 1960, there were still some questions being asked about Joe Kennedy.

Here, then, are six men who lived and worked in the United States at different times during the first two hundred years of the country's existence, and who under varying circumstances and in differing businesses, succeeded in amassing six of the greatest fortunes that America has produced. All did so effectively without any form of financial inheritance; some made their wealth whilst working closely with others who also made fortunes of their own, most notably Rockefeller and Carnegie, whilst others were more individualistic (in particular Astor and Kennedy). None doubted the morality of what they were doing although some tried to justify the existence of their fortunes in social or religious terms. None were predisposed to squander their hard won gains (a trait that was not invariably inherited by all of their descendants). Their legacies live on today, both in America and throughout the world. And as a consequence, their lives have entered America's financial folklore.

Wyn Derbyshire
St Albans, Hertfordshire – June 2008

John Jacob Astor

"A man who has a million dollars is as well off as if he were rich."
John Jacob Astor (1763 – 1848)

From Walldorf to New York

John Jacob Astor, destined to become the richest man in America, was born on 17th July 1763 in the village of Walldorf, near Heidelberg, Germany, not far from the Black Forest. His father, John Jakob Astor was a butcher, reputedly descended from Huguenot refugees who had fled from persecution in France in the sixteenth century. John Jakob, born in 1724, had married a local girl named Maria Magdalena Vorster in 1750 and together they produced six children, two daughters and four sons (John Jacob being the youngest) before Maria's death in 1766. John Jakob Astor remarried three years later, and his second wife produced another six children. The family home was therefore crowded and busy and John Jacob seems to have grown up without much parental attention or guidance. As a consequence he became particularly close to his elder brothers.

As Maria's children approached adulthood, they tended to leave home, the daughters to marry and the sons to seek their fortunes elsewhere. The first of the sons to leave was the eldest, George, who moved to London to join an uncle who was working in a firm making musical instruments. The second son, Henry, had been training as a butcher's apprentice with his father, and might well have stayed in Walldorf, but for the American War of Independence which broke out in 1776. Sensing an opportunity, he volunteered as a mercenary soldier to fight on behalf of the British, but on arriving in America, he soon deserted and by September 1776 had established himself as a small-scale merchant in New York, providing meat supplies to the British Army (and, according to legend, on occasions to the American forces as well). He also ran a meat stall in Fulton market. Henry was not the most scrupulous of individuals, and was not above indulging in stealing when he needed to secure supplies to fulfil his order book. Nevertheless, he was destined to thrive in the New World, and soon was writing back home trying to persuade the third son, John Melchior, to join him. Melchior decided instead to become the tenant farmer of a local aristocrat.

This left John Jacob, who by now had started work in his father's business. He continued to work as a butcher's boy until 1779, when George wrote from London, suggesting that Melchior should join him in the music business. Melchior did not wish to leave his farm and so it was decided that John Jacob should go in his place.

John Jacob spent four years in London. Such accounts of his life there that have survived suggest that he was a very serious youth, and he worked hard to try to better himself, notwithstanding the difficulties of being an immigrant of low birth with few connections and the handicap of having to learn English. (He later claimed to have learned English in six weeks, although throughout his life he always spoke it with a pronounced German accent.) However, his brother Henry continued to write from America, where the rebel colonists were now on the verge of defeating the British, stressing the advantages of living in a new country where (ostensibly at least) humble beginnings posed no obstacle, as was in fact demonstrated by Henry's own career. In the light of Henry's urgings, John Jacob decided to emigrate to America, and in November 1783, booked steerage passage to Baltimore on a ship called the North Carolina. He took with him a small selection of flutes that he hoped to sell, and £5 in ready cash.

The passage was dogged by bad weather and the North Carolina was eventually trapped in ice in Chesapeake Bay, a day's sail away from Baltimore. Whilst waiting for the ice to melt, John Jacob met another young German immigrant, who told him of opportunities in the fur trade, stressing the great profits that could be generated for relatively little capital outlay. John Jacob listened carefully but for the moment determined to continue in the music business.

When John Jacob Astor finally reached Baltimore in early 1784, he contrived to sell his selection of flutes to raise some much needed cash. He remained short of funds however, and for a few weeks took a job as a delivery boy for a local butcher, a fact which embarrassed him in later life and which he tried to suppress. He then made his way to New York and found his brother Henry, who promptly offered him a job. John Jacob, however, was not keen on becoming his brother's employee. He cherished long-term plans to open a shop specialising in musical instruments but for the time being lacked the money he needed to do so, and instead, on Henry's advice, he went to work for a bakery in the

Bowery, selling bread and cakes in the streets, which at least gave him the opportunity of learning his way around the city.

The Fur Trade

He had not, however, forgotten the siren call of the fur trade and after a few weeks at the bakery, he saw an advertisement by a fur merchant named Robert Bowne who was seeking to hire a clerk. He applied for the job and was appointed.

Astor's new duties included beating fur pelts to keep them free from moths, and learning how to separate the better skins from the poorer ones and how to distinguish a pelt's quality by touch alone. He also watched his employer as he negotiated prices, recognising the dramatic profits that could be realised by buying pelts from Indians and European trappers for pennies and shipping them back to Europe where the demand for pelts of all kinds for use in the clothing industry meant they could be sold for high prices. The idea of working as a fur trader himself continued to call to him, but he remained hesitant about abandoning his long term plans for a music shop until he met a man called William Backhouse.

William Backhouse was a powerful fur merchant. Exactly how Astor met him and how they became friends is not entirely clear; it seems however that Backhouse took a shine to young Astor. Before long, Backhouse had convinced Astor that his belief that there were opportunities in the fur trade was not misplaced and that if Astor wanted fame (and more particularly, fortune) he would be more likely to find it in the fur trade than in the music business. Astor was persuaded, and before long he in turn had persuaded Bowne to let him try his hand at negotiating directly with the Indian and European trappers for pelts.

This meant travelling up the Hudson River into the wilderness of Albany and beyond, deep into what was then Indian territory to negotiate with the Iroquois and other Indian tribes. At that time, the fur trade in North America was dominated by the British, who had retained control of Canada following their recognition of the independence of the United States. The Hudson Bay Company and the Northwest Company each maintained a string of forts and trading outposts in the region of the Great Lakes where Indians and other trappers congregated to trade pelts for manufactured goods (and frequently whiskey and other forms of alcohol, despite the fact this was forbidden by the British).

Notwithstanding the conclusion of the War of Independence, British colonial rules severely restricted the ability of fur traders to ship their pelts directly to New York, rather than via London. This was bitterly resented by the Americans who felt (understandably) that by being denied the opportunity to send their pelts directly to New York or any other American town or city, they were missing the opportunity to profit fully from the trade of furs, many of which were caught on American territory. Nevertheless, despite this restriction, the fur trade continued to provide financial opportunities for American traders and Astor soon became adept at trading for furs. By the time he returned to New York from his first trading expedition, he had acquired a cargo of fine pelts of such quality that Bowne raised his wages. Despite this, he decided that he would soon go into the fur trade business for himself.

1785 was notable in Astor's life not only because of his growing success in the fur trade. Shortly after his arrival in New York, he had met a young woman named Sarah Todd, who lived with her widowed mother with whom she ran a boarding house. Mrs Todd apparently approved of this hardworking German immigrant and the relationship between Astor and Sarah steadily blossomed until they married in September 1785, and Astor joined Sarah and her family in the boarding house. A shipment of musical instruments subsequently arrived, sent by Astor's brother George in London, and Sarah (with Astor's encouragement) converted one of the ground floor rooms of the boarding house into a shop in order to sell them. Astor had his music shop after all, and with the promised of financial security that this brought (musical instruments were in short supply in New York and the shop did well), Astor felt able to leave the employment of Bowne and to enter into the fur trade on his own behalf.

In the beginning, he made many forays into the wilderness to trade by himself, sometimes for months at a time, leaving Sarah to run the music business alone. These were long and hard journeys and sometimes dangerous, as traders, trappers and Indians fought between themselves as often as they traded in peace, but Astor was equal to the challenge. Over time, he became accepted by and built up a series of contacts with the independent traders and trappers who ranged through the wilderness. Even more importantly, he developed a friendship with one of the founders of the Northwest Company, which gave him an opportunity to see how that company organised its affairs.

Initially, he sold his pelts through established dealers; however, he realised the advantages of establishing his own network of trading posts, suppliers and traders that would allow him to trade in bulk. Before long, he was booking shipping space and sending his pelts directly to London on his own account. He also noted the growing friction between American and British trappers operating in American territory and recognised that there was an opportunity to break the British fur trade monopoly, at least in American territory, and to replace it with his own.

In 1795, President Washington sent emissaries (including the Chief Justice to the Supreme Court, John Jay) to London to negotiate a new treaty intended to address the various outstanding border disputes between Canada and the United States. The resulting treaty led to the dismantling of British forts and trading posts on American territory, free trade between Canada and the United States, and the consequential breaking of the British fur trading monopoly in the United States (although the influence of the British companies was far from eliminated). This gave Astor the opportunity to expand his fur trading activities. Although difficulties still remained, he could now concentrate his energies on importing his furs directly to New York, where there was a growing market and he could also ship them abroad as he wished. His wealth grew rapidly until, by the early 1800s, he was popularly supposed to have a fortune in the region of a quarter of a million dollars, a very substantial sum for the time. Even this however, may have been an underestimate; later in life, Astor is reputed to have told a friend that he had become a millionaire long before anyone suspected it.

The early 1800s were however, also the apogee of Napoleon's empire. The Napoleonic Wars made trade with Europe difficult and it became more difficult still after the British used their naval might to establish and enforce a blockade of continental Europe. Astor therefore began to look around for other markets and found one in China.

American ships had been trading for a number of years in Chinese waters, where there was a steady demand for American furs and other produce. Astor himself seems first to have become involved in the China trade in 1800, when he and a consortium of investors hired a merchantman called the Severn, loaded her with furs and other trade goods and dispatched her to Canton. She returned a year later with a large cargo of silks, chinaware, tea and other goods that were promptly sold at a substantial profit. Astor reinvested his share of the profits in the China trade, purchasing and ultimately building his own ships, the first of which was aptly christened the Beaver and the second the Magdalen, named after Astor's eldest daughter. These new ships could sail to China and back in less than a year – a quick passage for the time. Over the next few years, Astor grew even wealthier as a result of his investment in the China trade (as did several other American businessmen).

Astor also gained a reputation for miserliness and for never paying more than he needed to, for anything. This, coupled with a tendency to be reserved and to keep his plans to himself, meant that unflattering stories began to circulate about him. One story describes how one of Astor's ships arrived from China and how he was concerned about a shipment of wine which was on board, for he wanted it to be transferred to another ship which was shortly due to set sail for Europe. The problem was that the wine shipment was buried beneath cases of tea. Astor asked the captain to unload the wine without disturbing the tea, promising him a demijohn of the wine as a reward if the task was accomplished promptly. The captain and his crew worked for two days to accomplish the task and once they had done so, the wine was sent off to Europe on time. Astor made no mention of making good his promise to the captain however, and after a year had passed, the captain raised the subject, only to be told that "the wine is not ready yet". Some time later, the captain again raised the matter and was again given the same answer. The captain never did receive the promised demijohn.

Another story involves the captain of the Magdalen, a man called John Cowman. Cowman was ordered to insure the ship's cargo and told Astor that as a condition of the insurance, a new ship's chronometer (costing $500) would have to be installed. Astor demurred, insisting that the responsibility was that of the captain, not the owner. Eventually, Astor agreed that the chronometer should be installed but once it had been, he refused to pay. Cowman resigned, obliging Astor to appoint another (less experienced) captain, who then set sail for Canton. A few weeks later, Cowman was appointed as the captain of a ship owned by one of Astor's rivals and also set off for Canton. Although the Magdalen had a head start of several weeks, Cowman was by far the better navigator of the two captains, and both the Magdalen and Cowman's new ship returned to port in the United States with substantial cargoes of tea within a few days of each other. The result was a glut of tea, which caused the price to plummet. Astor is said to have lost over $70,000. However, he seems to have gained respect for Cowman as a result of this, for encountering

Cowman one day, he conceded he had been wrong, and promptly rehired him.[1]

As a sideline to his interests in the fur trade and shipping, Astor also began to invest in real estate, concentrating on properties on Manhattan. In this he was following the example of his brother Henry, who had begun to invest in land on Manhattan in the late 1780s.[2] As early as 1789, Henry had sold Astor some small plots of land and urged him to make further investments as he himself was doing. At the time, Astor had preferred to continue to focus on his own fur trading business; however, he appreciated Henry's argument that New York was expanding rapidly, and that there was money to be made by buying farm land on the edge of the city and waiting until the city's expansion made it worthwhile to develop it. He continued to make purchases of land whenever he had surplus funds to invest, particularly after 1800 when profits from his China ventures began to be realised. Indeed, between 1800 and 1819, he was to invest over $700,000 in Manhattan property.

In the meantime, there was plenty to keep him occupied at home. By 1802, he and Sarah had produced eight children, three of whom died in infancy. He named his eldest son after himself, but he was diagnosed in childhood as suffering from severe mental problems and eventually was forced to live a retired life under the care of personal physicians in a house built especially for him by Astor. John Jacob Astor II (as he became known) lived until 1869.

This meant that Astor's effective heir was his second son, William Backhouse, born in 1792 and who had been named after the fur trader who had encouraged Astor's decision to specialise in the fur trade. In the light of his elder brother's mental problems, William Backhouse Astor was effectively Astor's only son (another son, christened Henry, had been

---

[1] It is only fair to add that there is considerable doubt about whether this second story is true. Astor may have been reluctant to spend money without good reason (one of the reasons, after all, why he became so rich) but he was no fool and was an experienced businessman. It seems unlikely that he would have been prepared to run the risk of losing an uninsured cargo worth tens of thousands of dollars (not to mention the Magdalen herself) simply for the price of purchasing a chronometer for $500.

[2] Henry did well out of his investments. When he died, he left an estate in excess of $1 million.

born in 1797 but had died two years later and yet another died shortly after being born in 1802) and eventually William dutifully began to work in his father's business.

Of Astor's daughters, three survived to adulthood and all eventually married, the youngest to a European nobleman, Count Vincent von Rumpff, which was no mean achievement for the granddaughter of a Walldorf butcher. This marriage was probably one of the earliest examples of European nobility marrying American wealth.

The family had moved out of the Todd's boarding house in 1791 when Sarah had finally insisted that they should have a home of their own, and Astor had bought a three bedroom house, complete with a store into which Sarah moved the music business. Eventually, as Astor grew richer and richer, he and Sarah decided that it was time to dispense with the music business and it was sold in 1802. In that year too, the Astors bought a large house at 223 Broadway (formerly owned by New York Senator Rufus King) and a "country house" at Hellgate, near what is now 88th Street but then was pretty riverside farmland, from which vantage point Astor could watch schooners and other merchantmen making their way steadily towards New York harbour.

Astoria

In 1803, fate or rather international politics intervened in Astor's life in the form of the Louisiana Purchase, whereby for the sum of $15 million, the United States acquired the lands comprising the District of Louisiana from Napoleon. This transaction resulted in the United States almost doubling its territory at the stroke of a pen (at the cost of 4 cents an acre) and has justifiably been described as the greatest real estate deal in history. The natural resources of the lands west of the Mississippi were now (at least theoretically) open to exploitation by American merchants and Astor was not slow to recognise the possibilities. In 1808, two years after the epic Lewis and Clark expedition,[3] Astor established a new company – the American Fur Company – with the stated aim of ensuring that the fur harvesting opportunities within the new territories should be enjoyed by Americans rather than foreigners (principally Canadians).

---

[3] Between 1803 and 1806, Meriwether Lewis and William Clark led the first American overland expedition to the Pacific coast. The principal purpose of the expedition was to carry out an initial survey of the vast new territories acquired by the United States as a consequence of the Louisiana Purchase.

This appealed to American patriotic pride, and President Jefferson himself approved the project, and promised Government support, believing it would be open to various American trading companies. In reality, Astor was less concerned with benefiting his country than ensuring that he personally controlled as much of the fur trade in the new territories as he possibly could. This greed would lead to Astor making one of the greatest mistakes of his career.

Key to Astor's plans was the proposal to establish a string of trading posts across the continent, and most importantly, an American settlement on the Columbia River in the Pacific Northwest, to which all the furs collected in the area could be transferred before being shipped to China, where the demand for imported furs remained strong. The profits from this new trade route would then be used to purchase Chinese goods, which could be shipped back to New York for sale by Astor on the eastern seaboard. Modestly, Astor decided to name the proposed settlement Astoria.[4]

To achieve this aim he needed the cooperation of trappers who were familiar with the area. Unfortunately, the only trappers with the knowledge he needed were Canadian, the very people who Astor had declared should be expelled from the fur trade. This however posed no problems for Astor; he simply persuaded several of them to join him in setting up yet another company, the Pacific Fur Company. Astor's intention was that once Astoria was a success, he would persuade the American Government to pass legislation prohibiting foreigners from holding shares in American companies, thus leaving him in sole control of the fur trade in the Pacific Northwest, and with an immensely profitable Astoria-China-New York trading network.

Astor decided that the project would be initiated by sending two expeditions to the Pacific coast. One would go overland, setting up trading posts as they did so. The second would proceed by sea and would be responsible for establishing the Astoria settlement, which would thus be operational by the time the overland expedition arrived.

On paper, from the comfort of Astor's home in New York, the plan must have seemed simple enough. In practice, it turned into disaster.

---

[4] Once established, Astoria would be the first American settlement on the Pacific coast.

Setting off from New York in June 1810, the overland expedition had difficulties in recruiting experienced men (the expedition paused at Montreal for this purpose, where rival Canadian fur companies did their best to disrupt it) and dissension between the American and Canadian members of the expedition was rife. Progress was slower than anticipated and the expedition (or rather, its bedraggled remnants, for it had been ravaged by desertions, sickness, hunger and death) only reached the Columbia River in early 1812, and it did so without having established the network of trading posts across the West that had been the principal reason for the journey in the first place. However, when the survivors finally reached the Astoria settlement, they found that the seaborne expedition had, if anything, suffered even more than they had.

The problems had started early into the voyage. Astor had arranged that the seaborne contingent of his expeditionary force would sail on board a small ship known as the Tonquin, under the command of Lieutenant Jonathan Thorn, who at Astor's specific request had been seconded from the United States Navy. The Tonquin, with a crew of twenty in addition to the members of Astor's expedition, departed New York on 8th September 1810. Unfortunately, as events were shortly to prove, Thorn was totally unfitted to command such an expedition. He had a reputation as a strict commander (which no doubt explains his appeal to Astor); in reality he was a petty tyrant, wedded to the rule book and unable to demonstrate any element of the flexibility necessary for the commander of an expedition travelling far from home. He would brook no argument from anyone, not even fee paying passengers as illustrated by his threat to clap expedition members in irons when they protested his unilateral decision to order "lights out" at the early hour of eight in the evening. Thorn so antagonised his crew that several attempted to desert when the Tonquin arrived at the Hawaiian Islands in February 1811; before then, he had tried to abandon several of the expedition's members when the Tonquin had been forced to call in at the Falkland Islands because of a shortage of water.

The Tonquin finally reached the mouth of the Columbia River in March 1811 and, after losing one of the ship's boats (and five men) in an attempt to find a navigable channel in appalling weather, Thorn decided to anchor the Tonquin in Baker's Bay on Cape Disappointment. The expeditionary members, anxious to be rid of Thorn as soon as possible, decided to establish Astoria on land above Baker's Bay known as George's Point.

Once the expeditionary members and their equipment had been unloaded, the Tonquin sailed north to Newetee, Vancouver Island, where Thorn decided to try his hand at trading with the local Indians, despite the fact that he had little trading experience. It did not take the Indians long to sense the presence of a novice, and they were soon demanding returns in exchange for the furs they were offering on terms that Thorn considered outrageous. Thorn lost his temper, insulted them and threw them off his ship. His crew begged him to up anchor and sail away, but Thorn refused. The Indians returned the next day indicating that they were unarmed, willing to let bygones be bygones and wanted to resume trading. Incautiously, Thorn allowed them on board; incredibly he allowed them to trade their pelts for knives. Before long, all the Indians were armed and they suddenly attacked, slaughtering all the crew save for five who somehow escaped the massacre.

The Indians abandoned the ship for the night, but returned the next day, when they were greeted by one of the survivors, who motioned them aboard. It was a trap; the survivor had rigged the ship's powder magazine, and blew it when several hundred Indians were aboard. The other survivors had sought to escape in the night but were nearly all captured and killed; only the ship's Indian interpreter escaped to make his way back to the Astoria settlement where he reported the loss of the Tonquin.

In the meantime, the expeditionary members who had landed at Baker's Bay had been working hard to establish Astoria. In addition to building log cabins, storehouses and a defensive perimeter, friendly trading relations had been established with the local Indians, and an impressive number of pelts were beginning to accumulate. The arrival of the overland expedition strengthened the settlement and the subsequent arrival of Astor's ship, the Beaver, which he had dispatched to collect the first shipment of furs from Astoria and transport them to China appeared to confirm that the new settlement would be successful after all.

However, the arrival of the Beaver was overshadowed by the outbreak of the War of 1812 between Great Britain and the United States. The Canadians had been keeping a wary eye on Astor's activities in the Pacific Northwest and now seized the opportunity to persuade the Royal Navy to dispatch a warship to take control of Astoria. On hearing the news from emissaries of the Canadian North West Company of the imminent arrival of the warship, the Astorian settlers were persuaded to transfer control of Astoria to the Canadians (who promptly renamed it Fort

George), and sold their accumulated furs and other trade goods to the North West Company at heavily discounted prices. Astor lost several hundred thousand dollars over the failure of Astoria.

Astor was furious when he heard the news of the failure, but before long he was his old self again, shrewdly calculating how best to squeeze the maximum advantage for himself out of the situation in which his adopted country now found itself. America's fur and tea trades suffered as a result of the War of 1812, partly as a result of the British sea blockade and partly as a result of the United States' own Embargo Acts designed to prevent American merchantmen from falling into the hands of European combatants (and in particular, the British). As a consequence, most American merchants were forced to abandon their trading activities with Europe and Britain. Not so Astor, who still continued to purchase furs and sought about for ways to transport them to Europe, where they could be expected to be sold for immense profits.

Astor's solution to this problem involved utilising the services of a French General, General Moreau, who had been sent into exile by Napoleon in 1804. Now living in New Jersey, Moreau allowed himself to be persuaded to offer his services to Britain's ally Russia. Astor offered to carry Moreau across the Atlantic in one of his ships, the Hannibal and the British in turn were persuaded to allow the Hannibal to sail without interference from the Royal Navy. Needless to say, when the Hannibal did sail in the summer of 1813 she also carried a full shipment of furs, which were subsequently sold in London at prices which satisfied even Astor. "I have done very well on the voyage" he commented to a friend, ignoring the fact that he was in fact trading with the enemy. Moreau was less fortunate, for having joined the Tsar's forces, he was mortally wounded in action and died in September 1813.

Astor also made money during the war by subscribing to Government loans, purchasing two million dollars' worth of American war bonds. However, he also offered to lend money to the British forces in Canada and it has been suggested that he provided the Canadians with intelligence as to possible American surprise attacks across the border, actions which (if true) are difficult to characterise as anything other than treasonous.

Be that as it may, by 1815, when the Napoleonic Wars in Europe finally came to an end and the British and Americans formally made peace, Astor was widely regarded as one of the richest and most influential of the American merchant princes, whose trading ships traversed the globe in search of profit. Nevertheless, Astor was still not satisfied and sought to extend his power and influence further. Now that the wars were over, he turned his attention once more to Astoria and the possibility of establishing a fur monopoly in the Pacific Northwest by resurrecting the American Fur Company. As part of his campaign to achieve this goal, Astor actively lobbied the American Government to restrict Canadian traders from carrying out their activities on American territories. With feelings still running high following the end of the hostilities between the British and the Americans,[5] Astor had little difficulty in persuading President Madison that a bill restricting the ability of foreigners to trade with Indians on American soil (save with the express permission of the President) was a necessity. With Madison's support, a bill to this effect was passed by Congress in 1816.

Astor duly wrote to James Monroe, President Madison's Secretary of State and himself destined to become President in 1817, pronouncing himself satisfied with the new legislation. However he now had a problem, for if his plans to establish a fur trading monopoly in the Pacific Northwest were to bear fruit, the American Fur Company would need the skills of those Canadian trappers who, thanks in a large part to Astor's efforts, had been barred from American territory. Astor therefore petitioned the President (now Monroe) to grant licenses to the American Fur Company, enabling it to employ Canadian trappers notwithstanding the general prohibition. Monroe, who was himself in debt to Astor, prudently decided to delegate the decision to Lewis Cass, the Governor of the Michigan Territory. Cass (also in debt to Astor, although this was not made public for many years) duly granted the licenses and the American Fur Company began operations, moving into the territories which had been abandoned by the Canadian fur trading companies.

Astor still did not have his monopoly for there were a number of independent traders who still operated in the Great Lakes region (most of whom Astor eventually bought out or drove out of business). However, his greatest competitor was the United States Government itself, which had established a string of trading posts – or factories – throughout the

---

[5] Which had not, from the American perspective, been the series of unbroken military successes that they had been expecting, as exemplified by the burning of Washington City by the British in 1814.

territory in an attempt to promote a regime of fair trading with the local Indians by offering fair prices and eschewing the use of alcohol as a trading tactic. Astor was determined to eradicate the Government's trading posts and mounted a vicious and ultimately successful political and commercial campaign against them, leading to their abolition in 1822. Thereafter, the American Fur Company had an effective monopoly in the Great Lakes region and it expanded rapidly, and Astor's profits soared. In the process however, it gained an appalling reputation as a result of the way it treated the Indians it dealt with, in particular because the company's traders did not hesitate to provide Indians with copious quantities of cheap gut-wrenching whiskey and other spirits to induce them to trade their pelts on terms that were ruinously cheap. Indeed, selling whiskey to Indians became a most profitable sideline in its own right and the effect on the Indian communities was disastrous.[6] The company also treated its own employees harshly, forcing them to pay high prices for the goods which would they would then trade with the Indians for pelts, which in turn of course encouraged the traders to exploit the Indians even more rapaciously simply in order to survive.

Within a few years, even United States Government officials were becoming concerned about the effects that the use of alcohol was having upon relations with the Indian communities and a law was passed in 1832 prohibiting the importation of alcohol into the Indian territories. Unfortunately, it was a poorly drafted law, with many loopholes, and was widely ignored, to the continuing detriment of the Indians. Nevertheless, it was around this time that Astor decided to pull out of the fur trade (he had decided to abandon his overseas trading ventures a few years earlier).

There were probably several reasons for Astor's decision to abandon the fur trade after so many years. To begin with, by this time he was in his seventieth year and his health was beginning to fail, requiring him to travel to Europe on several occasions in order to consult doctors there. Furthermore, public disdain for the activities of America's fur companies was mounting and whilst Astor's latest fur trading activities had multiplied his fortune several times over, he may have felt that the days of

---

[6] The American Fur Company was not alone in using alcohol in their dealings with the Indians; the Hudson Bay Company had done so for years, and the practice was widespread amongst the small independent traders. However, it is doubtful whether any other trading company used alcohol as widely or as irresponsibly as did Astor's American Fur Company.

easy profits from furs were drawing to an end. Thirdly however, he had grown ever more interested in the possibilities offered by real estate, particularly in the light of the changes being brought about by the impact of the Industrial Revolution on the north eastern United States and now felt that the time had come to investigate such matters more closely. He also suffered several personal misfortunes during the early 1830s, including the death of his wife, his brother Henry, a half-sister, Elizabeth and his eldest daughter Magdalen and he may have felt a need to seek new challenges simply to distract him from the miseries of his everyday life. In any event, by 1834, he had sold out his interests in the American Fur Company and turned his full attention to the investments that would make him and his descendants famous for several generations – land.

Manhattan Landlord

There was of course nothing new about Astor's interest in land. As previously noted, he invested over $700,000 in Manhattan real estate between 1800 and 1819, generally purchasing land on the outskirts of Manhattan, the value of which would soar as the city expanded. In particular, in 1803 he bought a farm which lay between Broadway and the Hudson River, an area which in due course was to become 42nd Street and in 1809, he acquired another farm, which was destined to be buried beneath the buildings flanking 55th Street. Initially, Astor "bought by the acre and sold by the lot"; however, over the years he adopted the practice of retaining the freehold title to the land he bought and instead sold twenty-one year leaseholds to property speculators who would then erect the buildings they wished to build as quickly and cheaply as possible. Typically, these buildings were residential tenements and once the twenty-one year leases expired, the leaseholders were either obliged to negotiate new leases with Astor or to surrender the properties to him. Cash rich, Astor was also in a position to offer mortgages to speculators who lacked the necessary capital to finance the building of properties on Astor's land and any failure on the part of such speculators to meet mortgage payments as they fell due would inevitably result in Astor foreclosing on the property. Over the years, Astor's income from real estate increased dramatically and by the date of his death, it was estimated that his yearly rental income alone was close to a quarter of a million dollars. Much of this income arose from overcrowded, poorly planned, poorly built, poorly maintained and disease-ridden tenement blocks which soon degenerated into slum areas occupied mainly by poor immigrants who had been attracted to America's "promised land" but never escaped from New

York. The problem grew even worse under Astor's son, William, as New York's population exploded in the years following 1848, partly as a result of Irish refugees escaping the Potato Famine and then the arrival of masses of immigrants from Central Europe. Too many of these unfortunates had nowhere to go but into one of the Astors' tenement blocks. The existence of these slums disgraced the city and attracted increasingly vocal public condemnation of both the slums and the Astors, which culminated in a number of devastating public investigations and (eventually) the passage in 1867 of the first in a series of laws enacted by the New York legislature aimed at regulating the building and operation of tenement blocks. Despite these steps, the problems posed by the slums built on Astor-owned land persisted well into the twentieth century.

Be that as it may (and neither Astor nor William ever accepted that they bore any responsibility for the slums), Astor was proud of his real estate dealings. When asked in later years to describe his favourite property deal, Astor would usually refer to his acquisition of the Morris estate.

The Morris estate, comprising some 51,000 acres in Putnam County, New York, had originally belonged to a British Army officer, Major Roger Morris and his wife Mary. Upon the outbreak of the War of Independence in 1776, Roger and Mary Morris had fled to England, and the American authorities had confiscated their land and sold it in lots to various local farmers. So matters rested for a number of years, until 1809 when a lawyer working for Astor learnt that the Morrises had only held a life interest in the estate and that on their deaths, the property should have passed to their heirs. This called into question whether the confiscation of the land from the Morrises had in fact been legal since they had been dispossessed of more than they had actually owned to the detriment of their heirs, whose names had not been included on the confiscation order.

Naturally, it was extremely doubtful whether the Morris heirs were willing or indeed financially able to pursue any legal claim for the return of the property, not least because the land was now in the possession of several hundred farmers who had bought it from the state government in good faith. Moreover, there would have been political repercussions had the government been willing to simply order the return of the land to "foreigners" and British foreigners at that. Consequently, when Astor approached the heirs and offered to buy their "interest" in the land for $100,000, they were more than willing to agree to the sale.

Having acquired the reversionary title to the land (which was still subject to the life interest of Mrs Morris, who was still alive), Astor then approached the New York state government, offering to sell his interest for $300,000. The state government however was in no hurry to commit itself, reasoning that until Mrs Morris died[7], there was no particular urgency to the matter. When she did finally die (in 1825, at the age of ninety six), Astor promptly issued eviction notices to the farmers working the land and sought to enforce them through the courts. No lesser personages than Daniel Webster, a senator and future Secretary of State and future President Martin van Buren appeared for the defendants; nevertheless, Astor's claim to the land was upheld and the state government was forced to offer Astor a deal whereby he relinquished his rights in exchange for $520,000 of New York stock yielding an indefinite return of 5 per cent.

Astor's pursuit of the Morris estate did not prevent him from thinking about other possible real estate ventures and he became fixated on the idea of building a new hotel in New York. Inevitably, Astor was not satisfied with the idea of simply building a fine hotel; his hotel was to be the finest and most luxurious hotel in the United States. Such a hotel, he believed, would be profitable and at the same time confer some form of lustre upon his family name. He determined to build it on the site of the Broadway block where he himself had been living, which entailed obtaining possession of neighbouring buildings. This took some time to achieve since not all of his neighbours wished to move, but eventually the task was accomplished. The old buildings were then demolished and construction of the new hotel (to be called "Astor House", although for a while it was known as the "Park Hotel") began in July 1834. By 1836, it

---

[7] Mary Morris had an interesting life. Born Mary Philipse on 3rd July 1730, she was the daughter of Frederick Philipse, the speaker of the New York Colonial Assembly and one of the richest landowners in New York before the American Revolution. She is said to have numbered George Washington amongst her suitors although it is unlikely that Washington ever proposed to her. Following the Declaration of Independence and the confiscation of the Morris' property, Washington used their mansion in New York as his army headquarters in the autumn of 1776. Mary Morris was one of the very few women to be personally attainted for treason by the American Government during the Revolution.

was finished and regarded as "the marvel of the age". Six stories high, it possessed 300 rooms and no less than seventeen bathrooms (considered a major innovation at the time), with dark walnut furnishings throughout and a shopping arcade. The hotel soon acquired a reputation for serving fine food and wines and the great and the good flocked to visit. During the hotel's eighty years of existence, celebrities who stayed there included Davy Crockett, the opera singer Jenny Lind, William Makepeace Thackeray, Edgar Allen Poe, Abraham Lincoln, Jefferson Davis, the Prince of Wales and Charles Dickens.

1836 also saw the publication of a highly romanticised account of the attempt to found Astoria by no less a literary figure than Washington Irving. Irving, the author of the *Legend of Sleepy Hollow* and *Rip van Winkle*, was specifically recruited to the task by Astor who arranged for Irving to be housed in considerable comfort at one of his country estates while researching and then writing the book. By all accounts, Irving did not take the job too seriously and was therefore genuinely surprised when it promptly became a bestseller. The book (entitled *"Astoria: Or Anecdotes of an Enterprise Beyond the Rocky Mountains"*) painted a picture of Astor as a patriotic hero and carefully avoided imputing any blame to Astor for the debacle that actually occurred. Astor was pleased.

In the meantime, Astor had been forced to look for alternative accommodation for himself while Astor House was being constructed. He bought himself a brownstone mansion further along Broadway and invited his grandson, Charles Bristed to move in with him. Charles was the son of Astor's daughter Magdalen, who had married twice before she died, first to Adrian Bentzon, Governor of Santa Cruz in the West Indies, then Danish territory. When that marriage failed, Astor used his influence to secure a divorce for Magdalen and she subsequently married an Englishman John Bristed, a part-time journalist and lawyer. That second marriage also failed – by all accounts, Magdalen was spoiled and arrogant and one of her own cousins described her as a "lamb of Beelzebub" – but not before she had borne Charles. Charles was one of Astor's favourites and lived in great luxury with his grandfather.

As for Astor's other surviving children, John Jacob II had by now long been institutionalised. This left Dorothea, Eliza and William. Eliza of course had married Count Vincent von Rumpff, a Swiss diplomat, in 1825 and settled in Europe. Astor saw her fairly frequently in the course of his various trips across the Atlantic and there is no doubt that he particularly enjoyed the prestige of having a European nobleman as a son-in-law. Sadly, Eliza died in 1838.

Dorothea, on the other hand, caused her father considerable trouble and grief. Born in 1795 and having grown up to be rather fat, she was sometimes cruelly nicknamed "Plump Dolly". Astor had strong views as to who his children should marry (at one point, Eliza had apparently engaged the interest of a dentist called Eleazar Parmly[8] and it was partly in order to thwart that prospective romance that Astor took Eliza to Europe on the prolonged trip which led to her meeting and subsequent engagement to von Rumpff). Dorothea had her own views on such matters. In 1812, she met and eloped with a man five years older than herself, Colonel Walter Langdon, a man described by Albert Gallatin (Secretary of the Treasury under Presidents Jefferson and Madison and a close personal friend of Astor) as having "every recommendation except wealth". Astor was furious and disinherited Dorothea, who nevertheless settled into married life with Langdon.

The rift continued for a few years, but eventually, the Astors and Langdons were reconciled. A story as to how this occurred has entered Astor legend; apparently Astor was invited to attend a children's party and whilst there, he saw a pretty little girl who was looking at him. Astor asked her name and calmly she replied "Sarah Sherburne Langdon" whereupon Astor laughed and declared "For your sake, I shall have to forgive your father and mother." Dorothea was reinstated into Astor's affections and when Astor died, he left the Langdons valuable legacies. Dorothea lived a happy life, and produced eight children.

In the meantime, Astor's son William, born in 1792 and educated at a private school in Stamford, Connecticut and then at the Universities of Heidelberg and Gottingen, had started work in his father's business in 1816. It would seem that William accepted this development with a fatalistic resignation – left to his own devices, he would have preferred to live a scholarly life – but Astor's wishes in this regard were too overwhelming to ignore and in any event, it was certainly true that the family fortune had now developed to such a size that Astor was sorely in need of a dutiful junior partner whom he could trust. In any event,

---

[8] Parmly was not just any dentist, but widely regarded as one of the finest dental practitioners in America in his day. When he died, he left his descendants an estate valued at approximately $3 million.

William settled down to a life of office files and balance sheets and obeying his father's wishes and by all accounts could be very boring indeed when discussing business.

In 1818, he married Margaret Rebecca Armstrong, the daughter of General John Armstrong who had fought in the Revolutionary War and had subsequently served as Secretary of War in President Madison's administration. William and Margaret had six children who survived to adulthood, who in due course would carry the Astor legacy (and even more importantly, the Astor fortune) into the third and subsequent generations.

The year after Astor House was completed brought a sharp financial downturn in the form of the Panic of 1837. For many, the Panic brought disaster, as hundreds of businesses failed, property prices collapsed and paper money became virtually worthless. Astor's vast wealth protected him from the effects of the crash and allowed him to take advantage of the misfortunes of others, as he foreclosed on borrowers who could no longer meet their mortgage payments and bought land from sellers who were obliged to sell at the bottom of the market. His landholdings expanded enormously during the years of economic depression that followed the Panic of 1837, and he became generally recognised as the richest American and the greatest landowner in New York.

His reputation for meanness continued however. He had little or no interest in charitable works (although he could be financially generous to family members). A friend called Joseph Cogswell (who at one time acted as a kind of paid companion to Astor) tried to interest Astor in funding a public library in New York. Astor initially demonstrated some interest, but once some preliminary plans were drawn up and it became clear that the initial outlay would be in the region of $65,000, Astor locked the plans in a trunk and never looked at them again. (The plans were not wasted however. After Astor's death, it was found that he left $400,000 to commence work on a library, which in the fullness of time became part of the New York Public Library.)

Another story involves the great naturalist, John James Audobon. Audobon's masterpiece was his *Birds of America*, a work containing hundreds of exquisitely produced coloured prints of America's birdlife and which was published between 1827 and 1838. Astor promised to pay a subscription fee of $1,000, but whenever Audobon asked him for the money, Astor would plead poverty and advance one excuse after another for not paying. Eventually, on his sixth attempt, Audobon met Astor when his son William was also present. Again, Audobon asked for the money and again Astor pleaded poverty; however, this time Astor looked to William for support and asked him "Have we any money in the bank?" William presumably thought the question was serious, for he replied "Yes father. We have $220,000 in the Bank of New York, $70,000 in the City Bank, $90,000 in the Merchants' Bank…" Astor eventually managed to shut down William's flow, and Audobon was given his long awaited cheque.

Astor lived on for eleven years after the Panic of 1837. Living in considerable luxury at one or another of his homes, he nevertheless grew physically weaker as the years passed, suffering from palsy and a disordered digestion. Towards the end of his life he was wheeled around his mansions in a bath-chair. On doctor's orders, he was thrown about on a blanket in order to improve his circulation. Nevertheless, his grasp on his business affairs never diminished, and even in the last months of his life he was willing to order the expulsion of tenants who failed to pay their rents on time.

He died on 29th March 1848. Within hours, the news had been passed all over the United States and full page obituaries appeared in all of the major newspapers, all hailing him as the richest man in America, and one of the richest in the world. Some obituaries deplored his miserliness, but most were complimentary. America had already reached the stage where a man's wealth was regarded as a fairly accurate indicator of his moral worth.

Astor left an estate valued at $20 million. Under his will, he bequeathed $500,000 for charitable purposes (including the $400,000 he left for the Astor Library); the vast majority of his wealth he left to his family, and the greatest beneficiary of all was William, who overnight inherited his father's mantle as the "richest man in America". In the years to come, William and some of his descendants would make the fortune grow even further; others would devote their lives to the cult of conspicuous consumption long before that term was coined, spending their shares of the Astor fortune on palatial homes and other luxuries and convincing themselves and others that they were leaders of society.

In due course, the family would split into two strands, one remaining in the United States and the other transplanting itself to England, where in the fullness of time its members would become accepted as blue-blooded members of the British aristocracy, acquiring in the process a Viscountcy and a Barony, not to mention Hever Castle and Cliveden (and in Nancy Astor, the first woman MP to sit in the House of Commons). The Astor fortune would eventually diminish and be overtaken by even greater fortunes created by other tycoons and other families. Nevertheless, even today, the name of Astor is recognised on both sides of the Atlantic and whilst the fortune may have diminished, its influence can still, on occasion, be felt.

Cornelius Vanderbilt

"I have been insane on the subject of moneymaking all my life."
Cornelius Vanderbilt (1794 - 1877)

New York Harbour

Cornelius Vanderbilt – popularly known as "The Commodore" although he never served a day in any navy – was born on 27th May 1794 on a small farm near Port Richmond on Staten Island. By the time he died, on 4th January 1877, at the age of 82, he had amassed a fortune of more than $100 million, and generations of his descendants would come to epitomize the luxurious wealth of America's Gilded Age.

The fourth of nine children, Cornelius Vanderbilt was descended on his father's side from Dutch immigrants who had been amongst the earliest of the European settlers in North America, arriving in the middle of the seventeenth century, when New York was still Dutch and known as New Amsterdam. The Commodore's father, also named Cornelius, was a farmer, fisherman and boatman working in and around New York harbour. A harsh childhood resulting from the death of his parents at an early age had left Cornelius Senior semi-literate at best, unambitious, careless with money, and as often as not teetering on the edge of financial embarrassment. It was the Commodore's mother, born Phebe Hand, herself descended from a cultured New Jersey family of English ancestry, who was largely responsible for keeping the family together, often in difficult circumstances.

When Vanderbilt was one year old, his family moved from the farmhouse at Port Richmond to a somewhat larger house at Stapleton on the north-east side of Staten Island and close to the waterfront of New York Bay. Here, the Commodore grew into a big and vigorous boy, obviously clever, but with very little interest in attending school and obtaining anything approaching a formal education. He in fact attended school for more than six years, considerably longer than many of his contemporaries, but never developed more than a shaky grasp of English spelling and grammar, nor any aspect of arithmetic beyond addition and subtraction. He would however become famed for his ability for expressive profanity; years later, in old age a clergyman paid him a visit, and found him unaccountably depressed. When asked why, the

Commodore replied "Oh God-damn it, I've been aswearing again and I'm sorry".

He was also famed in later life for his self-reliance, and tendency to take matters into his own hands, rather than relying on the slow and often expensive machinery of the legal courts. The story is often told that later in his life, he was urged by a colleague to bring legal proceedings against a business opponent. "Law!" Vanderbilt is said to have exclaimed. "What do I care about law? Haven't I got the power?" Alas, the tale is almost certainly untrue.

In any event, when not haphazardly attending school, or working on the family farm, young Cornelius Vanderbilt prowled the waterfronts near his home, watching the sailing ships navigating their way through the narrow approaches to New York harbour and Manhattan Island, and learning the ways of a harbour boatman. By the age of eleven, whenever permitted, he worked with his father on his father's boat, a periauger, which was a substantial two masted barge of Dutch design, capable of transporting goods and passengers in shallow waters such as those of the New York waterfront.

By May 1810, he knew he wanted a boat of his own. He found a periauger for sale, and asked his mother to lend him $100 so he could buy it. His mother, no soft touch when it came to negotiating, even with her own son, drove a hard bargain, telling him that before she would lend the money, he would have to plough, harrow and plant a previously uncultivated eight acre plot of land before his sixteenth birthday, which was in a few weeks' time. When Vanderbilt told the story in later life, he used to say that his mother had thought he would fail to complete the job in the time available, but he enlisted the help of some of the neighbourhood boys and completed the task on time and to his mother's satisfaction. She lent him the $100, and he bought the boat.

In the years to come, he would recall his feelings when he first took charge of his boat and sailed her though the waters of New York harbour.

"I didn't feel as much real satisfaction", he said "when I made two million dollars in that Harlem corner as I did on that bright May morning sixty years before when I stepped into my own periauger, hoisted my own sail, and put my hand to my own tiller." Before long, Vanderbilt was busy ferrying cargo passengers to and fro across New York harbour, vigorously competing with the other ferryboats for business. It was at this time that he was first nicknamed the Commodore in jest by the other boatmen, but demand for his services grew as he developed a reputation for fairness and capability and by the end of his first year, he had paid back to his mother the $100 loan, and another $1,000 as well.

The Commodore's business really expanded during the War of 1812. The British blockaded New York harbour and the US army needed someone completely reliable to supply provisions to the fortifications protecting the city, and to carry the workmen and supplies needed to construct new defences. The contract was awarded to Vanderbilt, even though he had not, in fact, submitted the lowest bid. Vanderbilt delivered the cargoes required under the contract largely at night, continuing his regular business by day.

Vanderbilt soon found that the business of a boatman was not solely a matter of contract, but rather required him to seize opportunities to work as they presented themselves, and to make the most of those opportunities often in the face of considerable opposition. The story is told that one day he was carrying a detachment of soldiers across the bay when a rival boat carrying an army officer came alongside and the officer ordered the soldiers to transfer boats. Vanderbilt, realising this was nothing less than attempt to hijack his cargo on the open water, knocked the officer to the deck and hastily sailed away.

As this story demonstrates, Vanderbilt was no physical weakling. He was over six feet tall, tall indeed by the standards of the time, physically strong and broad shouldered, with an erect carriage he maintained all his life.

Vanderbilt worked hard and lived frugally, saving the profits from his business to build his capital, which he in turn invested in other boats. By the end of 1813, he was sufficiently established to marry his eighteen year old neighbour and cousin Sophia Johnson. Marriage did not blunt his business ambitions however; the day after his marriage he was again down at the docks seeking cargoes to carry. By 1818, he was worth $9,000 by his own estimation, and had invested in several sailing ships. Moreover, he had begun to interest himself in ship design and over the years proposed modifications and design changes which attracted the attention of other boat builders.

Gibbons v Ogden

It was around this time that steamboats began to appear in serious numbers in New York harbour, following Robert Fulton's introduction of the North River Steamboat (later called the Claremont), the first commercially viable steamboat, on the New York to Albany run. The Claremont attracted popular attention by being able to complete the run from New York to Albany against the current, faster than any sailing ship, and much faster than was possible on land. At first, Vanderbilt, like most boatmen of the time, had his doubts about the use of steampower, but before long he had noted the commercial advantages steamboats enjoyed by being independent of wind and tide. Vanderbilt soon concluded that the future belonged to the steamboats, sold his schooners, placed his periaugers in the charge of his father and set out to teach himself all he could about this modern mode of transport.

He did this by going to work as a captain for Thomas Gibbons, a wealthy 60 year old attorney and planter who had established a small steamboat ferry service as little more than a hobby, originally running a steamboat from Elizabethtown Point up the Raritan River to New Brunswick, New Jersey and back again. Gibbons and Vanderbilt negotiated a deal under which Gibbons agreed to pay Vanderbilt $60 a month plus half the profits from the ship's bar. In addition, Gibbons also allowed Vanderbilt and his family to stay rent free in a small but rundown wayside inn located by the New Brunswick landing stage (the Bellona Hall), on the understanding that Sophia would manage the inn and share any profits with Gibbons. Before long, Sophia had turned the Bellona Hall's business around, so that it became famous for its food and service and ultimately profitable, and this despite Sophia bearing Vanderbilt thirteen children between 1815 and 1839.

Once Vanderbilt had learned all he needed to know about operating a steamboat, he and Gibbons decided to expand the scope of Gibbons' steamboat operations by establishing a ferry service from New York to New Jersey. This was, on the face of it, illegal, for the New York state legislature had granted a monopoly of steamboat navigation in New York waters to Robert Fulton and one of his financial backers, Robert R Livingston. Moreover, in doing so, the New York legislature had defined New York waters as running to the high tide mark on the New Jersey shore, and any steamboats operating in defiance of this monopoly were liable to seizure and confiscation. Needless to say, this action by the New

York legislature proved highly unpopular with just about everybody (except, of course Robert Fulton and Robert Livingston), regardless of whether they lived in New Jersey or New York. The New Jersey legislature retaliated by declaring that any persons who tried to enforce the monopoly would themselves be jailed if they fell into the hands of the New Jersey legal authorities.

Gibbons and Vanderbilt determined to break the monopoly. Gibbons financed the building of a new and large steamboat, designed and commanded by Vanderbilt and christened the Bellona. Before long, Vanderbilt was openly operating the Bellona in New York waters without any authorisation, and moreover had cut his passenger rates to undercut those of his competitors. In compensation, he raised the prices of the food and drinks served at the Bellona's bar.

From the outset, Vanderbilt played cat and mouse with the New York state authorities who tried to enforce the monopoly. Every day, New York constables tried to arrest him. Every day, by one means or another, he escaped their attentions, much to the delight of his passengers who openly enjoyed the contest. The New York authorities never knew when the Bellona would arrive in New York harbour, or at which pier, or how long she would remain tied up. Eventually, despairing of capturing Vanderbilt on dry land, they attempted to seize the Bellona in open waters. Their attempt failed, for when the authorities boarded, they found a woman passenger at the helm but no sign of Vanderbilt, who was hiding in a secret compartment, and the authorities had to suffer the derision of the Bellona's passengers as they departed empty-handed.

After failing to catch Vanderbilt by land or by sea, the monopoly then tried to bribe him, offering him $5,000 a year to join their side. Again, to no avail, for Vanderbilt declined their offer, adding that he would stay with Gibbons "till he is through his troubles". This demonstrates an admirable facet of the Commodore's personality, for although capable of extremely tough, and on occasions vengeful behaviour, particularly when he believed himself betrayed by an erstwhile business ally, Vanderbilt was a man of his word and was in the eyes of many of his contemporaries, a man of honour.

The contest between Vanderbilt and the New York authorities might well have continued indefinitely. However, in 1819, another New Jersey steamboat owner named Aaron Ogden (a Revolutionary War veteran, a former Governor of New Jersey and at one time a business partner of

Thomas Gibbons) who had purchased a licence from the monopoly to run a ferry service in New York waters, brought legal proceedings against Gibbons, seeking an injunction to close down his operations on the New York to New Jersey run. Gibbons fought the case through the courts for five years, at first in the New York state courts (where he lost) before finally reaching the United States Supreme Court in February 1824. Gibbons hired Daniel Webster and Willard Wirt to plead his case (interestingly, Wirt was at the time the Attorney General of the United States, a fact which appears to have concerned nobody at all) and Webster's closing argument challenging the constitutionality of the monopoly before the Supreme Court took an entire day to deliver. It is still regarded as one of the most impressive legal arguments ever delivered to a court.

The Supreme Court's decision, when ultimately given by way of written ruling, was unanimous in declaring the monopoly to be unconstitutional. Chief Justice John Marshall declared that the federal government alone had the power to regulate interstate commerce and today, the Supreme Court's decision in the case of Gibbons v Ogden is recognized as one of the most important decisions reached by that court, one that had profound effects upon the development of the United States as a unified country, and upon the growth of the US economy. The practical effects of the ruling did not take long to manifest themselves. Within a few years of the decision, the number of steamboats operating in New York waters had increased dramatically, with Gibbons' line (the Union Line) alone expanding its operations so that by 1829, it had over 70 steamboats in operation.

Thomas Gibbons died in 1826, having had the satisfaction of seeing his erstwhile legal opponent Ogden bankrupted by the costs of the court case and ultimately imprisoned for debt.[9] He bequeathed the Union Line to his son William Gibbons, for whom Vanderbilt worked for several more years, acting as general manager and ship's captain.

By 1829, Vanderbilt had worked for the Union Line for eleven years. He was now 35 years old and having accumulated approximately \$30,000 of

---

[9] Ogden was released from prison in 1829 thanks to the efforts of former Vice President Aaron Burr, a childhood friend, who persuaded the New York legislature to pass a statute prohibiting the imprisonment of Revolutionary War veterans for debt.

capital, he decided that he wanted to work for himself again and resigned from William Gibbons' employment. Shortly thereafter, Gibbons sold the bulk of his steamboat interests to the Stevens family of Hoboken, who themselves already had interests in steamboats and railroads.

Self-employed, Vanderbilt started by acquiring two steamboats, and designing and building a third, which he put to work on the New York to New Jersey run and later the New York to Philadelphia run. He was soon engaged in a fierce price war with his competitors, including the Stevens family who had bought the Union Line. Eventually, several rival lines came together and paid Vanderbilt substantial amounts not to compete against them.

Vanderbilt then turned his attention to the Hudson River, and in particular the New York/Peekskill run where he established a monopoly service. It was not long however before he was challenged by a man, with whom he was destined to have dealings of one sort or another for much of the rest of his life. That man was Daniel Drew.

Uncle Daniel

Daniel Drew - Uncle Daniel, as he would come to be known in the newspapers - was born in 1797 on a poor farm in the backwoods of New York State. He received even less formal education than the Commodore, but was taught a severely fundamentalist version of Christianity by his mother the effects of which would remain with him, one way or another, for the rest of his life, although in a strange, compartmentalized way. He dressed and spoke like a country parson of the fire-and-brimstone variety and later in his life endowed a seminary and several churches. At the same time, he was one of the sharpest operators on Wall Street, one whose religious beliefs by no means precluded the making of money, if necessary at the expense of other people.

Drew began his career as a barker in a circus, where he learned many of the skills that he would put to such profitable use in later years. After the War of 1812 (during which time he volunteered to join the New York militia so as to gain a $100 bonus), he became a cattle drover, one of those who bought cattle from country farms and drove them to the slaughterhouses of New York City. There is a story – almost certainly untrue, but one which is recounted whenever Drew's name is mentioned – that on one occasion, on the night before the end of a drive, he had the idea of allowing his cattle all the salt they wanted, but denied them water.

The next morning, the thirsty cattle reached a stream and Drew allowed them to drink their fill, so that when they reached the cattle yards in Harlem where the buyers awaited, they were full of water and therefore much heavier, albeit only temporarily. As the price of the cattle was calculated by reference to their weight, Drew's ploy netted him a tidy profit and gave rise to the term "watered stock".

By the time Vanderbilt encountered him, Drew had established a successful brokerage firm on Wall Street and his cattle driving days were behind him. He was now rich and like Vanderbilt, he too had seen the commercial advantages of steamboats and had acquired an interest in a small steamboat, the Water Witch, which he now put to work in direct competition with Vanderbilt. Inevitably a price war ensued, one that was expensive for both sides and eventually Vanderbilt found it was simpler just to buy the Water Witch from Drew, who thereafter temporarily withdrew from the Commodore's life. But Drew would be back.

In the meantime, Vanderbilt was also seeking to extend his influence on the New York to Albany run. This attracted the attention of a cartel of steamboat owners known as the Hudson River Association who had banded together to discourage competition. In this case, the resulting price war lasted several years, with Vanderbilt continually cutting his rates, until eventually he was offering free passage on his boats steaming between New York and Albany (although the costs of food and drinks on his boats were increased in compensation). He was losing money, but so was the Association; the question was who could afford to lose money for longest? Eventually, it was the Association who blinked first and Vanderbilt was offered $100,000 cash, together with a yearly payment of $5,000, in order to induce him to leave the Hudson River for a period of ten years. Vanderbilt was delighted to accept.

Over the next few years he focused his steamboat interests elsewhere, competing vigorously and establishing lines around Long Island Sound and on the North and East Rivers, extending into Connecticut, and reaching as far north as Boston, and as far south as Charleston and even Havana in Cuba. By the middle of the century, his business interests stretched across the Atlantic and as far afield as Central America and he was worth several million dollars. He was recognized as the greatest ship owner in America.

In the meantime, he and his wife Sophia were raising their family, although in the light of the Commodore's frequent absences, it would be more accurate to say that Sophia alone was raising the family. Of their thirteen children, ten ultimately survived him, eight daughters[10] and – more important from the perspective of the Vanderbilt dynasty – two sons. Of the two boys, William, commonly called Billy, was the eldest; the youngest son was named Cornelius after the Commodore himself.

Billy was a disappointment to the Commodore, at least to begin with. By all accounts, he grew to become a stocky, coarse-looking young man, slow-moving and clumsy. Some thought he was of limited intelligence; certainly his father did, making no secret of his contempt for his son.

After leaving school, and following a brief spell working for Daniel Drew in his brokerage business, Billy married and became a farmer. The Commodore was unsurprised by this move; he had long before concluded that Billy was good for little else, and he provided the money to enable Billy to buy a small farm on Staten Island. Vanderbilt also gave him an annual allowance of $3,000.

However, Billy had his merits. He was hard-working, often beginning his work on the farm at five in the morning. Before long, he had extended his farm, and turned it into one of the most profitable on Staten Island. He raised eight children in all, and saw to it that they received excellent educations. Slowly, Billy rose in the estimation of his father, although the Commodore would never offer him a post with his profitable steamship lines.

The Commodore was also fated to be disappointed with his second son, Cornelius Jeremiah. Vanderbilt initially judged that Cornelius "had more brains" than Billy, and he may have been right. Although he was bright, Corneel, as he was popularly known, was also confrontational and aggressive, particularly in relations with his father. He also suffered from epilepsy from the age of eighteen, a malady which the Commodore regarded as a sure sign of weakness. When Corneel was nineteen, Vanderbilt had him committed to an insane asylum for three months, the first of several such admissions. Vanderbilt eventually concluded that his second son would be unable to support himself, and so arranged for him to receive a monthly allowance. The effect on Corneel was disastrous - he

---

[10] The Commodore would have difficult relationships with his daughters for many years and he was fundamentally uninterested in them, although he ultimately employed several of his sons-in-law in his various businesses.

effectively gave up any pretence of working for a living, and instead set about gaining what advantage he could from being his father's son - borrowing money from friends and relations and strangers with little or no intention of repaying the sums borrowed, gambling and on occasions forging his father's signature on cheques. He seldom kept any job for long – and he had several – and his father soon despaired of him. Eventually, he too was found a farm by his father – in his case, a small fruit farm in East Hartford, Connecticut, far from the Commodore's presence.

Salvation of a sort, or at least the semblance of a brake upon Corneel's personal downwards slide, came when Corneel was 25, as a result of his marriage to a young woman called Ellen Williams, the daughter of a minister. Although her family was not particularly wealthy - certainly not as wealthy as the Vanderbilts were in the process of becoming - she seems to have been a sensible and tactful woman, and before long, she established a positive relationship with her new father-in-law. He must have approved of her, for he raised Corneel's allowance several times, and gave them money to build a new house.

However, notwithstanding Ellen's support, and unlike his brother Billy, Corneel could never make his farm pay. He continued to borrow money, living well beyond his means and gambling wildly and on several occasions was committed to debtors' prisons from where his mother had to bail him out. Eventually the Commodore refused to provide any further financial help, and Corneel Vanderbilt was forced to file for bankruptcy in 1868.

There was one more son – the Commodore's thirteenth child and youngest son. Named George Washington Vanderbilt, he was born in 1839 and for many years, the Commodore had hoped that he would be the worthy heir for whom he had been waiting, Billy and Corneel being so obviously unsuitable. George trained at West Point, where he excelled, and served as a lieutenant in the Union Army during the American Civil War. Unfortunately, George contracted tuberculosis whilst on active service and died in 1864, at the age of 25, depriving the Commodore of his desired heir.

As for the Commodore himself, he retained the dockside habits of his youth. Polite society did not fall over itself to admit him or his family to their ranks; as far as most wealthy New Yorkers were concerned, the Commodore was uncultured and crude, and somehow his rapidly increasing wealth only made matters worse.[11] He for his part showed little or no wish to be invited to the dinners and balls organized by people who considered themselves his social betters and more often than not, he managed to offend whenever he did accept a social invitation.

Instead of seeking the delights of high society, he continued to amuse himself as he had always done. His pleasures included harness racing (admittedly a pastime he shared with many of New York's elite) and drinking and womanizing, often visiting the dockyard haunts of his youth. He had innumerable affairs throughout his life, unconcerned about popular opinion (or indeed the opinion of his wife and family). Unsurprisingly, he largely disdained organized religion, although he showed an interest in spiritualism and psychic healing (particularly later in life). Nor did he ever show much interest in works of charity. To the end of his life, his primary concerns were himself and his fortune, and he made no pretence of hiding this aspect of his personality.

To The Pacific

In the meantime, the United States was in the grip of gold fever, occasioned by the discovery of gold in California, which gave rise to the Gold Rush, with thousands of people seeking to move west hoping for a better and richer life. However, this was easier said than done in the days before the transcontinental railroads, when the writ of the United States did not automatically run across the plains. Many would-be gold tycoons did not in fact seek to cross the continental United States at all; rather they either sailed around Cape Horn, at the southern tip of South America – a trip which could easily take six months or longer – or they sailed to Panama, battled their way across the fever ridden jungle to the Pacific coast, and then took ship to San Francisco.

The Commodore, with his usual instinct for competition, felt that there had to be a better route. His attention was drawn to Nicaragua, where the San Juan River connects Lake Nicaragua with the Atlantic. If a steamboat could sail up the river and across the Lake, the route to the Pacific would be much shorter and less arduous than any of the alternatives and for such advantages, the Commodore speculated, people would be willing to pay.

---

[11] It would be two generations before the Vanderbilts were generally considered to occupy the pinnacle of East Coast polite society.

The Commodore, not for the first or last time, decided to back his own instincts. He arranged for the construction of a special steamboat capable of overcoming the rapids, sand bars and rocks of the San Juan River, and by the early 1850s, Vanderbilt's new line was in operation. It was an immediate success – albeit that conditions aboard the steamships of Vanderbilt's Nicaraguan line were notoriously dreadful – and Vanderbilt's profits from his Nicaraguan venture alone were soon more than $1 million a year.[12]

By now, Vanderbilt was 60 years old, and he estimated his personal wealth to be in the region of $11 million. He therefore decided to do something he had never done before – he would take a vacation in Europe (together with most of his immediate family, whom he simply ordered to join him), and he would do so in a style befitting America's greatest ship owner.

He commissioned a new steam yacht, the North Star, to be built by a Long Island boatyard. Costing over half a million dollars, the North Star was a 270-foot paddle steamer, with two auxiliary masts and four coal-burning boilers, and was the first oceangoing steam yacht built for a private individual. The American popular press paid a great deal of attention to both the yacht – which was of course fitted out in a style suitable for royalty – and to the trip itself, which ultimately involved the North Star sailing as far as St Petersburg and Constantinople, as well as extended visits to England and France.

However, before the voyage was over, the press was anticipating trouble on the Commodore's return. Vanderbilt had arranged for two business colleagues, Charles Morgan and Cornelius Garrison, to watch over his Nicaraguan interests in his absence. No sooner had Vanderbilt sailed over the horizon than Morgan and Garrison effectively double-crossed him, deliberately failing to make agreed payments to Vanderbilt's agent.

Upon his return to America, it did not take Vanderbilt long to learn of Morgan's and Garrison's duplicity. He penned them a letter, and saw to it that the press received a copy. The letter read:

---

[12] For a time, Vanderbilt had also been interested in the possibility of digging a canal from Lake Nicaragua to the Pacific, thus making the passage even easier, but political and logistical problems rendered the proposal unfeasible.

"Gentlemen

You have undertaken to cheat me. I won't sue you, for the law is too slow. I'll ruin you.

C. Vanderbilt."

In September 1853, Vanderbilt organized yet another new shipping line to California, this time by way of Panama and, as usual, immediately initiated a rates war with his erstwhile colleagues. By September 1854, Morgan and Garrison were forced to meet Vanderbilt's terms, which included meeting all outstanding payments and purchasing ships from the Commodore (including the North Star) at prices set by Vanderbilt himself. Still later, when the Nicaraguan line suffered losses due to political difficulties in Central America, Vanderbilt bought a controlling interest in the company which now ran it and unceremoniously sacked Morgan and Garrison. They never bothered the Commodore again.

Meanwhile, Vanderbilt's competitors in Central America were less than enthusiastic to see him returning to the fray. They agreed to pay him $40,000 a month – the sum was soon raised to $56,000 a month – in exchange for him agreeing not to compete with them. Once again, the Commodore was delighted to be paid handsomely for doing nothing.

Vanderbilt's Nicaraguan adventures represented perhaps the apogee of his shipping interests. Slowly but surely, and to some extent, reluctantly, Vanderbilt's attention was being drawn away from steamboats and towards the latest transportation miracle of the new industrial age – the railroad.

Railroads and Corners

Vanderbilt had long been doubtful as to the desirability of investing in the American railroad network. Trains lacked the easy mobility of steamboats; they required the laying and maintenance of railroad track, which was expensive and sometimes posed complex engineering difficulties, and the construction of stations and marshalling yards and other forms of infrastructure that could eat away at potential profits. Undoubtedly, Vanderbilt's early views were somewhat coloured by his involvement in a railroad accident in October 1833, when he was taking his first train ride. The train he was on had jumped the tracks, crashing into a ravine and killing many of its passengers. Vanderbilt escaped with serious injuries, including broken ribs which penetrated his lungs, requiring him to endure over a month's bedrest.

Nevertheless, even Vanderbilt was eventually forced to modify his views of railroads, especially when he foresaw, in the last years before the American Civil War, that the time was fast approaching when railroads would start to compete directly with shipping lines, instead of merely carrying passengers to embarkation ports from where they would be borne away to their destinations by steamships. This was a time when the American railroad network was expanding at an ever increasing rate, with railroad companies vigorously competing with one another. Some of the competition was legitimate; however much of it involved obtaining support in corrupt state and city legislatures and thus was most certainly not. It was also an age when railroad companies sought to raise capital on Wall Street – capital supposedly necessary to finance future expansion plans. Undoubtedly some of the capital raised was indeed ploughed back into the railroad companies, but a substantial proportion was siphoned off by one means or another by railroad promoters and investment speculators – many of them supposedly investing on behalf of British and European investors – for less legitimate purposes. Nevertheless, the public's attention was captured by the railroad companies' activities on Wall Street – railroad companies were the hot stocks of the 1850s and the 1860s.

To date, Vanderbilt's involvement with Wall Street had been limited, although he was not quite the Wall Street innocent that he has sometimes subsequently been depicted as being, or indeed as he himself liked to pretend. However, he had generally kept his distance from the machinations of Wall Street. This was about to change.

The Commodore's attention was drawn to a small, poorly run railroad company known as the New York and Harlem Railroad. The Harlem's route – all 131 miles of it – lay through poor farming country, and generated little in the way of passenger and freight revenues. There was little interest in Harlem stock on Wall Street when there were richer pickings to be gained from other more substantive railroad stocks.

Vanderbilt observed that the New York and Harlem Railroad did have one major advantage that it shared with only one other railroad company, the Hudson River Railroad. These were the only railroad companies with direct access to Manhattan. The Commodore convinced himself that properly run, the Harlem could be very profitable indeed, and that he was the man to accomplish that task. In 1857, Vanderbilt began to buy Harlem shares for between $8 and $15 a share. A few months later, when a fall in the market led to severely reduced share prices, Vanderbilt hastened to increase his holdings. Over the next few years, the share price recovered, giving Vanderbilt a satisfying paper profit.

It was through the Harlem that Vanderbilt again encountered Daniel Drew, former cattle driver and steamboat rival of the Commodore. Drew, by now a millionaire in his own right, was a director of the Harlem. Experience was to show that Drew had lost none of his old tricks or his ability for mischief.

One of the reasons why Harlem's share price had risen and was continuing to rise was that the Common Council of New York – the equivalent of today's City Council – was expected to authorize the Harlem to build and operate the franchise for a streetcar line along Broadway to the Battery. Once constructed, this line would mean that the Harlem would have the only line running the length of the Island of Manhattan. As soon as this point was appreciated – and it didn't take long - the price of Harlem shares leapt, reaching $75.

This was an opportunity for Drew that he found impossible to refuse. By all accounts, he approached the mayor and other members of the Common Council, and drew their attention to the rapid rise in the value of Harlem shares. If, perchance, the Common Council did not in fact grant the Harlem the authority to build the streetcar line, or if the authorisation was granted, and then rescinded, the price of the shares could be expected to fall, and fall rapidly. Moreover, if anyone had had the foresight to sell the stock short – that is to borrow shares they did not own, sell them in the market at the current high prices, and then subsequently redeem the borrowed shares with shares purchased after the price had fallen – any such person could be expected to make a rather satisfying profit.

The Common Council of New York was not at that time a body famed for its moral or financial probity and if the mayor and aldermen raised any objections to Drew's proposals, they were purely short-lived and nominal. Before long, the Council's members together with a ragtag collection of professional speculators were selling Harlem stock short in anticipation of a future fall in the share price. And all the time, Vanderbilt and his allies were continuing to buy the stock and the share price was continuing to rise, eventually reaching more than $100 a share, before falling back somewhat.

The bill authorizing the construction of the streetcar line was passed on 23rd April 1863. By now, the Council members were selling short as never before. Vanderbilt, it seems, had some idea of what was happening and warned the Council members most forcefully of the folly of their actions. To no avail, the Common Council rescinded the streetcar line franchise on the afternoon of 25th June 1863. When the news was released, it was too late to affect the regular stock price that day;[13] however, it was widely anticipated that the price would fall "like a shot partridge" on the next day of trading, and that Vanderbilt would rue the day he had become embroiled with Wall Street.

However, that didn't happen. Far from falling, the price of Harlem stock rose the next day, reaching $97 a share, and then over the next few days rising even further to $106 a share. It did not take long for the reason for this to become apparent to the public and to the members of the Common Council. As the newspapers of the day gleefully reported, Vanderbilt and his associates had cornered the market by effectively acquiring all the available shares in Harlem. For the Council members to meet their contractual obligations, they would now have to buy Harlem shares, and there was in practice only one person who had any to sell - Vanderbilt. And it would be Vanderbilt who would set the price. Financial disaster was staring the Council members in the face.

The Commodore forced the price of Harlem stock up and up, ignoring the pleas of Council members and professional speculators alike that he allow them to purchase the shares and meet their obligations. On the 29th June 1863, the Council met in desperation to rescind their rescission of the streetcar line franchise (to much public derision, it must be said), and still the price went up, until it reached $180 a share and Vanderbilt finally allowed those who had shorted the stock to buy the shares they needed to meet their obligations. By the time the Harlem corner was over, Vanderbilt had increased his worth by more than $5 million. It had cost the speculators, and Drew, a fortune. Drew at least, was philosophical. He composed a short rhyme that ran: "He that sells what isn't his'n, must buy it back or go to prison." He knew there would be other opportunities to make money.

---

[13] Although the price of Harlem stock on the curb plummeted to $72.

The Commodore's victory in the Harlem corner did not mean that all his troubles with the Harlem's streetcar franchise were at an end. Various legal challenges were mounted in the courts and in October 1863, the New York Supreme Court[14] ruled that the Common Council of New York City had exceeded its authority in granting the streetcar franchise to the Harlem. Vanderbilt was therefore obliged to approach the New York state legislators in Albany in order to obtain fresh legal sanction for the construction of the streetcar line. It was at this time that history sought to repeat itself.

Daniel Drew appeared in Albany and, essentially, made the same proposition to the state legislators as he had previously made the members of New York's Common Council. If it seemed that the proposed legislation would pass, the price of the Harlem stock would rise. And if at the last moment, the legislation were to be voted down, the stock price would fall, again giving knowledgeable parties the chance to make a fortune – if they shorted the stock.

Like the Common Council, the New York state legislature was not exactly a body of social rectitude. Indeed, it was widely regarded as a disgrace to the state and to the country. In 1857, the famous author and lawyer George Templeton Strong wrote on behalf of many of his countrymen when he observed in his diary: "Heaven be praised for all of its mercies, the Legislature of the State of New York has adjourned", whilst in 1860, the journalist Horace Greeley commented that he doubted that "another body so reckless, not merely of right but of decency – not merely corrupt but shameless – will be assembled in our halls of legislation within the next ten years." Shameless and corrupt the New York state legislature of the time undoubtedly was; however, it seems incredible that the legislature's members – and the professional speculators who again flocked after them – could have believed that Vanderbilt would fall victim to Drew's machinations bearing in mind what had happened in the case of the first Harlem corner. Yet believe it they certainly did, and they began to sell Harlem stock short.

Part of the reason why they did so was due to the fact that they believed that following the Harlem corner, the Commodore was short of cash. And this was an impression that Vanderbilt (who was of course aware of

---

[14] Despite its name, actually a court of first instance rather than a court of appeal.

the activities of the legislature's members and their cronies) did nothing to contradict. Indeed he encouraged this view.

Unfortunately for the speculators, the Commodore and his allies – who included Leonard Jerome, Winston Churchill's American grandfather - had considerable cash reserves which they used to buy up as many of the outstanding Harlem shares as they could. Even more unfortunately, in selling the stock short, the speculators were effectively selling Harlem stock – stock they did not actually own – to intermediaries acting on behalf of the Commodore.

In the meantime, from the perspective of the speculators, matters appeared to be proceeding according to plan. The state legislature debated the proposed legislation and it seemed likely to pass and the stock price duly rose, rising from approximately $90 at the start of the year to $149 by 16th March 1864. Then, the legislative committee considering the draft legislation reported unfavourably, and the stock price fell back to $101. The speculators waited expectantly for further falls – but strangely these didn't occur – indeed the price started to climb back up – to $150, to $235 and by 17th May, the price had reached the dizzying height of $280. Once again, Vanderbilt and his allies had purchased all the stock available, so that when the time came for the speculators to meet their contractual obligations – that is, to deliver the stock they had been selling short – Vanderbilt was the only seller. It was almost a complete re-run of the first Harlem corner.

The state legislators begged Vanderbilt to stop – this time however, he wasn't inclined to. "Put it up to a thousand!" Vanderbilt is said to have exclaimed.

Fortunately for members of the state legislature, after some counseling from Leonard Jerome, who pointed out that if the price of Harlem reached a thousand, half the financial houses on Wall Street would be insolvent, Vanderbilt relented to the extent of allowing the legislators to escape from the financial trap with the price at $285. Vanderbilt was delighted with the result. He exclaimed: "We busted the whole Legislature and scores of the honourable members had to go home without paying their board bills!" Vanderbilt made several million dollars more on this second Harlem corner. The whole episode is estimated to have cost Daniel Drew more than one million dollars.

In the meantime, the Harlem wasn't the only railroad company in which the Commodore was interested. He also regarded the Hudson River Railroad – the other company with direct access rights into Manhattan – as a company worthy of his attention. Like the Harlem, the Hudson was also a poorly run company, with a laughably short track – only 140 miles long – although it was in a somewhat better financial position than the Harlem. Vanderbilt considered that combining the Harlem and Hudson railroads would enhance the prospects of both, and so he had been buying Hudson stock. By the beginning of 1864, having seen off an attempt by speculators to short the Hudson stock, Vanderbilt was a major shareholder and a director of the company and was in the process of acquiring yet more stock.

Vanderbilt now effectively controlled two railroad companies – the Harlem and the Hudson. He was now casting his eye at a third – the New York Central, a more substantial railroad company than either the Hudson or the Harlem. With over 510 miles of track, it was an important transport link for the towns and cities lying along the Erie Canal, and together with the Harlem and the Hudson, it connected Manhattan with the interior of the country. By 1867 – not without some initial difficulties – Vanderbilt was named president of the New York Central, which subsequently merged with the Hudson. The Commodore was now ready to take the next step – to deal with the issues posed by yet another railroad company – the Erie.

The Erie Railroad Wars

The Erie, like the New York Central, connected New York with the American mid-west, albeit by a less advantageous route. It was also poorly run, and had over the years required support from public funds on a number of occasions. Nevertheless, it had from time to time engaged in sporadic rates war with the New York Central, and from the Commodore's perspective, acquiring effective control of the Erie would remove a troublesome competitor and allow Vanderbilt to improve the efficiency and scope of his railroad empire. Almost inevitably, one of the directors of the Erie was Daniel Drew, who not infrequently manipulated its stock price to make money at the expense of gullible investors.

Vanderbilt himself had been appointed a director of the Erie in 1859; but had resigned in 1866. Now he determined that he needed a louder voice in the affairs of the company and an opportunity arose in October 1867 when there was an election of directors to the Erie board.

It was generally anticipated that Drew would be kicked off the board by Vanderbilt and his allies; after all, Vanderbilt had been loudly criticizing Drew all over Wall Street ever since the days of the first Harlem corner. Strangely, however, although Drew was indeed defeated in the elections, one of the newly appointed directors promptly resigned and Drew was then elected to replace him, and appointed treasurer as well. Drew's election apparently had Vanderbilt's blessing; exactly why Vanderbilt changed his mind and decided to sanction Drew's re-election at the eleventh hour is unclear. It may have been that Vanderbilt felt that it was better to have Drew on the board, where it might be hoped that some degree of control might be exercised over him. It may also have been that Vanderbilt believed that Drew could be useful in dealings involving investors from elsewhere in the United States. Whatever Vanderbilt's reasoning, expecting Drew to behave himself following re-election was one of the very few naïve actions of the Commodore's life. And this time, Drew was not alone; also elected to the board were two men who were virtually unknown to the general public – and to Wall Street – at this time. They were Jay Gould and Jim Fisk. Before long, they would be working very closely indeed with Drew, and they would be known throughout the city.

Gould and Fisk, for all that they worked together successfully and apparently with a great deal of mutual respect, were almost completely unalike. True, they were each a generation younger than the Commodore and Drew, Fisk having been born on 1st April, 1835 and Gould on 27th May 1836. Neither came from a wealthy background – Fisk's father was a peddler of household goods whilst Gould's family were farmers descended from New England puritans. And they both had deep-seated desires to become rich. However, there the similarities between them ended. Fisk had an exuberant – indeed a theatrical - approach to life, with a well-developed sense of fun and enthusiasm which made him popular. He enjoyed women, food, wine, the theatre and all the other good things in life and although he undoubtedly had financial talents, fundamentally he was a financial showman – and he loved it.

Gould, in contrast, seems to have inherited all the seriousness that his puritan forebears could bestow, although apparently he could be good enough company when he wanted to be. Gould's health was not good and constantly aware of the passage of time, he seems to have devoted all of his mental energies and attention to the pursuit of his fortune to the exclusion of any other interests. He was essentially a very private man, with few close friends outside his family, and not given to dramatic displays – a total contrast to the expansive, high living Fisk. There was, however, no doubting his financial abilities.

Different characters they may have been; nevertheless, they seem to have recognized kindred spirits in each other when they first met, thought to be sometime in 1865 although the details of their first encounter are sketchy at best. What is clear is that they determined that their chances of making money would be enhanced if they worked together, with Gould supplying the financial acumen and Fisk the powers of his persuasive personality. Their opportunity to make serious money came in 1867 when they were both elected to the Erie board.

The first evidence of mischief-making came not long after the new board of directors took office. Vanderbilt had proposed a plan whereby the New York Central, the Erie and another railroad – the Pennsylvania – would divide the New York railroad business between them, so as to avoid a ruinous rate war. He – and just about everyone else – expected the Erie board to vote in favour of the proposals. It may be that this had formed part of the agreement whereby Drew regained his seat on the board. Consequently, Vanderbilt was less than pleased when the Erie board voted against the proposals, declaring that they were not in the best interests of the Erie. Vanderbilt immediately recognized that this was a declaration of war by Drew and his allies on the board and that if he wanted to control the Erie, he would have to buy a controlling interest in the company's shares.

This was no easy task, even for a man with the financial resources of the Commodore. The Erie had more than a quarter of a million shares outstanding, with a market capitalization of more than $17 million. Acquiring a controlling interest could easily have cost Vanderbilt more than $10 million. Moreover, Vanderbilt knew that Drew and his allies could be counted upon to pull every trick they knew to oppose him.

The situation was complicated still further by the existence of phantom or convertible shares. In 1866, the Erie had, not for the first time, found itself short of money. Drew had helpfully offered to lend the company several million dollars – just less than $3.5 million in fact – for two years at an interest rate of 7 per cent. As security, however, the company was obliged to pass to him 28,000 unissued shares and bonds worth $3 million. Those bonds could be converted at will into 30,000 further shares, and those shares could in turn be converted back into bonds.

Very curious financial instruments indeed – they made it possible for Drew to increase or decrease the number of Erie's shares outstanding whenever it suited him to do so.

Moreover, as treasurer, Drew was in a position to manufacture still further convertible bonds, which could then be converted into yet more shares. This potentially made it impossible for Vanderbilt to acquire a controlling interest in the company – whenever it looked like this might happen, Drew could simply arrange for more shares to be created and dumped into the market.

Therefore, if Vanderbilt wanted to control the company, he would not only have to deal with the existing phantom shares, but prevent any more shares being created.

This was one time when Vanderbilt decided he had no choice but to seek the assistance of the courts – and he sought injunctions from Judge George G Barnard of the New York Supreme Court forbidding the Erie company from converting bonds into stock and forbidding Drew personally from "selling, transferring, delivering, disposing or parting with" any Erie shares under his personal control. The injunctions were duly granted on 17th February 1868 (and extended a few weeks later); however, if Vanderbilt had anticipated that this would bring Drew under control, he was doomed to disappointment. Drew, now openly working with Fisk and Gould, simply ignored the injunctions and carried on converting bonds into shares as he saw fit. In the meantime, Vanderbilt ordered his brokers to buy every Erie share they could.

Judge Barnard's injunction was just the start of a flurry of court actions over the next couple of months. Drew, Fisk and Gould persuaded an out-of-town judge to grant an order suspending Frank Work – Vanderbilt's nephew and personal representative on the board of directors – from office, whilst almost simultaneously, another judge forbade the board from attending to company business without the presence of Frank Work. To add to the legal chaos, a judge named Gilbert sitting in Brooklyn issued an order overturning Judge Barnard's injunction, and ordering the Erie to continue to convert bonds into shares, to be followed by Judge Barnard issuing yet another order voiding all previous injunctions except for his own.

Meanwhile, 50,000 new shares had been issued by Drew and released onto the market. Fisk, at least was enjoying himself. "If this printing press don't break down" he is said to have exclaimed, "I'll be damned if I don't give the old hog all he wants of Erie!"

Wall Street was in uproar – news of the new shares spread like wildfire, and the price of Erie shares, which had stood at $80, fell "like lead" to $71. Vanderbilt's position was perilous, to say the least, and if he had then failed, not only he but perhaps thousands of other investors would have suffered grievous losses. But the Commodore did not fail. Betting his whole fortune, Vanderbilt ordered his brokers to keep buying regardless of price, and the Erie share price recovered somewhat. Before long, Vanderbilt and his allies owned nearly 200,000 shares. No-one knew whether this was sufficient to give them control of the company and Vanderbilt couldn't even sell his newly acquired shares – the New York stock exchange ruled that Erie shares dated after 7th March 1868 would not be capable of constituting "good delivery".

The operation had so far cost Vanderbilt $7 million – and most of that money ended up in carpetbags clutched by Drew, Fisk and Gould and their allies, for they had promptly converted the share proceeds into cash, an action which temporarily drained New York of much of its money supply, causing local interest rates to rise sharply. Vanderbilt was now furious and his lawyers persuaded Judge Barnard in the middle of the night to issue warrants for the arrest of Drew, Fisk and Gould.

Until now, Drew and his companions had perhaps understandably been feeling pleased with themselves, holding court in high spirits and higher style in the Erie's New York offices. However, this party mood rapidly evaporated when they learnt that the New York county sheriff and his officers were on their way to clap them behind bars. Once in jail, they knew, Vanderbilt would have them at his mercy.

Drew and some of the other directors immediately headed for Jersey City, out of the jurisdiction of the New York legal authorities. Gould and Fisk and one or two other directors stayed behind at first, dining that evening in Delmonicos, with lookouts stationed in the street outside. Inevitably, the authorities heard of this and sent officers to arrest them. On hearing this news, Gould and Fisk fled the restaurant, heading for the Hudson River, where they persuaded a boatman to row them over to New Jersey. Their passage was perilous, but they made it across and before long Drew, Fisk and Gould, together with the Commodore's $7 million and a small army of hired thugs, were safely together in Taylor's Hotel on the

Jersey City's waterfront out of reach if not out of sight of the New York police.

It soon became plain the two sides were at a standoff. With the support of the New Jersey state legislature, Drew, Gould and Fisk were for the moment safe in Taylor's Hotel – soon dubbed Fort Taylor by the ever present press who were covering the story with relish. On the other hand, with Vanderbilt in New York, and with outstanding warrants for their arrests, the Erie directors couldn't return home.

This was particularly a problem for Drew, who by now was 70 years old, missed New York and disliked being cooped up in a small New Jersey hotel. He also disliked being in the constant presence of his fellow directors who, well aware of Drew's capacity for troublemaking and double-dealing, were watching him like hawks. Steadily, power was shifting from Drew to Fisk and Gould and before long Drew was effectively removed from office as treasurer of the Erie.

In the meantime, and in the full glare of press publicity, there was another flurry of activity in the courts and the state legislatures. Judge Barnard appointed one of Vanderbilt's sons-in-law as receiver of the proceeds of the sales of the Erie shares which had taken place, an appointment that was promptly overturned by an upstate judge at the request of lawyers acting for the Erie company. Just as promptly, Barnard voided the upstate judge's ruling, whereupon the son-in-law decided not to accept the appointment after all – eventually Barnard appointed a New York Tammany politician called Peter Sweeney to the post. As the proceeds of the share sales were sitting in carpet bags in a safe in the Taylor Hotel in New Jersey, there was little for Sweeney to actually do – not that this prevented Judge Barnard from awarding Sweeney $150,000, to be paid by the Erie railroad company as "recompense" for Sweeney' efforts.

Fisk and Gould decided that the only way for them to escape the legal quagmire in which they found themselves was for them to petition the New Jersey legislature for a charter, making the Erie a New Jersey company – they hoped this would prevent the New York courts from granting Vanderbilt control of all the Erie property in New York state. The members of the New Jersey legislature, always keen to demonstrate their independence from New York, approved the charter with indecent speed, and sent it for ratification by the Governor. Vanderbilt sent supporters to Trenton with the intention of defeating the bill, whereupon at least some of the New Jersey legislators realized that in their haste in submitting the bill, they had thrown away the opportunity of being bribed by both sides – the legislators then tried to withdraw the bill but failed, and the New Jersey Governor subsequently signed the bill into law.

Meanwhile, a most extraordinary bill was introduced into the New York state legislature in Albany – essentially, the bill was designed to ratify all the acts of Erie's board of directors, and to allow them to do pretty much anything they liked in the future without the pesky inconvenience of considering the interests of the shareholders. Judge Barnard – not exactly the most impartial of public servants himself – declared it to be "an act to legalize counterfeit money". The press reported that the purpose of the bill was to elicit bribes from both sides, which was almost certainly the case. And the bribes were flowing freely – the Erie directors sent one John E Develin to gather them support – but Develin miscalculated the greed of the legislators, who spurned the bribes being offered as being "too cheap" and by way of warning Gould and Fisk of this, refused to support the bill.

Gould went to Albany to try to repair the damage. Installing himself in a leading hotel in Albany, he rapidly set about suborning the state legislators and began to succeed – within a few weeks the bill was reintroduced into the senate and this time it looked like it might pass. Of course, as soon as he arrived in Albany, Vanderbilt's supporters learned of it, and informed the sheriff, who promptly arrested Gould pending bail for half a million dollars. To the astonishment of those watching, Gould coolly produced the money – almost certainly using some of the proceeds the Erie directors had extracted from the Commodore – and was soon a free man, albeit that he was scheduled to attend a court hearing for contempt in a few weeks time.

But by now, the momentum behind the various court antics was beginning to diminish. Initially, public opinion in the matter of the Erie Wars had largely and vociferously been on the side of the Commodore. However, in a masterstroke, Gould had begun to encourage the idea that allowing Vanderbilt to control both the Erie and the New York Central was not in fact in the interests of the public. Within a few weeks, the newspapers – particularly the *New York Herald* – began to support this idea and slowly public support for Vanderbilt's position began to ebb away.

Vanderbilt had never been particularly concerned about public opinion. However, neither was he inclined to fight battles that he could not easily win and he no doubt foresaw that even if he could secure ultimate victory, it could easily cost him millions more to do so. Moreover, he had his other interests – most notably the rationalization of the New York Central and the alignment of its operations with the Hudson and the Harlem – to consider, and the Erie was proving to be an expensive distraction. So the Commodore arranged a meeting with Drew and indicated his willingness to talk terms. Effectively the Commodore wanted three things: to be reimbursed for the losses he had sustained in acquiring worthless Erie shares, for compensation to be given to those of his allies on the Erie board who had supported him and suffered at the hands of Gould, Fisk and Drew, and (most importantly of all) for Drew to agree to play no further part in the management of the Erie. All along, Vanderbilt had been more concerned about ensuring that the Erie was properly and reliably run than gaining control and with Drew removed from power, Vanderbilt might well have concluded that he had gained something from the conflict after all.[15]

The negotiations took some time to complete. However, Drew had many reasons for wanting to reach terms with the Commodore. Drew wanted to come home and he knew that the other directors would never allow him to gain control of the company again. Gould and Fisk, for their part, were initially less inclined to support the deal, but eventually were brought on board. As part of the deal, Vanderbilt immediately sold 50,000 shares to Gould and Fisk at $70 a share, received another $1 million for a four month call on a further 50,000 shares, received $1,250,000 worth of bonds and an additional $1 million in cash. Vanderbilt's supporters were paid more than $450,000 in compensation and Drew resigned from the board. Gould and Fisk were awarded control of the Erie, Gould being appointed president and Fisk becoming treasurer. The cost of the settlement – about $9 million in total – was effectively borne by the Erie's longsuffering shareholders, who (as a result of the subsequent release of the 100,000 shares Drew had printed to prevent the Commodore from taking control of the company) saw their equity in the company substantially diluted.

---

[15] Nevertheless, as many writers have observed, in failing to gain control of the Erie, he cannot be said to have won the Erie Wars. On the other hand, neither had Drew. The real victors were Gould and Fisk. And Vanderbilt, for one, knew it. "From now on," he concluded, "I'll leave them blowers alone."

After the Erie Wars

The Erie Wars were over by October 1868 and had cost Vanderbilt several million dollars. They also represented the beginning of the end as far as Drew was concerned – once Gould and Fisk were safely in control of the Erie, he began his old game of speculating on the Erie share price movements, but was outmanoeuvred by Gould and Fisk, ultimately losing over one million dollars. He was never really a force on Wall Street ever again, was forced into bankruptcy in 1876 and died in September 1879, at the age of 82.

As for Gould and Fisk, they still had several tricks up their sleeves so far as the manipulation of the Erie's shares were concerned and steadily made money at the expense of the Erie's longsuffering shareholders. They also attempted – and very nearly succeeded - in cornering the New York gold supply, with the unwitting help of no less a personage than President Ulysses S Grant himself. Fortunately, Grant realized that he was being manipulated in the nick of time, forcing Gould and Fisk to curtail their activities, but not before they had made yet more money speculating on gold, and triggering a financial crisis on Wall Street which would become known as Black Friday.

Fisk, meanwhile, did not have long to live. Although a married man, he had for several years enjoyed the charms of a woman known as Josie Mansfield; however Josie had become enamoured of Edward Stokes, the manager of the Brooklyn Oil Refinery that was largely owned by members of his family. Eventually, Josie left Fisk for Stokes and by way of revenge, Fisk had Stokes arrested on charges of embezzlement. Stokes was held overnight in the cells, but was released the next day by a sympathetic judge who agreed that Stokes was innocent of the charge. Stokes then counterclaimed against Fisk for malicious prosecution, with Josie as an enthusiastic witness on Stokes' behalf. This matter eventually settled, but not before Stokes threatened to release to the public a series of letters Fisk had previously written to Josie. By all accounts, those letters weren't in fact very compromising in nature, but Fisk - often a sentimentalist in matters of the heart – was keen to avoid their publication. Fisk offered $15,000 for return of the letters, and Stokes accepted the offer. He also accepted the money but then refused to return the letters.

Fisk then brought a prosecution against Stokes for blackmail. On hearing the news, in January 1872, that the grand jury had decided to indict him

Stokes, according to an eyewitness, rose from his table in Delmonicos, where he had been dining and made his way to Fisk's office, and waited for him. When Fisk arrived and was making his way up the stairs, Stokes stepped out of the shadows and shot him twice, once in the stomach and once in the arm. Stokes was promptly arrested; Fisk died several hours later, much mourned at least by the popular press. Stokes subsequently stood trial for Fisk's murder and was sentenced to death. However, he came from a rich family who hired the best criminal lawyers in New York and, ultimately, he was convicted only of manslaughter and served four years in Sing Sing prison, on the Hudson River. He died in 1901.

After the murder of his partner, Gould carried on business on Wall Street. He eventually lost control of the Erie, largely as a result of a clampdown on corruption in public offices that had belatedly been initiated by the courts and the politicians, but kept his fortune intact. He diversified his interests into other railroad companies and invested heavily in the Western Union Telegraph Company. Over the years, as he became richer, he became more and more mysterious and reclusive. His wife died in 1889, and thereafter his will to live seemed to ebb away. His health was never good, and he succumbed to tuberculosis in 1892. At his death, his fortune was estimated at $60 million.

But what of the Commodore? He continued to consolidate his railroad empire, unifying the Harlem, Hudson and New York Central lines and thereby creating a railway system that linked the industrial centres of the north eastern United States. He introduced innovations such as replacing the old iron tracks – which rusted easily – with new steel tracks imported from the steel refineries of Great Britain – and parallel tracks, allowing more trains to run more frequently and in greater safety. His railroads offered all that modern engineering science could devise: freight trains capable of carrying twenty tons, Pullman sleeping cars for greater passenger comfort and Westinghouse air breaks, a major step forward so far as safety was concerned. And he built the Grand Central Depot in Manhattan, which became the largest railroad terminus in the world. Needless to say, he made lots of money.

There were changes in his personal life too. His wife Sophia died in 1868 and the following year, he married Frankie Crawford, a distant and much younger relative – he was 75 when they married; she was just 30. She received half a million dollars as part of the marriage settlement.

So far as the children by his first wife were concerned, the Commodore was fundamentally a disappointed man. For years he had been looking for a worthy heir - male of course, his daughters didn't count, and anyway they had by now married and moved out of the family home. For years he had hoped that his youngest son George Washington would prove to be the heir he needed, but George's early death had ended this possibility, leaving the Commodore with the choice of Billy or Corneel. Neither choice initially appealed to Vanderbilt.

Billy, the eldest son had for years been the object of the Commodore's derision. Exiled to his farm on Staten Island, he nevertheless had worked hard to make a success of his life and to show his father that he was in fact a worthy son. He did so well that slowly, over many years, the Commodore's attitude towards him gradually softened. The Commodore began to involve him his business affairs, at first only in relation to the most trivial matters, but as time went by, Billy became involved in more and more important aspects of his father's financial empire. Eventually, Vanderbilt named Billy as vice-president of the Harlem and Hudson, allowing him to become involved in the day to day management of Vanderbilt's railroad lines – although for so long as the Commodore remained alive, the Commodore alone retained the right to set company policy.

Billy was lucky compared to his brother. Corneel, the second son, was still the black sheep of the family and Vanderbilt wanted little to do with him and did nothing to prevent his bankruptcy in 1868.

Time was now running out for the Commodore himself. He continued to try to dominate all who were around him, including Frankie, and his relationships with most of his children and grandchildren (whom he suspected, probably correctly, of only being interested in his money) were strained, unsurprising considering the disdain with which he had treated them over the years. As the years passed, he became more and more physically enfeebled, his mental powers varied from one day to another, and he relied more and more on Billy to run his business affairs.

He was taken ill in May 1876 and retired to his bed in his townhouse at 10 Washington Place. He went into a slow decline, never leaving the house again whilst he was alive and on 4th January 1877, he died, at the age of 82. The doctors carried out an autopsy and discovered that virtually every organ in his body was ravaged by illness of one form or another.[16]

He was buried in the family vault in the Moravian Cemetery on Staten Island, following which his family gathered in New York to hear the reading of his will. Much of its contents were uncontroversial. Frankie, his second wife, received half a million dollars and the townhouse at 10 Washington place. His married daughters each received a few hundred thousand dollars. Corneel, the bankrupt, received the benefit of a trust fund of $200,000. Several of his grandsons each received a few million dollars.

But the residue of the estate, calculated to be worth in excess of $95 million, was left to Billy. Billy was now one of the richest men in the world, and went on to double the fortune he inherited, so that when he died six years later, the Vanderbilt fortune was estimated to be worth $200 million. Corneel tried to challenge his father's will, which resulted in many embarrassing stories about Corneel's gambling activities being presented to the court in the full blaze of publicity. Eventually, by way of settlement, Billy paid Corneel an extra $600,000, a sum which must have been almost trivial to a man in Billy's position. Corneel did not live long to enjoy his inheritance. He committed suicide in April 1882, when he was 52 years old.

After Billy died (also in 1882), the Vanderbilt fortune continued to be passed down the family from generation to generation – but after Billy's death, there was no member of the family with the ability or the inclination to ensure its continued growth. In consequence, it was divided and squandered by Vanderbilts who were primarily interested in maintaining their position in society by prodigious spending. Even the Vanderbilt fortune was ultimately unequal to the extravagance of the Commodore's grandchildren and their successors. By the second half of the twentieth century, there was little of the original fortune left.

For generations after his death, Vanderbilt symbolized the very image of an American robber baron – incredibly rich, a hard and sometimes ruthless businessman who sacrificed everything for his fortune and cared

---

[16] It has been suggested by Vanderbilt biographer Edward J Renehan Jr. that he suffered from advanced syphilis and this would certainly explain the physical and mental symptoms of his last few years.

for little or nothing apart from his dollars and his own pleasures. There is some truth to this picture. However, one senses that his contemporaries were perhaps less censorious of the Commodore than were some of his biographers in later years - and many of the Commodore's fellow citizens, in addition to understandable feelings of envy, may also have felt a quiet measure of pride as to what the Commodore achieved in his life – certainly he received less criticism from his contemporaries than other financial magnates of his time or after – much less, for example, than John D Rockefeller had to endure. Perhaps it is because many of Vanderbilt's contemporaries recognized that his achievements benefited his country and the lives of ordinary citizens – by rationalizing much of the transportation system of the eastern seaboard of the United States, both on water and by rail, he laid some of the essential foundations for the emergence of the United States as an industrial superpower at the close of the nineteenth century. And he simply made it easier, cheaper and more comfortable for ordinary people to travel. At the end of the day, that's not a bad epitaph.

SIX TYCOONS

Andrew Carnegie

"Surplus wealth is a sacred trust which its possessor is bound to administer in his lifetime for the good of the community."
Andrew Carnegie (1835 - 1919)

The Bobbin Boy

Andrew Carnegie, steel tycoon, author and public benefactor, was born in a small two room cottage in the Scottish town of Dunfermline on 25th November 1835. Andrew's father, William, a skilled linen weaver like his father and grandfather before him, was born in 1804, and had moved to Dunfermline in search of work in the mid-1820s. Andrew's mother, Margaret, whom William had married in 1834, was six years younger than her husband and was the daughter of Tom Morrison, a cobbler who held what were for the time radical political views[17], advocating universal suffrage, the abolition of aristocratic privilege, the redistribution of wealth and the protection of workers by organized unions. In the fullness of time, Andrew would express some (but by no means all) of his grandfather's radical socialist views, views that many observers would later find hard to reconcile with the pay and working conditions of the men and women who would toil for Carnegie in his great steel plants and in so doing help him to create one of the greatest fortunes in America.

Popular myth recounts that Andrew was born in poverty and that his story is a tale of a boy and young man who clawed his way to wealth and fame through talent, cunning, sheer hard work and a modicum of luck, and for once at least, popular myth is broadly correct. What popular myth nearly always refrains from mentioning, however, is that the dire poverty that Andrew and his family endured in his earliest days was a relatively new experience for the Carnegies. The 1820s and early 1830s had seen a great demand for delicate linens and fabrics of all types, particularly from America. At this time, whilst the Industrial Revolution was well underway and many skilled artisans were finding that they could not compete with

---

[17] So did William's father, Andrew, commonly known as "Professor Andra", an intelligent man who enjoyed reading, writing, thinking, arguing and drinking far more than he did weaving, and who eventually suffered financial difficulties as a consequence.

the new factories and steam engines, fine linen weaving still remained a skilled labour-intensive cottage industry, for the new machines could not easily reproduce the delicate designs produced by the weavers' hands. Consequently, William and his fellow weavers initially had all the work that they could desire, and in the years immediately before his marriage, William had reason for considering himself satisfied with his financial situation.

Such satisfaction evaporated abruptly less than two years after Andrew's birth, as the Panic of 1837 struck first the United States and then began to make its effects felt overseas. Banks failed, share prices fell, unemployment rates soared and the demand for luxury linens and other fabrics disappeared almost overnight. The effect on the weavers of Dunfermline was catastrophic; within months nearly half of the town's weavers were unemployed. Some weavers were forced to accept such work as there was at severely reduced rates of pay, and this led to conflict between weavers who were willing to accept the reduced rates and those who were not. To make matters worse, the Industrial Revolution was finally making its impact on linen weaving as powered looms were gradually introduced into the mills of Scotland and the north of England, reducing even further the need for skilled manual weavers such as William.

By the mid-1840s, the Carnegie family's financial situation had become precarious indeed, for William was now virtually unable to find any weaving work at all. He retreated into himself, becoming a silent and beaten man, selling his looms. As he did so, it fell to Margaret to try to bring in enough money to enable the family to survive, and she sold items of food such as potted meats, home made pastries and other confectionaries from the front room of the family's cottage. She also helped her brother who had become a cobbler like their father, but the money she earned for all her efforts was barely enough. By this time, Andrew was no longer the family's only child, for another son, christened Tom after his maternal grandfather, had been born in 1843. From time to time, Margaret would consider whether it might not be better for the Carnegies to leave Dunfermline and start a new life in America, as her twin sisters Annie and Kitty and a number of other relatives had already done, but the news she received intermittently from Annie convinced her that economically, life in the United States, still suffering as it was from the after-effects of the Panic of 1837, was no better than in Scotland.

The harsh winter of 1847 finally led Margaret to determine that the family had no choice but to seek a new life on the other side of the Atlantic Ocean. The Carnegies sold almost everything they owned to pay for their passage, but were still short of funds. At the last moment, one of Margaret's childhood friends, Ella Ferguson (who had helped at Andrew's birth, when Margaret had been unable to afford to pay for the services of a midwife) lent her £20, which was enough for Margaret to book the family's passage across the Atlantic on a former Maine whaler called the Wiscasset.

The Wiscasset set sail from Glasgow in early July 1848, bound for New York, from where the Carnegies planned to make their way to Allegheny City in Pennsylvania, where Annie and Kitty and their respective families had already settled. After an uneventful if boring and uncomfortable voyage of 42 days (during which, by all accounts, Andrew was befriended by several of the ship's crew, for whom he performed errands, leading to his adoption as the ship's unofficial mascot) the Wiscasset arrived in New York harbour. After complying with the disembarkation formalities (which at this time in the United States' history, were fairly perfunctory) the Carnegies elected to travel to Allegheny City by the cheapest route available: by steamboat up the Hudson River to Albany and then along the Erie Canal by canal boat to Buffalo. From Buffalo, they sailed by steamboat on Lake Erie to Cleveland, and then by a variety of canal and riverboats until they finally reached Allegheny City in the middle of September 1848.

The Allegheny City they found was at that time a dirty and dreary manufacturing town, in the process of becoming yet another suburb of Pittsburgh, which itself had the unenviable reputation of being the ugliest city in the United States. Located at the junction of the Allegheny and Monongahela rivers, Pittsburgh was already famous for its mills, factories and foundries, as well as for the poor quality of its air, heavily laden as it was with industrial soot and dust, and for the frequency with which the city suffered from flooding. Making matters worse, Pittsburgh's infrastructure was almost non-existent, and the lack of sewers and reliable fresh water supplies led to waves of cholera epidemics. Nevertheless, despite these problems, Pittsburgh was a bustling and expanding city, thanks in part to its location at the heart of America's canal and river transportation system, which meant it was well placed to supply the needs of the new settlements that were springing up all over the West. Here, unlike Dunfermline, there was work, if a person was willing to go out and find it.

On arrival in Allegheny City, the first task for the Carnegies was to join their relatives. Margaret's sister Annie had recently been widowed, and she shared a house with Kitty, Kitty's husband Thomas Hogan, and their four children. The property, located at 336 Rebecca Street, included a small cottage at the back of the lot, the ground floor of which was rented by Thomas Hogan's brother Andrew, who like William Carnegie was a weaver. The cottage also had two rooms upstairs, into which the Carnegies moved on a rent-free basis until they found their feet.

William tried to set himself up as a weaver once more, but he had little more success in selling his wares in Pittsburgh than he had enjoyed in Dunfermline. Once again, the burden of earning a living fell on Margaret's shoulders and she went to work for a neighbour, Harry Phipps, an English immigrant who was a cobbler, for which she was paid four dollars a week. That was barely enough to live on and, reluctantly, Margaret had to agree that it was time for Andrew to go out and earn a living. Andrew was barely thirteen years old, and seemed small for his age (he would be sensitive about his height all his life). He had however, the benefit of some education in Scotland before the move to America, and of course, he came from a family that valued education as a means of improving the lot of the working classes. He was moreover eager, quick on the uptake, willing to work hard and (as he had already demonstrated with the Wiscasset's crew during the voyage across the Atlantic, and as would become even more obvious in the years to come) he had a remarkable ability to make himself popular with people who were in positions to help him without seeming (or being) obsequious.

An opportunity shortly arose when both Andrew and his father William were offered work at a nearby cotton mill owned by another Scottish immigrant, whom Andrew referred to in his *Autobiography* as "Mr Blackstock". Andrew was hired as a "bobbin boy" at a wage of $1.20 a week, in exchange for which he worked twelve-hour shifts. The work was hard and monotonous, but Andrew drew some satisfaction from the thought that at least now he was contributing something to the family's finances.

Andrew had not been working for long as a bobbin boy when a new opportunity came his way, in the shape of yet another Scottish immigrant, John Hay. Hay owned a small workshop that manufactured cotton bobbins, and he hired Andrew to run the small boiler in the basement and the steam engines that turned the workshop's machinery. This was not a particularly happy time for Andrew,[18] not least because he had no great love for the new machinery that had impoverished his family, but he carried out his duties as best he could, and things began to improve when Hay discovered that thanks to his education, Andrew could assist with the workshop's clerical work. This entailed a move out of the basement and onto the factory floor, where he was expected to help to soak the bobbins in barrels of oil, the smell of which made him nauseous.

Andrew decided that the way to escape the drudgery of the workshop (and the stench of the oil) was to become a bookkeeper and with this in mind, he began to attend accountancy courses at night school in the company of several local lads from Rebecca Street who also were determined to better themselves. However, before he had finished his studies, yet another opportunity presented itself, once more thanks to the intervention of a Scotsman. Andrew Hogan, who by now had vacated the cottage on Rebecca Street and passed his looms to William, was a friend of David Brooks, the manager of the O'Rielly Telegraph Company. Brooks happened to mention to Hogan that he needed the services of a good messenger boy; Hogan suggested Andrew, and undertook to discuss the post with Andrew's parents.

Andrew was keen to take the job, which paid $2.50 a week, considerably more than he was earning working for John Hay and Margaret agreed that he should go for an interview the next day. William was less enthusiastic, and insisted however on accompanying Andrew when he went to the telegraph company's Pittsburgh offices the next day; when they arrived at the offices, Andrew made his father wait in the street and went in alone. He had a short but successful interview with David Brooks, and when asked when he could start work, replied that he could begin immediately, and did so.

Telegraphs and Railroads

The telegraph business in which Andrew Carnegie now found himself working was one of the wonders of the age. Only five years had passed since Samuel Morse had persuaded Congress to pay for the construction

---

[18] About this time, William Carnegie gave up his job at Blackstock's cotton mill and retreated to his looms, more out of touch with reality than ever.

of America's first commercial telegraph line between Washington and Baltimore, and telegraph companies were now vying with one another to spread networks of telegraph cables across the continent. The telegraph was the first method of communication that permitted the reliable electrical transmission of information over long distances, and already it was having a profound effect upon America's economy and upon America's perception of itself, as hitherto distant towns and cities found themselves instantaneously able to exchange messages which only a few years before might have taken days or even weeks to deliver. Suddenly, places that were connected by telegraph cables no longer seemed so far apart and in time, together with the railroad, the telegraph would help to bind America together as a single nation. In the meantime, Pittsburgh, situated as it was as one of the gateways to the West, was clearly destined to become one of the most important hubs in the country's ever expanding telegraph network.

One of Andrew's primary duties in his new job was of course to deliver the messages received at the telegraph offices to their intended recipients. This required a detailed knowledge of the streets and alleys of Pittsburgh, which Andrew rapidly acquired thanks to his excellent memory. He also learned the names and faces of Pittsburgh's most prominent businessmen, which not only helped him to make his deliveries efficiently, but also thanks to his polite and cheerful manners meant that many of them became aware of him as an individual, something that would prove useful in later years.

Andrew Carnegie was not the only messenger boy employed by the telegraph company, but soon became known as one of the most reliable, and he took a lead in organizing his fellow messengers so as to ensure that work and tips were shared equally. His reputation for reliability and honesty rose when he found a bank draft for five hundred dollars (a considerable sum of money at the time) in the street and handed it in to the authorities, a story which was reported in the local newspapers. Before long, he decided that bookkeeping was no longer the future he wished for himself, and instead, he kept his eyes open for ways to progress in the telegraph business. He set about learning how to operate the telegraph machinery in the office, and taught himself Morse Code, a skill which he put to good use on one occasion when a message began to be transmitted to the Pittsburgh office early one morning when no telegraph operator was present to receive it. Andrew took it upon himself to transcribe the message into English and formally acknowledge receipt.

Fortunately David Brooks regarded this as an example of initiative rather than unauthorized meddling (which could have had serious consequences if Andrew had made a mistake in translating the message) and before long, Andrew was acting as a standby telegraph operator, sitting at the telegraph keys when the other operators were absent. His skill increased to such a point that he was able to understand the sound made by the telegraph receiver as a message was received, rather than being obliged to wait for a printed slip bearing the dots and dashes of the Morse-encoded message that then had to be translated into English, as was common practice with most operators. Being able to decipher a message from sound alone was a skill mastered by only the most gifted operators, and increased Andrew's reputation with his employers even more.

Andrew's next opportunity came in June 1851, a few months before his sixteenth birthday, when a telegraph operator in the nearby town of Greensburg was granted a leave of absence of two weeks. Andrew was sent as a temporary replacement and performed admirably, although he was nearly electrocuted when he insisted on remaining at his post during a thunderstorm and a lightning bolt struck the telegraph cables outside his office, sending a burst of high voltage current to the telegraph keys. He was thrown off his chair, but survived, and when he returned to Pittsburgh, he was promoted to the post of full-time telegraph operator.

For the next few years, Andrew worked for the O'Rielly Telegraph Company. During his spare time, he continued to try to improve himself, reading as many books as he could obtain. In those days, books were not cheap (and in any event, the Carnegies had little spare money to spend on books) and free public lending libraries were unknown, and so Andrew was delighted when he learned that a local businessman called Colonel James Anderson had established a small library for the benefit of local working boys. In due course (after Anderson had passed the ownership of the library to the Allegheny City authorities) it was felt necessary to impose an annual subscription charge of two dollars upon all library users other than formally apprenticed working boys. On learning this, Andrew protested against this decision to charge a fee in a series of letters which were published in the local press until the decision was withdrawn and he was allowed to borrow one book a week free of charge.

Andrew's determination to improve himself led him to participate in a local debating society, and at the same time, he was engaged in a long (and on occasions, heated) correspondence with relatives still in Scotland.

In particular, he corresponded frequently with his uncle George Lauder, the widower of one of Margaret's sisters, and Lauder's son, also called George. Andrew by now identified strongly with his adopted country, and in his letters he often praised America and all things American whilst criticizing Britain, something that his relatives still in Britain (even though they themselves held radical views and wanted to change Britain's political and economic systems) sometimes found irritating and condescending.

Andrew was also involved for a time in the local Swedenborgian church, which his father also attended, a somewhat obscure sect founded in the eighteenth century by a Swedish nobleman who claimed to have been visited by Jesus Christ. It seems likely that Andrew attended more for the social opportunities the church offered (he particularly enjoyed the musical aspects of church membership) rather than for any deeply held theological beliefs. He would eventually allow his membership to lapse and throughout his life showed little real interest in organized religion.

In the early 1850s, Andrew met Thomas Scott, an official of the Pennsylvania Railroad, a railroad company that was laying down tracks to connect Pittsburgh to the railroad network of the eastern coast. Scott, in his late twenties when he met Andrew, was a rising star of the company, and during the course of his duties, he had many occasions to use Andrew's telegraphic services and was impressed by Andrew's expertise. When Scott was promoted to the post of western superintendent in charge of the new track shortly before Pittsburgh's rail link was opened in December 1852 (no mean feat for a self-educated man of relatively humble beginnings, as Scott was), he decided to establish his headquarters in Pittsburgh. He also decided that the company needed its own telegraph service to increase the efficiency and safety of its single track railroad, and succeeded in gaining the approval of company president J. Edgar Thomson to this proposal. The necessary telegraph equipment was obtained and installed, and Scott offered Andrew the post of clerk and telegraph operator. For his part, Andrew realized that he had risen as far as he was likely to go in the O'Rielly Telegraph Company, and decided to accept Scott's offer, which promised not only more money than he was receiving but also greater chances of future promotion. Andrew started to work for the Pennsylvania Railroad in February 1853.

His duties as a telegraph operator were relatively light, but Andrew also acted as Scott's personal secretary and aide, and did so with his usual enthusiasm and dedication, and once again, he succeeded in impressing his superiors. Before long, he was carrying out highly responsible tasks for Scott notwithstanding that as yet he knew little about the railroad business, and on occasions, he acted as Scott's deputy when Scott was away. During one of these times, news of an accident involving a ballast train reached him. Acting entirely on his own authority and without the knowledge or sanction of any of his superiors, Andrew established a "court martial" (as he himself described it) to investigate the matter, which resulted in the dismissal of one man and the suspension of two others. By the time Scott returned to the office, Andrew was wondering whether he had in fact been a little harsh, but in any event, he was grateful that Scott did not seek to override his decision and Andrew's rulings were confirmed.

1855 was a significant year for Andrew Carnegie. By now, the Carnegies' financial circumstances had improved markedly as compared to seven years earlier, although they were certainly not yet wealthy. They had repaid the money they had borrowed from Ella Ferguson that had enabled them to pay for their passage across the Atlantic and moreover, they had become property owners, having purchased the house on Rebecca Street from the Hogans in 1853. Nevertheless, Margaret still worked as a cobbler's assistant for four dollars a week and money remained in short supply. Tom, Andrew's brother, was attending a local school and William was still hand weaving linen that nobody wanted to buy.

And then, in late September 1855, William was taken ill and died on 2nd October 1855 at the age of 51. The death of William had little obvious effect on the daily lives of the surviving Carnegies and in later life, Andrew would seldom make reference to it, although he spoke warmly (if sparingly) of his father in his *Autobiography*. In any event, financial necessity meant that Margaret and Andrew had to continue working, and Tom continued to attend school.

A few weeks after William's death, Tom Scott offered Andrew the opportunity to buy ten shares in a private company, Adams Express, which specialized in the delivery of documents. Scott himself held an interest in the company (which had recently entered into a contract with the Pennsylvania Railroad), as did several others of the railroad company's executives, and Scott's offer reflects the high regard in which Andrew was held, and the almost magical willingness of Andrew's superiors to assist in his career. Andrew recognized the offer as a good one, for Adams Express paid generous dividends, but he lacked the $500 needed to buy the shares. Scott, on learning of Andrew's financial dilemma, agreed to lend him the money.

The Budding Capitalist

Ownership of shares in Adams Express meant that Andrew could now experience the delight of receiving dividend payments. In his *Autobiography*, he waxed lyrical about the feelings he experienced upon receiving his first dividend cheque of $10, money for which he had not had to work. "Eureka!" (he later wrote). "Here's the goose that lays the golden eggs." The experience opened his eyes to the possibilities of investment capital, and he resolved to look for other investment opportunities.

In January 1858, Scott was promoted to general superintendent, which entailed moving to the Pennsylvania Railroad's offices in Altoona, and Andrew, who was appointed as Scott's secretary at a salary of $50 a month, accompanied him. The Carnegies had originally intended that Margaret and Tom would accompany Andrew, but they had to remain behind until they could either sell the Rebecca Street house or find a tenant willing to rent it. Tom Scott was by now a widower, with two small children, and he too left his family behind in the care of his niece, Rebecca Stewart, until he could find suitable accommodation. In the meantime, he and Andrew shared a room in a hotel, and grappled with the responsibilities that Scott's new job entailed. Eventually, Scott acquired a suitable house and his children and niece joined him. Rebecca, a little older than Andrew, appears to have taken rather a shine to him, and took it upon herself to provide a degree of polish to his social skills, which at that time were somewhat rough and ready.

Andrew too acquired a house and, the Rebecca Street property having been sold, Margaret and Tom Carnegie joined him. He was now sufficiently prosperous that he could afford to hire a servant to help in the house, something that Margaret initially found difficult to accept, though she soon adapted. For the first time in her life she no longer had to work to support her family, and the contrast between the Carnegies' current prosperity and the poverty they had endured only a few years before was sharp indeed.

Later that year, another investment opportunity arose in the form of railroad sleeping cars, a much needed innovation on America's railroads. An inventor named Theodore T Woodruff had patented a design for a sleeping car in 1856 and subsequently entered into a number of contracts to supply cars built according to his designs to various railroad companies, including the Pennsylvania Railroad. In those days, when the concept of a conflict of interest was less recognized (or at least less susceptible to legal action) than is the case today, it was not uncommon for individuals negotiating on behalf of a company to themselves take financial interests in the investment under consideration. Woodruff's deal with the Pennsylvania Railroad was negotiated (on behalf of the railroad company) by J Edgar Thomson and Tom Scott. In exchange for agreeing that the Pennsylvania Railroad should purchase sleeping cars from Woodruff's company, Thomson and Scott themselves took shares in the Woodruff Sleeping Car Company. In order to disguise the nature of these investments, it was agreed that Thompson and Scott's shares should be held in Andrew's name, and Andrew himself was offered the chance to invest on his own behalf in exchange for his agreement to this arrangement.[19]

In his writings, Andrew gives a completely different account as to how his investment in sleeping cars came about. Carnegie claims that Woodruff first approached him and it was he who raised the possibility of buying sleeping cars with Scott and Thomson, claiming moreover that as a result of the deal, "sleeping cars [came] into the world." Sleeping cars had, in fact, existed in one form or another since the late 1830s (indeed Woodruff had sold sleeping cars to several railroads before approaching the Pennsylvania) and when the account was first published in 1886 in Andrew's book *Triumphant Democracy*, Woodruff angrily challenged Andrew's account. Andrew claimed that he had only mentioned the investment incidentally, and he had not intended his account to be an accurate history of the development of sleeping cars. The simple fact is that Andrew was only involved in the negotiations with Woodruff to a limited degree and his investment came about largely because he was in the right place at the right time, being perceived by Thomson and Scott as being a reliable "front man" for their investments.

---

[19] Many of the later (and very profitable) business dealings between Thomson, Scott and Carnegie would also take place in circumstances of conflicts of interest, a fact which appears not to have troubled any of them in the slightest.

In any event, Andrew Carnegie was allowed to pay for his shares in Woodruff's company in instalments. He borrowed money from a bank to pay for the first instalment; thereafter, dividends from his investment allowed him to pay the remainder. Within a few years, the dividends amounted to several thousand dollars a year and for the first time in his life, Andrew had a secure and respectable private income.

1859 saw further promotions for both Andrew Carnegie and Tom Scott. Scott was promoted to be a vice-president of the Pennsylvania Railroad, which meant yet another move for him, this time to Philadelphia. Andrew, now in his twenty-fifth year, had hoped to accompany Scott (but feared that he might be left behind in Altoona with a new boss who might prove less congenial than Tom Scott); in fact Scott surprised him by offering him the post of western superintendent, Scott's old position in Pittsburgh, at an annual salary of $1,500, with the promise that this would be raised to $1,800 if Andrew proved successful in his new role. Andrew accepted with eagerness and the Carnegies moved back to Pittsburgh, renting a house on Hancock Street, which was close to Andrew's new office. Tom Carnegie, having left school, was appointed his brother's secretary. Andrew's promotion took effect on 1st December 1859.

Although Hancock Street was in a respectable part of town, the Carnegies soon found that there were drawbacks in living there, thanks largely to the poor quality of the air which was so laden with smoke and soot produced by Pittsburgh's heavy industries that it was virtually impossible to keep anything clean. David Stewart, Rebecca Stewart's brother, with whom Andrew discussed the problem, recommended that the Carnegies should move to the nearby upmarket suburb of Homewood, where the air was cleaner, and the land was still relatively green and undeveloped. The Carnegies travelled out to Homewood, liked what they saw, and rapidly acquired a fine two-storey house with large gardens, in which Margaret busied herself growing flowers and raising chickens.

Andrew inevitably flung himself into his new duties as western superintendent, which required him to work closely with the railroad workers who laboured to keep the trains running on the tracks for which he was responsible. Those tracks had often been hurriedly laid and were becoming inadequate to the demands made of them as the railroad's business grew and grew. Andrew had to deal with a series of train wrecks, track breakages and other technical calamities and finding himself on call virtually 24 hours a day, he arranged for a telegraph connection to be established between his office and the house in Homewood. He not only worked himself hard but also the men working for him, and since he himself claimed not to know fatigue, he had difficulty in recognizing it in others and judging the limits of their endurance. Partly as a consequence of this, he was not a great supervisor of the men working for him and found it difficult to relate to them.[20] He had the sense to recognize his limitations in this regard, and in later life, when he had thousands of employees working for him, he always took care to ensure that someone else was responsible for the day-to-day supervision of his workforce.

The Civil War and After

In the meantime, great events were unfolding elsewhere in the nation. On the very day after Andrew's appointment as superintendent took effect, John Brown, who in October 1859 had led an abortive raid upon the federal arsenal at Harper's Ferry in Virginia in an attempt to incite a rebellion of southern slaves, was hanged for treason against the United States, becoming a martyr to the abolitionist cause. November 1860 saw the election of Abraham Lincoln as President, to the horror of the southern states. Talk of secession was heard everywhere, and in December 1860, as Lincoln, now President-elect, awaited his inauguration which was due to be held in March of the following year, South Carolina became the first of the southern states to formally declare that its links with the Union were at an end. South Carolina's declaration of secession was swiftly followed by similar declarations by Louisiana, Mississippi, Alabama, Georgia, Florida and Texas and in February 1861, the seceding states announced that they had established a new union – the Confederate States of America. On 12th April 1861, barely a month after Lincoln had taken his oath of office, Confederate forces fired upon the federal garrison at Fort Sumter in Charleston harbour, thus initiating the American Civil War.

Andrew Carnegie was a fervent abolitionist and shared fully his fellow northerners' feelings of fury and outrage at the news of Fort Sumter's capture by the Confederacy. Nevertheless, he did not rush forward to join up when, on 15th April, President Lincoln called for 75,000 volunteers for the US Army. Instead, a few days after Lincoln's call to arms, Lincoln's

---

[20] It was at this time he acquired the nickname of "Little Boss" which he retained all his life.

secretary of war, Simon Cameron, asked J Edgar Thomson and Tom Scott to assist the army in the transportation of volunteer troops to their training grounds and thereafter to the front (which, from the perspective of the North, was ominously close to the White House, thanks to the secession of Virginia shortly after Lincoln called for his volunteers). Scott was immediately dispatched to Washington to supervise matters there[21], but before he left, he recruited Andrew as his assistant and representative in Philadelphia.

One of the principal difficulties facing the North was that in order to transport troops from Pennsylvania to Washington by rail, they had to pass through Baltimore in Maryland. Maryland's loyalty to the North was by no means certain and indeed, the first Union troops to pass through Baltimore had been assaulted by a hostile mob of southern sympathizers. On 19th April, the railroad link through Baltimore was cut (upon the orders of Baltimore's chief of police, a southern sympathizer) and the telegraph service disrupted by secessionists, effectively isolating Washington from the northern states and leaving it vulnerable to a swift Confederate attack. President Lincoln was unwilling to countenance an attack on Baltimore by Union forces, fearing that this might drive Maryland to secession; it was vital that an alternative route to Washington be established as soon as possible.

An alternative route was rapidly found. Troops under the command of Benjamin Butler of Massachusetts, a politician and lawyer who had been appointed brigadier general in the militia, raised in response to Lincoln's call to arms, travelled to Perryville in Maryland, where they boarded steamboats and sailed to Annapolis. Upon arrival at Annapolis, they found that the railroad track from Annapolis to Washington had been ripped up. Luckily, several of Butler's troops were railroad men and they were able to repair the tracks so as to allow the passage of thousands of troops to Washington, with the first arriving (much to Lincoln's relief) on 25th April 1861.

In his *Autobiography*, Andrew claimed a great deal of the credit for reopening the rail link to Washington, declaring that it was railroad workers under his leadership who repaired the tracks, with some belated assistance from Butler's troops. He also claimed to have been injured in the cheek by a recoiling piece of telegraph wire, which (he said) meant

---

[21] Ultimately he would become Assistant Secretary of War.

that he could justly claim to have shed blood for his country in the Civil War. Indeed, he claimed to have been amongst the first to do so and that he accompanied Butler's troops as they entered Washington. Whether or not he did suffer such an injury is unknown; however, as Carnegie biographer David Nasaw has pointed out, there is no real evidence (apart from Andrew's own testimony) to support his claim that he was in large part responsible for reopening the Annapolis-Washington railroad track. Some reports suggest that he was still in Pittsburgh when Butler's troops reached Washington, and it would appear that, as in the case of his description of the role he claimed to have played in the introduction of sleeping cars, this is an example of Carnegie's imagination at work.

As to why he felt the need to exaggerate his role, it may be that he felt he had to justify his failure to join the army as so many of his friends and contemporaries did.[22] Be that as it may, there is no doubt that in the months following the reopening of the railroad link to Washington, Andrew Carnegie provided a valuable service to his country, helping to supervise the building of railroad and telegraph links across the Potomac and subsequently through Union-occupied portions of northern Virginia, links which were needed for the efficient transportation of northern troops and supplies. Whilst Andrew was so occupied, the first major clash between Federal and Confederate forces occurred on 21st/22nd July 1861, at the Battle of Bull Run (or Manassas, as the southerners named the battle). The result was a Confederate victory and panic in Washington, but Confederate forces lacked the resources to pursue the retreating Union survivors and capture Washington itself. Andrew himself took the view that the defeat at Bull Run was a blessing for the North, since it drove home the seriousness of the North's situation, and would ensure that the North's war effort was pursued with greater vigour in the future. However, it was becoming clear that his work in Washington was done, and a few weeks after Bull Run he returned to his duties in Pittsburgh and his personal business interests.

---

[22] In February 1864, Andrew Carnegie received a notice from the US Government informing him that he was to be drafted into the US Army. In order to avoid conscription (and as was quite legal at the time), he paid $850 to a draft agent who arranged for his place to be taken by an Irish immigrant, which exempted Carnegie from the draft for three years. By the time his exemption expired, the Civil War was over.

On his return to Pittsburgh, when not attending to his railroad duties (which were important, for the Pennsylvania Railroad played a key role in the northern war effort), he sought out various investment opportunities for himself. In this task, he was helped by one of his wealthy neighbours in Homewood, William Coleman. Two years before, Edwin Drake had drilled the first oil well at Oil Creek, Pennsylvania, and Coleman had grown interested in the burgeoning oil industry. In 1861, whilst Andrew Carnegie was busy in Washington, Coleman formed the Columbia Oil Company with a view to drilling for oil on various tracts of land he had acquired in the Oil Regions of Pennsylvania, and when Andrew returned to Pittsburgh, Coleman invited him to join him in his oil venture. Coleman took Andrew on a tour of the Oil Regions, following which he agreed to invest in Coleman's company. It was a wise move. Within a few years (and admittedly after a somewhat shaky start, when Coleman and Andrew sought to store oil in a reservoir, anticipating a future shortage of oil which never materialized, a misjudgement which eventually obliged them to sell the stored oil at a loss) the Columbia Oil Company was paying out substantial dividends to its shareholders. Andrew promptly invested much of his share of the dividends in other oil companies, but his attention was now swinging from oil to iron.

Thanks to his work for the Pennsylvania Railroad, Andrew had developed a firm understanding of the importance of the iron industry to America's railroads. Due in part to the demands of the war, and the dramatic expansion of the North's industrial capabilities, northern railroads and their rolling stock were showing signs of wear and tear and were in need of continuous upkeep and maintenance. In particular, many of the bridges that carried railroad tracks across valleys and ravines had originally been built out of timber; these were now proving inadequate and needed to be replaced by new bridges constructed of iron. Andrew now spotted an opportunity to establish a new company that would build iron bridges for railroad companies. Together with (inevitably) Tom Scott and J Edgar Thomson, Andrew approached three engineers, Jacob Linville, John Piper and Aaron Shiffler and together in February 1862 they established a new company, the Piper & Shiffler Company, which was soon successfully obtaining contracts to build iron bridges. Andrew took a one-fifth interest in Piper & Shiffler (which in 1865 would be reorganized and called the Keystone Bridge Company), his first major investment foray into the realm of heavy industry and a very successful one.

In March 1862, shortly after the formation of Piper & Shiffler, Andrew was taken ill and his doctors recommended a period of rest for several months. The Pennsylvania Railroad granted him a leave of absence of three months, and he decided to go back to Scotland with his mother and a friend, Tom Miller. They travelled in some style, boarding the steamship Etna in New York on 28th June 1862 and on arrival in Liverpool two weeks later travelled up to Dunfermline by train.

It was a proud and emotional time for both Andrew and his mother. Fourteen years earlier, they had been forced by poverty to emigrate to an unknown future in the United States. Now, they were returning with more wealth than they or their relatives could possibly have hoped for only a few years before, and Andrew was conscious of financial gulf that separated him, a successful American businessman who was still only his mid-twenties, from his cousins who had remained in Scotland, and for whom the heights of success meant being able to own a shop in the High Street. Nevertheless, it was a highly enjoyable visit for them all, marred only by a recurrence of illness that confined him to his bed for several weeks. Once he was convalescent, Andrew, Margaret and Tom Miller sailed back to America, and by the time their ship docked in New York, Andrew had fully recovered his health and was eager to return to work.

The autumn of 1863 saw a new investment opportunity for Andrew Carnegie. Tom Miller was a shareholder in a small iron foundry business established in 1859 by two German immigrant brothers called Andrew and Anton Kloman. Miller, who worked as a railroad agent, had arranged for his shares in the business to be held by Henry (or Harry, as he preferred to be called) Phipps, another of Carnegie's friends (the younger son of Harry Phipps, the cobbler for whom Margaret had worked upon first arriving in America) who was also a shareholder in the Klomans' business in his own right. Together, Phipps and Miller controlled a third of the shares and Phipps acted as bookkeeper. The business had been moderately successful until the start of the Civil War, when orders from the US Government began to pour in. Before long, the Klomans had been obliged to reorganize the business as Kloman & Co and to acquire more land and to construct an iron mill which they called the Iron City Forge in order to satisfy the increased demand.

As time went by, Andrew Kloman found it increasingly difficult to work with his brother and in 1862, they had a serious disagreement which led to Anton wishing to leave the business. Miller agreed to purchase Anton's

few times in his life that he did so) and thereafter, was noticeably suspicious about investing in radical new inventions. "Pioneering" he would later conclude, "don't pay."

Radically new industrial processes were not the only matters that concerned Andrew in the years immediately following his return to the United States. He indulged in a flurry of investment wheeler-dealings, often in partnership with J Edgar Thomson and Tom Scott, which gained him substantial interests in a succession of telegraph companies that were eventually consolidated into the Western Union Telegraph Company, to Andrew's considerable profit. A dispute between the shareholders in Union Iron Mills gave him the opportunity to buy out Tom Miller, meaning that he acquired effective control of the company. Patent disputes between the Central Transportation Company (the successor to Woodruff's sleeping car company) and George Pullman, the sleeping car magnate from the Mid-West, gave him the opportunity to gain a substantial shareholding in Pullman's sleeping car business, which proved valuable indeed after the tracks of the Union Pacific and the Central Pacific railroads were joined by means of a golden spike at Promontory Summit near Ogden, Utah in May 1869, establishing America's first transcontinental railroad. In the meantime, he was actively helping Keystone Bridge to secure valuable bridge building contracts across the country, and helping to sell corporate bonds and stocks. And all the time the flow of dividends from his investments grew and grew.

By the autumn of 1867, his business interests meant that he was spending more and more time in New York, and in October of that year, he decided to move there, taking his mother with him. They moved to the St Nicholas Hotel on Broadway, one of the most luxurious hotels in the city at that time, renting a suite of rooms.[23] Andrew opened up a business office nearby. The house in Homewood was taken over by Tom Carnegie, who now married Lucy, the daughter of William Coleman with whom Andrew had invested in the oil business five years earlier.

At the end of 1868, having just turned 33, Andrew Carnegie seated himself at a desk in the sitting room of his suite in the St Nicholas Hotel to take stock of his investments and his life. He made a list of his assets, liabilities and investment income, estimated his net worth as being

---

[23] In 1874, they moved to even more splendid quarters in the Windsor Hotel situated on Fifth Avenue.

$400,000 and calculated his annual income as being about $50,000. He then wrote himself a note, in which he declared that if he took the next two years to carefully arrange his investment affairs, he could maintain this level of income for the rest of his life. And that, he decided, would be sufficient for him and any income he earned beyond that should be spent "for benevolent purposes". Describing the amassing of wealth as a form of idolatry, he resolved that he would "cast aside business forever, except for others." Concerned that the single-minded pursuit of money to which he had so far dedicated his life was degrading his character, possibly irreparably, he also decided that he needed to widen his spiritual and cultural horizons. He would devote the afternoons of the next two years to "instruction and reading systematically", before retiring from business at the age of 35. Thereafter, he would seek an education from Oxford University and make the acquaintance of literary men, paying particular attention to learning the art of public speaking. This, he estimated, would take three years. He would then settle in London, acquire a controlling interest in a newspaper or similar publication, and devote himself to public affairs, and especially to matters concerned with the education and improvement of the poorer classes.

This was quite a remarkable life plan for a self-made and wealthy young man of 33. A willingness to admit that there could exist a point beyond which the accumulation of wealth was not an attractive proposition was (and is) an unusual trait in itself, and was certainly not a common characteristic of the men growing rich during America's Gilded Age. Moreover, this willingness seems not to have been prompted by religious belief or similar motivating factors, but rather something deeply personal in Andrew Carnegie's own character. In the note, we see Andrew openly refer to use of personal wealth for benevolent purposes, with an emphasis upon education and improvement for the poor, something which surely had its roots in the radical views of Andrew's grandfathers, with their emphasis on the self-education and self-improvement of the working classes.

Then too, the note is silent as regards Andrew's ambitions of a personal nature and in particular there is no mention of the possibility of him marrying, or raising a family. In this regard, Andrew was somewhat unusual, for to date he had shown little interest in women other than as relatives or family friends. He enjoyed the company of women, socially at least, but he still lived with his mother. She was the unquestioned lady of his household and for the moment at least, he was content with this and seems to have felt no need to search for an alternative.

He never publicly admitted the existence of the note or discussed its details during his lifetime. There were key aspects of the plan that he failed to satisfy; for example, he never studied at Oxford University[24]. Nor did he ever move permanently to London or retire from business at 35. That aside, the remainder of Andrew's life reflected, to a considerable extent, the principles he laid down that evening in December 1868.

The Panic of 1873

The early 1870s saw Andrew continuing to act as a bond trader, promoting the sale of corporate bonds issued by railroad and bridge companies both in the United States and overseas, particularly in London. He was by all accounts, a very good salesman, and when in London, he frequently used the services of Junius Morgan, an American banker who had moved permanently to London in 1854 and who was now the senior partner of J S Morgan & Co. Morgan's son, J P Morgan, was to have momentous dealings with Carnegie in the future.

Notwithstanding his earlier debacle involving the Dodds' Process, he had retained his interest in the iron and steel business, and had heard with interest the claims associated with a new process for producing steel invented in England by Henry Bessemer. The product of Bessemer's process, Bessemer steel, was highly malleable but strong, with many advantages over the wrought iron which was then being produced in so many of America's foundries. The production of Bessemer steel required specialized converters and (crucially) iron ore low in phosphorus, a fact that was not immediately appreciated when the process was first announced. In 1872, whilst on a trip to England, Andrew visited Bessemer's first steel plant near Sheffield. Recognizing that there was, for the moment, no comparable steel plant in Pittsburgh[25], he and William Coleman (who had independently decided that the future lay with steel, not wrought iron) decided to set up a business to exploit the new process. Coleman located suitable land some twelve miles outside Pittsburgh on which a new steel plant might be built. The land was well situated, having good railroad links (thanks to the nearby Baltimore & Ohio Railroad) and

---

[24] Although he was eventually awarded an honorary doctorate by Oxford.
[25] At that time, America imported much of its steel from Great Britain.

being reasonably close to supplies of coke and iron ore containing little or no phosphorus. Coleman and Andrew were careful as to whom they asked to join them as shareholders in their new business, inviting well regarded businessmen such as David McCandless and David Stewart (Tom Scott's nephew). Harry Phipps, Andrew Kloman and Tom Carnegie also were invited to join the new enterprise. The new firm, called Carnegie, McCandless & Company, was incorporated in November 1872, and Andrew was the largest shareholder. Andrew invited both J Edgar Thomson and Tom Scott to join the venture, but neither invested more than nominal amounts, neither having free funds available at that time.

Andrew Carnegie was naturally hoping to secure large orders for steel tracks from the Pennsylvania Railroad, and with this in mind, shamelessly suggested that the new steel plant should be named after J Edgar Thomson. Thomson, after a little deliberation, agreed, and the new plant soon became known as the "ET Steelworks". By the late summer of 1873, construction of the new plant was well underway and Andrew and his mother, together with Tom and Lucy and various friends went on vacation to the upmarket holiday resort of Cresson Springs in the Allegheny Mountains. It was while he was there that he received disturbing news from New York. On 18th September, Jay Cooke & Co, one of the most important - and most respected - banking houses in New York and Philadelphia, announced that it was bankrupt.

America had enjoyed eight years of astonishing economic growth following the end of the Civil War.[26] This boom now came to an abrupt halt as the failure of Jay Cooke & Co led to collapsing stock prices (forcing the New York Stock Exchange to suspend its business indefinitely for the first time in history) and a string of business and banking failures and the nation entered a period of sharp economic depression. As the news spread across the Atlantic, courtesy of the newly completed trans-Atlantic telegraph cable, prices fell sharply in London and elsewhere in Europe, depressing business activities there as well. The Panic of 1873 (as it inevitably became known) had arrived.

---

[26] This notwithstanding the events of Black Friday, 24th September 1869, when Wall Street suffered the greatest bear panic in its history, thanks at least in part to the gold speculations of Jay Gould and Jim Fisk. Black Friday led to several investment houses suffering considerable losses on Wall Street, and a subsequent period of economic uncertainty.

Andrew's first reaction on hearing the news was to suspend all new investment ventures in the hope of keeping his existing businesses (including the ET plant) afloat. He called an immediate halt to his bond trading activities (he no longer had the time and, in any event, the Panic would have scared away most of his potential customers), sold some stock, and called in his debts whilst seeking to delay payments to his creditors. Somehow, he managed to keep his businesses afloat during the first difficult months following the Panic when so many others failed, although he was obliged for a while to halt construction work at the ET steel plant and to lay off some workers at the Union Iron Mills. By December 1873 for Carnegie at least the worst effects of the Panic were over, and he was able to look cautiously towards the future once again.

The ET plant finally came into operation in the summer of 1875. Despite the harsh economic climate, it was successful from the start, thanks in large part to Andrew's efforts as a steel salesman.[27] Brash, confident, enthusiastic (and, in the eyes of some, arrogant), Andrew Carnegie was remarkably successful in securing orders for the new plant, from the Pennsylvania Railroad and elsewhere, and he had no hesitation in entering into "working relationships" with other would-be competitors in the steel industry so as to minimize the possibility of wealth-damaging competition. By the end of 1875, having only been in operation for four months, the new plant was already showing a healthy profit, with the promise of more to come.

Andrew Carnegie did not, of course, run the new steel plant himself. He had not forgotten the lessons of 1860, when it had become apparent that he lacked the requisite skills to personally lead and motivate workers of the Pennsylvania Railroad, and in any event, he had little desire to spend his days on the floor of the plant, or indeed in Pittsburgh. He instead took care to appoint tough and able lieutenants to carry out such tasks, and to act as both buffer and conduit between himself and the steel workers. Two names in particular stand out in the history of the early days of Carnegie's steel business. The first was William Shinn, who was appointed by Andrew to act as general manager of the plant. An ambitious accountant and businessman who had previously worked as a

---

[27] The new business was also helped by the decision of the US Congress in 1870 to impose high tariffs on imported steel, creating a golden opportunity for US domestic steel manufacturers at the expense of foreign (particularly British) steel makers.

senior official of the Allegheny Railroad, Shinn had a reputation for keeping a close eye on business costs and for ensuring they did not spiral out of control (a particular concern of Andrew Carnegie).

One drawback was that Shinn lacked direct experience of the steel industry and so in order to compensate for this lack, Andrew procured the appointment of William (Bill) Jones as the ET plant's general superintendent. Jones, a Pennsylvanian of Welsh descent, had served in the Union army during the Civil War (and been awarded a captaincy, a title which led to his nickname, "Captain Bill", by which he was almost universally known). More recently, he had recently been employed as a supervisor at the Cambria Iron Works. Passed over for promotion at Cambria, he joined the ET plant and assumed responsibility for the hiring and day-to-day supervision of the plant's workforce. Robust and volatile, Captain Bill did not mince his words, and was prepared to argue with anyone, including Andrew Carnegie himself. If a worker crossed him, he was quite willing to fire him immediately. If Carnegie irritated him too much, he was prepared to resign on the spot (which often happened – indeed, he is said to have carried resignation letters with him at all times just for use in such eventualities), but would always allow Carnegie to persuade him to retract his resignation. He was nevertheless (from Carnegie's perspective) the ideal man to deal with day-to-day matters involving the workforce. Together, Shinn and Captain Bill contributed a great deal to the early success and profitability of the new steel plant.

The Panic of 1873 and its after effects allowed Carnegie to extend his control of Carnegie, McCandless & Co, as several of his fellow shareholders were forced to surrender their investments in the company, and Andrew seized the opportunity to buy their shares. Amongst the shareholders who sold out to him in this way was William Coleman, who found himself financially stretched and (after some initial reluctance) eventually accepted Andrew's offer for his shares in May 1876. Andrew Carnegie was now by far the largest shareholder, and he used the opportunity of Coleman's departure to reorganize the business, dissolving Carnegie, McCandless & Co and establishing the Edgar Thomson Steel Company in its place.[28]

---

[28] Another casualty of the Panic was Andrew Kloman, who unwisely had speculated in a rival iron business (to Carnegie's fury when he learned of it) which ultimately led to Kloman's bankruptcy and eventual departure from both

Tom Scott too ran into difficulties at this time, largely thanks to his enthusiasm for establishing a new transcontinental railroad running from Texas to Pacific . Carnegie had been dubious about its prospects but had agreed to purchase $250,000 worth of shares, upon which he had paid a ten percent deposit. When the Panic struck, Scott called upon him to pay the balance and Andrew did so, but steadfastly refused to advance any more money to the beleaguered railroad or to advance any money to Scott himself. Despite such lack of support, both Scott and the Texas & Pacific ultimately survived the Panic, and Scott eventually sold his holdings to Jay Gould for more than $2 million. The episode marked a turning point in the relationship between Tom Scott and Andrew Carnegie, and whilst they would successfully work together again in the few years remaining before Scott's death in 1881, they would never again be as close as once they had been.

With the Edgar Thomson Steel Company showing the potential of becoming even more successful than his earlier business ventures, and the worst effects of the Panic now behind him, Andrew Carnegie now felt able to relax a little and indulge in some of his other interests. He had by now adopted a working style that he would retain for the rest of his life, which involved whenever possible attending to business matters in the morning, leaving the rest of the day free for other concerns such as reading, writing or socializing. So long as his subordinates retained his confidence (and if they did not, they did not tend to remain his subordinates for long), he was happy to be absent from his businesses, supervising them (via the telegraph, often using code) from a distance. Given that he was usually at least several hours' travel from his principal businesses (and sometimes much further away than that), he managed to keep a very close eye on his business interests, and demanded regular updates of the costs of raw materials, wages, new equipment, plant maintenance and similar matters. He firmly believed that the way to maximize profit was to minimize costs, and ensured that his subordinates put his beliefs into practice.

As far as his workers were concerned, he took a distant, somewhat paternalistic but limited interest in them as a body rather than as

---

Union Iron Mills and Edgar Thomson. Kloman complained bitterly to the end of his days that he had been cheated by Andrew Carnegie, but given that Andrew allowed him to continue as a (highly paid) employee for several years after he signed away his shares, such accusations seem unjustified and unfair.

individuals. In principle, he believed that workers should be paid a fair wage, arguing that such an approach was not only consistent with the social and moral lessons he had learned as a child in Scotland, but also made good business sense, and in this, he was supported by Captain Bill at the ET plant. In practice, he had no hesitation in demanding that workers accept savage wage cuts during economic downturns, or dismissing workers if a way could be found to maintain the same level of productivity with fewer men. Moreover, he had established the ET plant with non-union labour and was initially opposed to the introduction of organized labour there, albeit that he accepted its presence in the Union Iron Mills and he strove to maintain good relations with union leaders.[29] And in the event of a labour dispute, he avoided direct contact with his workers, allowing subordinates such as Captain Bill to engage in the fray and to bear any odium that might result.

Of his interests outside the business arena, the one that principally attracted him in the late 1870s was writing. He had previously submitted articles to journals and newspapers on a variety of topics but now decided it was time to pursue his writing ambitions in earnest. He concluded that his writing skills would be improved if he widened his experience of the world, and what better way to do so than to travel around it? Consequently, in October 1878, he set off abroad once more with his old friend John Vandervoort, leaving his various business interests in the hands of his subordinates.

This time, rather than crossing the Atlantic, Andrew and Vandervoort set off cross-country to San Francisco, where they boarded a steamship bound for Japan, from where they travelled (again in some luxury) to China and then to India, where Andrew and Vandervoort spent a considerable amount of time before eventually heading for Scotland where he met his mother who had in the meantime sailed across the Atlantic to join him. From Scotland, Carnegie and his party headed back to New York, having been absent for nearly a year. Whilst on his travels, he kept detailed notes of his experiences, and after he returned to the United States, he converted them into a book entitled *Around the World*. This was the first of several books that he wrote and once published by

---

[29] He eventually allowed the Amalgamated Association of Iron and Steel Workers to establish a presence at Edgar Thomson, much to Captain Bill's dismay. The decision did much to promulgate the myth that Carnegie was a friend of labour.

Charles Scribner, it was reasonably successful, much to his pleasure. He was delighted to be an "author" and sent copies of his books to his friends and business associates.

The Industrialist

Carnegie returned to find the Edgar Thomson Steel Company flourishing[30], as were many of his other interests, and his dividend income steadily increasing. There were some changes in personnel at Edgar Thomson, for William Shinn resigned shortly after Carnegie returned to the country, but Tom Carnegie moved effortlessly to assume most of Shinn's duties at the ET plant, and Captain Bill continued to supervise its workers, and these events impinged little on Andrew's everyday life. He continued to live in New York with his mother, supervising his businesses at a distance, and by now his reputation of a rich bachelor meant he was frequently invited to all manner of social events. He enjoyed the social whirl, and generally accepted the invitations, particularly enjoying the female company afforded by such occasions. But he remained single.

The first hint that this situation might be susceptible to change came shortly after his return from his trip around the world, when he renewed his acquaintance of a 23 year old woman called Louise Whitfield. Andrew had met Louise's father, a fairly successful businessman in the clothing industry, some years before and had grown friendly with the whole family. Now he began to pay particular attention to Louise (who was 21 years younger than him), and before long he was calling upon her regularly, going riding with her[31] and to all appearances courting her, albeit that her mother in particular had some concerns about the age difference between them.

It was a strange courtship. He was frequently away, either on business or on vacation (sometimes abroad), and despite a stream of letters between them it was often difficult for Louise to gauge exactly what Andrew wanted, or indeed, what she wanted herself. One thing seemed fairly clear, namely that Andrew was extremely unwilling to commit himself matrimonially, and it has generally been accepted that this was due to his relationship with his mother. Whether she was unwilling to see Andrew

---

[30] Indeed, it was at this time that America's production of steel began to surpass that of Great Britain.

[31] Andrew Carnegie had a particular fondness for horses.

married at all, or only unwilling to accept Louise as a potential daughter-in-law is unclear (although Margaret apparently also worried about the age difference), and indeed, it may be that the reluctance was more on Andrew's part rather than Margaret's, for she seems to have raised no objections when Tom married Lucy Coleman. Be that as it may (and it should be noted that Louise for her part always believed that Margaret was opposed to her marrying Andrew), for the immediate future, Andrew and Louise's relationship seemed to be locked in a holding pattern leading nowhere and each of them at various times despaired of it ever developing into anything more permanent.

In the meantime, Andrew had his businesses to attend to. The Edgar Thomson works had been so successful that it now made sense for Carnegie to consolidate all his steel and iron interests in one business, and with this goal in mind, he organized a new company known as Carnegie Brothers & Co. The new company was formed on 1st April 1881, and Andrew Carnegie held more than 50 per cent of the shares, with Tom Carnegie and Harry Phipps each controlling nearly 17 per cent. Such was the demand for the steel from Carnegie's foundries that by the end of its first year of operation, the new company had generated profits in excess of $2 million.

The demand for steel products, and particularly for steel railroad tracks, which had contributed much to Andrew Carnegie's profits in 1881 and 1882, began to fall in the years that immediately followed, as the country experienced an economic downturn, and railroad companies placed fewer orders for replacement tracks, which in turn led to a fall in the price of steel. Carnegie's businesses were fairly well placed to withstand such economic pressures, thanks in part to his financial astuteness, and also to his reputation with union leaders, which helped when Captain Bill sought to persuade workers to accept wage reductions. Other competing steel producers were not so fortunate, several of whom went bankrupt, and this created opportunities for Andrew Carnegie. One such opportunity involved the Homestead steel plant, situated a few miles from the ET plant and owned by the Pittsburgh Bessemer Steel Company, a company that had been established a few years before by several Pittsburgh businessmen with a view to competing with the Carnegies. Unfortunately for them, the Homestead plant had been riven with industrial unrest for several years, culminating in a vicious strike in 1882 that had seriously damaged the financial position of their company. Unable to recover thanks to the 1883 recession, Homestead's owners agreed to sell the plant to Carnegie, under whose ownership it was soon operating smoothly. Andrew ordered that the Homestead plant be converted so as to be able to produce girders and other structural products rather than rail tracks, a decision that proved financially prescient as American architects began to design the first skyscrapers creating a new demand for steel. Within a few years, Andrew was counting the profits from the Homestead plant in millions of dollars.

Andrew Carnegie's ostensible good relations with union leaders, and in particular the leadership of the Amalgamated Association of Iron and Steel Workers did not mean that he was exempt from labour problems. As steel prices continued to fall during the years of 1883, 1884 and 1885, he regularly encouraged Captain Bill to reduce costs and maintain profits by cutting wages and on the whole, workers and union leaders accepted this, albeit with some resistance. In 1885, however, Carnegie and his fellow shareholders sought not only to cut wages but also to lengthen the working day of their men from eight to twelve hours, which would enable them to dispense with the services of an entire shift of workers. This step flew in the face of fifty years of attempts by working men and women to reduce the length of their working day and if implemented would leave them with very little time to do anything other than work, eat and sleep. Moreover, even eight-hour shifts left the men physically exhausted, not to mention that the work was frequently dangerous; twelve-hour shifts would be far worse. Nevertheless, Carnegie was adamant that the step was necessary, and Captain Bill implemented it by the simple method of closing the ET plant for repairs and maintenance, laying off the workforce and then only rehiring workers who were prepared to accept the new terms. Workers were horrified but had little choice other than to accept Carnegie's terms; the price paid by Carnegie and his fellow shareholders was a collapse in workers' morale and palpable industrial unrest. Captain Bill bore the brunt of the workers' hatred for the introduction of twelve-hour shifts as Carnegie hid behind his subordinates. Union leaders fared almost as badly as workers blamed them for failing to protect them and Amalgamated temporarily withdrew their officials from the ET plant.

Steel prices began to recover in early 1886, and whilst Andrew ensured that his workers received a modest pay increase, furnace workers threatened a strike if the working day of eight hours was not restored and promptly made good their threat when their demand was refused. The strike crippled production, and although Captain Bill tried to hire new workers, he (and Carnegie) were eventually forced to accede to the workers' demands and to restore the eight-hour day.

To be fair to Carnegie, several of his competitors operated their iron and steel plants on the basis of twelve hour shifts and operating on an eight hour system represented a competitive disadvantage for Carnegie Brothers. However, it is hard to avoid the conclusion that this whole episode demonstrates a ruthless side to Andrew Carnegie's character. For all his espousing of (some) socialist values and his proclaiming of the need for a just and fair relationship between labour and management (as he did in various press interviews), in practice he regarded the men who worked for him as little more than components in a machine, to be forced to perform at whatever level was necessary to produce the profits he required, regardless of the human cost. It is not a pleasant characteristic.

Aside from industrial problems, 1886 was yet another significant year in Andrew Carnegie's life. His mother, now elderly, had been suffering from increasingly poor health for a number of years, and Andrew spent much of his free time caring for her and worrying about her. Then in October, he himself suffered from an attack of typhoid, which confined him to his bed for over a month and which for a time seriously threatened his life. At almost exactly the same time, Tom Carnegie, whose health had been undermined by years of heavy drinking,[32] succumbed to pneumonia at his home in Homewood and died on 19th October 1886 at the age of 43. A few days later, whilst Andrew lay in his sick bed, Margaret died lying in the room next to him. At a stroke, Andrew had lost his two closest relatives, and the shock sent him into a deep depression and delayed his recovery from typhoid.

The sudden deaths of Margaret and Tom had two immediate consequences for Andrew. The first was that after having finally recovered his health, he now determined to marry Louise Whitfield (they may have been secretly engaged before Margaret's death but it now became official). The wedding took place on 22nd April 1887 and was held in the Whitfields' house in New York, after which the couple departed on honeymoon, first to England (during which time they visited

---

[32] Unlike his brother, Andrew Carnegie rarely drank.

former Prime Minister William Gladstone) and then to Scotland.[33] They spent several months on honeymoon, finally returning to the United States in late October 1887, where they moved into a mansion Andrew purchased on New York's West 51st Street. They were to enjoy a long and happy marriage.

The second consequence of the family tragedies of 1886 was Andrew Carnegie's deepening relationship with Henry Clay Frick, a man who was to play a pivotal role in the development of Andrew's steel empire. Frick, born in 1849 in Westmoreland County, Pennsylvania, had entered the coke manufacturing business with two cousins in 1871, and after a somewhat shaky start thanks to the Panic of 1873, his business had flourished. Coke being essential to the process of steel manufacturing, it was inevitable that Frick would cross paths with the Carnegie brothers, and they first met in 1881. At that time, Frick was looking for outside investors who could supply capital to enable his company to further expand and the Carnegies agreed to invest in Frick's company in exchange for a regular and reliable supply of coke. Initially, the Carnegies acquired 11 per cent of the shares of H C Frick & Co, but over the next few years, they increased their shareholding, until by the late 1880s, Carnegie Steel (as Andrew's combined steel businesses would come to be known) controlled nearly three quarters of the shares.

Tom Carnegie's death meant that Andrew had to find a new reliable lieutenant capable of taking over Tom's duties, and he decided Frick was the man for the job. He offered Frick a two percent interest in Carnegie Brothers, and Frick accepted, and before long had proved himself to be one of Carnegie's ablest executives. Carnegie needed all the able advisers he could get, for a new wave of industrial unrest was about to strike.

Labour unrest had arisen at H C Frick & Co's coke fields in 1886, as workers sought higher wages. Frick, adamantly opposed to wage increases, resisted the workers' demands and was quite prepared to ride out any strike; Carnegie, mindful of the need to keep his steel furnaces

---

[33] Immediately prior to the commencement of the wedding ceremony, they signed a pre-nuptial agreement, under which Louise waived her rights to her soon-to-be husband's estate in exchange for an annual income of $20,000. The agreement noted that Andrew intended to devote the bulk of his estate to benevolent purposes, clear evidence that Louise knew of, and approved, Andrew's plans for his fortune.

operating at full capacity was not. Using his influence as H C Frick & Co's major shareholder, he ordered Frick to settle with the workers and Frick, with some reluctance and against his better judgment did so. The following year (while Carnegie was on honeymoon), the coke workers struck again, and again Frick was ordered to come to terms with the strikers. This time, Frick obeyed but then tendered his resignation and promptly left on vacation to England. On arriving in London, he found a message awaiting him inviting him to join the Carnegies who were now visiting Scotland. After initially refusing the offer, Frick agreed when the invitation was pressed, and he and his wife travelled to Kilgraston, near Perth, where the Carnegies had rented a restored castle. Whilst he was there, Carnegie persuaded him to retract his resignation, and by October 1887, Frick was back in the United States working in Carnegie's interests once again. In January 1889, he was appointed chairman of Carnegie Brothers.

Industrial problems next arose at the ET plant. In 1886, Andrew Carnegie had published an article in which he urged the use of arbitration and sliding wage scales as a means of avoiding industrial strikes. In 1888, at a time of falling steel prices, and concerned that wage costs meant his steel plants were less competitive than those of his rivals elsewhere in the country, he sought to put these ideas into practice by requiring that workers at the ET plant accept a sliding wage scale (which would entail an immediate reduction of pay) and (again) a lengthening of the working day. ET's workers and union leaders from the Knights of Labor (which had swiftly moved to fill the vacuum left when the Amalgamated Association of Iron and Steel Workers had withdrawn their officials from the ET plant) rejected the proposal, and were locked out of the plant. After several months, the two sides had still not reached agreement and eventually Captain Bill hired agents from the Pinkerton National Detective Agency, a private security guard and detective agency, to protect the plant, and prepared to hire non-union labour in place of the striking workers. This was sufficient to demoralize the workers, who by now were suffering financially as a consequence of not having been paid for many weeks. Slowly most of the strikers returned to work, being obliged to accept a sliding scale of wages[34] and a twelve-hour day.

---

[34] Theoretically, a sliding wage scale should have meant that workers' wages could rise as well as fall, depending upon the price of steel in the market. In

Andrew Carnegie and Captain Bill had crushed the Knights of Labor at the ET plant as surely as they had crushed the Amalgamated Association of Iron and Steel Workers in 1885, and for the next few years, the plant would effectively be union-free.

Carnegie's behaviour during the ET lockout had shocked many of the workers. Until then, there had been a widespread belief that the hard line adopted by management during work and pay negotiations was largely a result of Captain Bill, and that Andrew Carnegie was fundamentally on the side of the workers. The lockout of 1888 had clearly shown that Carnegie was capable of being at least as ruthless as his deputy when it came to maintaining the profitability of his steel plants (indeed, possibly more so), and if any worker had any lingering doubts (and there were some), those doubts would be robustly dispelled by events that took place four years later at the Homestead plant.

In June 1889, the pay contracts of Homestead workers (many of whom were represented by Amalgamated or the Knights of Labor) were due to expire, and Carnegie (who as usual was on holiday in Europe) took this opportunity to seek to impose a sliding wage scale on the Homestead workers and hoped that this would allow him to demonstrate the impotence of the union representatives much as he had done at Edgar Thompson. Inevitably, the Homestead workers rejected Carnegie's proposal, and at first it looked as if the previous year's events at Edgar Thomson would be repeated at Homestead, as the plant's managers locked out workers and prepared to hire non-union labour under the protection of Pinkerton agents. On this occasion however, William Abbott, chairman of Carnegie Phipps (which owned the Homestead plant) entered into direct negotiation with the union leaders that swiftly resulted in a settlement being reached. A sliding wage scale would be introduced which would remain in force for three years, but the company would recognize the unions. When the news of the settlement reached Carnegie, he was not happy, but recognized that there was now little he could do to alter its terms. Ironically, the workers believed that the settlement was the result of pressure being brought to bear by Carnegie on his managers, and his reputation with the workers rose accordingly.

---

practice, increased steel production meant that steel prices were likely to continue to fall for the foreseeable future, and Carnegie knew this.

Carnegie blamed Abbott for surrendering to the unions, and decided that henceforth, Frick (who had always advocated taking a firm line on matters of pay and working conditions) should be his primary representative in Pittsburgh.[35] Another man who met with Carnegie's approval at this time was Charles Schwab, then a young man of 27, who eight years earlier had approached Captain Bill for a job and commenced work at the ET plant as an engineer assisting in the construction of new furnaces. Thanks to hard work, enthusiasm, a dedication to self-education, a determination to prove himself invaluable and the fact that he caught the eye of Carnegie himself, Schwab enjoyed rapid promotion and in 1886, he was appointed general superintendent at Homestead. He proved invaluable in getting the Homestead plant back into full production following the ending of the 1889 dispute and Carnegie was pleased.

A few weeks after the end of that dispute tragedy struck, when a blast furnace at the ET plant suddenly exploded on the evening of 26th September 1889. Caught in the blast was Captain Bill, who had been touring the plant, and he died two days later without regaining consciousness. Carnegie moved swiftly to appoint Schwab in his place as general superintendent at Edgar Thomson.

The Homestead Strike and its Aftermath

The Homestead pay settlement negotiated by William Abbott was due to remain in force until the end of June 1892, and Carnegie took some comfort from the fact that Abbott had at least secured three years of relatively peaceful industrial relations at the Homestead plant. This did not however mean that Carnegie's businesses were strife-free during these years, for a series of strikes and lockouts struck his other steel and coke plants during the course of 1891, as workers demanded better pay and (particularly in the case of the ET plant) a shorter working day. In each case, Frick and Schwab threatened to hire unskilled immigrant workers (who would have little choice but to accept the company's terms) to replace the striking workers, and arranged for local sheriffs, posses of armed deputies (many of whom were handpicked by Schwab) and

---

[35] That same year, Frick proposed that Carnegie's various steel businesses, which until then had been divided into two divisions, Carnegie Phipps and Carnegie Brothers, should be reorganized into a single group: Carnegie Steel. Andrew Carnegie agreed and in 1892, Frick was appointed president of Carnegie Steel.

Pinkerton agents to protect the plants and intimidate the workers. All the disputes were called off without any concessions to the workers' key demands, and Carnegie, Frick and Schwab began to think that they could always triumph in any dispute with their workers.

The spring of 1892 saw both Homestead's management and Amalgamated preparing to negotiate a new pay settlement. Amalgamated wished to extend the current settlement for another three years. Andrew Carnegie was, however, determined to use the negotiations as an opportunity to rid his businesses of unions once and for all, arguing that the creation of Carnegie Steel, and the fact that most workers were still not represented by any union, made such a step a necessity. He drew up a note to this effect just before he departed for his usual annual vacation in Europe and confidently left the actual negotiation of the settlement in Frick's hands. Frick met with union representatives in May and presented the company's demands (which included yet another round of wage reductions) as being non-negotiable, demanding acceptance by 24th June. Failure to accept the company's terms, warned Frick, would result in the company no longer dealing with the unions and instead negotiating with workers on an individual basis. Unsurprisingly, these terms were firmly rejected by Amalgamated. Further talks yielded little or no progress, and as the 24th June deadline approached, Frick took steps to secure the services of 300 Pinkerton agents and arranged for the Homestead plant to be protected by high fences and powerful searchlights. The workers dubbed the fortifications "Fort Frick".

The workers, still convinced that Carnegie was fundamentally on their side, tried to contact him, but he remained mysteriously unavailable somewhere in Scotland. On 28th June, two days before the existing settlement was due to expire, Frick gave orders to begin to shut Homestead down and by the end of the next day, the lockout was complete. Frick was confident that Homestead's workers would accept the company's demands, not least because Homestead was a company town and there was little or no alternative work available, but on the afternoon of 29th June, nearly 3,000 Homestead workers met and agreed to support the union's stance. Having heard of the imminent arrival of the Pinkerton agents, they organized teams of men with the intention of themselves guarding the plant and preventing anyone from entering it until the dispute was resolved, and they foiled several attempts by sheriffs' deputies to enter.

The Pinkerton agents, armed with pistols and Winchester rifles, were due to arrive in Homestead by barge on the Monongahela River at midnight on 5th July. News of their arrival preceded them, and when their barges arrived, they were met by thousands of striking workers and sympathizers, many of whom were also armed. Strike leaders warned the Pinkerton men not to disembark, but their leader, Captain Frederick Heinde, disregarded the warning and began to stride down the gangplank. A striking worker stepped forward to stop him, and he and Heinde struggled. Several shots suddenly rang out, one of them striking Heinde in the hip. This was the signal for more shooting from both sides, during the course of which three workers were killed and many more injured. Several Pinkerton agents were also injured (one of whom later died) and, outnumbered, the agents retreated into their barges, where the furious crowd kept them pinned down for hours, threatening to kill them all. Eventually, strike leaders managed to regain a modicum of control over the situation, and agreed to a plea from the now desperate Pinkerton agents that they should be allowed to surrender to the local sheriff and be held on charges of suspicion of murder.[36] As they were escorted away to the local opera house to await the arrival of the sheriff, they suffered merciless beatings from the still infuriated crowd and their barges were burnt, all of which was observed by newspaper reporters. Within hours, news of Homestead had flashed around the world.

For the next few days, the striking workers effectively controlled the town of Homestead and its steel plant. Finally and belatedly, on 12th July, Governor Robert Pattison sent a division of the Pennsylvania National Guard to restore law and order. Outnumbered and outgunned, the strikers and their supporters had little choice but to back down and within a few days, the Homestead plant was operational again, this time using new employees hired from elsewhere. The company announced that striking workers could reapply for their old jobs, although some, principally the strike ringleaders, were blacklisted. One condition for returning to work was that the workers had to agree that the plant would be union-free. Only a few initially responded to this invitation, but as the winter approached, more and more did so, compelled by the simple necessity of earning a living. Amalgamated finally and officially called the strike off on 21st November 1892.

---

[36] The Pinkerton agents were never indicted of any crime as a result of the events at Homestead.

However, before that happened, there was one further drama to be played out. On 23rd July, whilst Frick was in conversation with one of his subordinates, John Leishman, a young man called Alexander Berkman burst into Frick's office, pulled out a revolver and shot two bullets, wounding Frick in the neck and the back. Leishman and Frick managed to wrestle Berkman to the floor before he could fire again, but Berkman managed to pull a knife and further wound Frick in the hip and leg before assistance belatedly arrived in the form of Frick's clerks who had been working in the outer office.

Berkman was overpowered and arrested by the police, whilst Frick was hurried to the local hospital, where the doctors operated (without anaesthetic) to remove the bullets, after which he was sent home to recuperate. Frick recovered rapidly and within days was back at work, telegraphing Carnegie that he was fit for duty.[37]

It was later learned that Alexander Berkman, who had recently emigrated to the United States from Lithuania (then part of the Russian Empire), was a self-proclaimed anarchist who had fled Russia to avoid the attentions of the Tsar's police. He had no connection with anyone at Homestead, and appears to have decided to kill Frick of his own volition after having read reports of the Homestead strike in the newspapers. In due course, he was found guilty of attempted murder and sentenced to 21 years imprisonment, although he in fact only served thirteen before being paroled. Ultimately, he was expelled from the United States as an undesirable alien in 1919.

The Homestead strike cost Carnegie an estimated $2 million[38] but the power of the unions in his steel plants was finally broken. The rest of

---

[37] Tragically, whilst Frick recovered from the shooting, his baby son, who had been born prematurely only two weeks earlier, died on 3rd August.

[38] Nevertheless, Carnegie Steel's profits for 1892 exceeded $4 million. Carnegie Steel's profits would rise to $7 million by 1897, notwithstanding a sharp recession in 1893 that lasted four years and a continuing fall in the price of steel, thanks in part to Carnegie being able to retain a firm grip on wage costs, a task that must have been made easier by a lack of effective union representation. After 1897, as the economy recovered, Carnegie Steel's profits began to rise faster than ever, reaching $11 million in 1898, $21 million in 1899 and $40 million in 1900. It must be added that Carnegie's workers did not benefit from this remarkable financial performance; thanks to the introduction of the sliding wage scale, their wages were determined by reference to the price of steel (which

America's steel industry soon followed Carnegie's lead in dispensing with recognized unions and henceforth there would be no effective union representation in any of America's steel plants until the days of Franklin D. Roosevelt.

There was much public criticism of the events at Homestead, both in the United States and abroad. Much of the blame for the tragedy initially fell on Frick's shoulders (although news of his attempted assassination markedly lessened criticism of him), but what the press wanted to know most of all were the views of Andrew Carnegie. But Carnegie was still in Scotland on vacation at an undisclosed location. Eventually, he was tracked down by a New York reporter and issued a statement to the effect that he was no longer in day-to-day control of his business, had no wish to interfere in the management's activities and that management's handling of the situation at Homestead had his "full approbation and sanction". Such an attitude did not read well in the nation's newspapers and for once, the press was disapproving of Carnegie, to such an extent that his reputation as a friend of the working man never fully recovered. Nevertheless, he left affairs at Homestead in Frick's hands and elected to stay out of the United States until January 1893, a decision that did nothing to lessen the continuing criticism of Carnegie Steel and Andrew himself in the press.

Carnegie Steel

1893 saw the advent of another economic recession that lasted several years. Despite this, Andrew and Louise spent much of their time abroad, often in England and Scotland, but also visiting Europe, and in 1894 they toured Egypt, a popular destination for wealthy Americans and Europeans. Whilst they were away, Frick continued to run Carnegie Steel in Pittsburgh and with the enthusiastic and efficient assistance of Charles Schwab, who by now had responsibility for day-to-day operations at both Edgar Thomson and Homestead[39], he ensured that Carnegie Steel remained profitable. By the mid-1890s, Carnegie Steel was producing over a quarter of America's steel.

---

continued to fall much as Carnegie had predicted) rather than Carnegie Steel's rising profits.

[39] Where he continued to pursue cost-cutting measures with a vengeance, to Carnegie's satisfaction.

Andrew, still Carnegie Steel's largest shareholder by far, continued to control his companies from a distance as he had always done. Over time, though, Frick began to resent Carnegie's long-distance interference in day-to-day affairs, particularly when it involved H C Frick & Co, the coke business that Frick had established, and which in his heart of hearts he still regarded as "his" business, but whose principal shareholder was now Carnegie Steel. Carnegie for his part, concerned that Frick's loyalties were divided between the steel and coke businesses, wanted Frick to step aside from the management of H C Frick & Co and to concentrate solely on Carnegie Steel, something that Frick adamantly refused to contemplate. The two men also disagreed about the price at which H C Frick & Co supplied coke to Carnegie Steel (a sensitive matter for Andrew, who was always extremely conscious of the need to ensure a cheap and reliable supply of fuel for his furnaces) and about a possible merger between H C Frick & Co and one of its rivals, something Andrew was keen to pursue against Frick's wishes. By the end of 1894, relations between the two men had grown sufficiently tense for Frick to write to Carnegie announcing his intention of resigning from Carnegie Steel in January 1895, a resignation that, after a fairly acrimonious exchange of correspondence, was accepted.

John Leishman, who had helped to wrestle Alexander Berkmann to the ground during the abortive attempt on Frick's life in 1892, replaced Frick as president of Carnegie Steel.[40] This did not however mean the end of Frick's involvement with Carnegie Steel. He retained a substantial interest in the company (amounting to 6 per cent of the outstanding shares) and with Andrew Carnegie's approval he agreed to serve as chairman of the board of managers, where he remained involved in planning the company's long term strategies.

---

[40] Leishman did not survive long in his post. In early 1896, Carnegie discovered that Leishman was not only speculating in pig iron, and incurring considerable personal debts in the process (something Andrew regarded as reprehensible, particularly bearing in mind the similar episode involving Andrew Kloman a few years earlier), but had also purchased two bankrupt furnaces without appropriate authorisation. By the end of 1897, Leishman had been removed from office, and replaced as president by Charles Schwab. Leishman went on to have a distinguished career in the US diplomatic service, serving at various times as American Ambassador to Switzerland, to Turkey, to Italy and to Germany. He died in 1924.

One major problem facing Carnegie Steel in the 1890s was the need to ensure regular and reliable supplies of high quality iron ore at reasonable prices. A decade earlier, vast deposits of iron ore had been discovered in the Mesabi Range in Minnesota. At the time Andrew Carnegie, convinced that iron ore would remain cheap, had shown little interest in obtaining a financial stake in the new finds; indeed, he had (initially) turned down an opportunity to enter into a joint venture with just that aim in mind, although he had eventually changed his mind and so was not totally excluded from the Mesabi iron ore bonanza. Nevertheless, ownership of much of the Mesabi ore fell into the hands of the Merritt family, local pioneers in the area; however, they ran into financial difficulties in 1893, and had to be rescued by none other than John D Rockefeller of Standard Oil, who invested in their business. In time, and thanks largely to the advice of his close colleague Frederick T Gates, who would later play a pivotal role in Rockefeller's philanthropic activities, Rockefeller gradually extended his interest in the Merritt's iron ore business until by 1895, he effectively owned vast tracts of ore-bearing land in the Mesabi Range, together with a railroad and a fleet of ships on the Great Lakes which would allow him to transport his newly acquired ore to customers. At a stroke, Rockefeller controlled much of the country's supply of iron ore. The press speculated that Rockefeller was about to enter the steel business, and Andrew Carnegie realized he had made a mistake.

Andrew Carnegie had always been somewhat dismissive of John D Rockefeller – he persistently misspelled Rockefeller's name, Reckafellow or Rockafellow being typical examples – notwithstanding that Rockefeller had made his fortune before Carnegie had made his, but he now realized that he would either have to reach some form of accommodation with Rockefeller or face the possibility of a ruinous business war with someone whose financial resources and business skills were even greater than his. Fortunately for Andrew Carnegie, John D Rockefeller was reaching the stage in his life when he was contemplating retiring from active business, and he had little taste for a fight. In December 1896, Carnegie and Rockefeller reached an agreement whereby Carnegie Steel would purchase all the ore produced by Rockefeller's mines at a rate of 25 cents per ton, which was below the current market rate. In exchange, Carnegie Steel agreed that all the iron ore it acquired from the Lake Superior area (whether from Rockefeller's mines or elsewhere) would be transported on Rockefeller's railroads and ships, and that it would not seek to acquire any more mines in the Mesabi Range. Rockefeller similarly undertook not to establish any steel mills of his own.

It was a good deal for both sides, and for Carnegie it ensured a reliable low cost supply of iron ore for his furnaces. Typically, once the dust had settled, Carnegie decided that he had obtained the best of the bargain, and claimed as much publicly in 1912 before a congressional committee. "Don't you know," he said, "it does my heart good to think I got ahead of John D Rockefeller on a bargain." In fact, Carnegie had been seriously concerned that Rockefeller was about to enter the steel business on a massive scale, and was relieved to discover that Rockefeller had no appetite for a contest.

Skibo Castle and the Gospel of Wealth

Andrew Carnegie was 62 in 1897. He and Louise had now been married for ten years, and although in many ways they made an odd-looking couple (not least because of the age difference, and the fact that Louise was taller than Andrew),[41] it was nevertheless a happy relationship. To date, however, they had not produced any children, and as Louise approached her fortieth birthday, it may well have seemed that this was destined always to be the case. However, in the autumn of 1896, Louise found herself pregnant, and on 30th March 1897, she gave birth to a daughter, Margaret, who was to be the Carnegie's only child. At the time, Andrew was recovering from a serious bout of pleurisy, and his convalescence took several months. Nevertheless, Margaret's birth prompted the Carnegies to decide that they needed to purchase their own home in Scotland which they could use during the summer vacations; until now they had rented estates whenever they had visited Scotland, frequently Cluny Castle in the Cairngorms, which they both adored.

Andrew tried to buy Cluny from its owner, the Chief of the Clan Macpherson, but he refused to sell his ancestral home. Consequently, the Carnegies spent much of the summer of 1897 searching for a Scottish highland estate they could buy for themselves. They eventually identified Skibo Castle, near the town of Dornoch in the county of Sutherland as being the most suitable for their needs. The property comprised an estate of several thousand acres, with spectacular views of the Highlands and

---

[41] Andrew Carnegie was only five feet two inches tall, about which he was always sensitive, and in photographs, he invariably tried to arrange his pose so as to disguise the fact.

Donoch Firth; however the castle itself was falling into disrepair, and would need considerable (and very expensive) work before it could be considered fully habitable. Moreover, its last owner had been declared bankrupt and the estate was now in the hands of the trustee-in-bankruptcy. Nevertheless, the Carnegies agreed initially to rent the property for a season, and then in the summer of 1898, purchased it and set about the substantial task of renovating and enlarging the castle and the estate. Fortunately, Carnegie's profits from Carnegie Steel meant that he had the funds to pay for the costly and luxurious renovations, which would take several years to complete, and once the task was done, it was generally agreed that Skibo Castle was a most suitable residence for one of the richest men in the world.[42]

Business interests and family life were not the only matters that occupied Andrew during the 1880s and 1890s. He continued to write and enjoyed the company of other writers, and of intellectuals generally, whenever he could. He was particularly impressed by the work of Herbert Spencer, an English sociologist who proposed a philosophical theory in which he tried to apply scientific principles, and in particular evolution, in order to explain the development of human societies and cultures, notwithstanding that the theory of evolution was and is most ill-suited to such an application. Spencer (essentially) argued that humans continually compete with each other for money and power, and that inevitably some succeed and others fail, and that those who succeed in amassing great fortunes are simply examples of the "survival of the fittest" (a phrase which Spencer popularized). Andrew Carnegie found this reasoning very persuasive.

One of the (many) problems with Spencer's philosophy was that it could be used as an argument against providing any form of assistance for the poor and needy; after all, if Spencer was right, the poor were poor simply because they were unfit to be rich, and there was therefore little point in helping, for example, the unemployable because any attempt to do so would be to seek to resist an inevitable natural law and thus be doomed to failure. Similarly, Spencer's theories could be used to justify almost any business practice, no matter how disreputable or immoral, so long as it

---

[42] A few months after they acquired Skibo Castle, the Carnegies also purchased a plot of land (an entire city block in fact) on Fifth Avenue in New York, upon which they built themselves a new mansion, which replaced the mansion on West 51st Street as their New York home.

succeeded in generating money. It was also only a very small step from Spencer's ideas to such appalling concepts as racial cleansing and eugenics (although to be fair, Spencer did not pursue this line of reasoning as far as some of his disciples did). Nevertheless, Spencer's theories were very popular indeed with many of the millionaires of the Gilded Age, for whom it provided an instant justification of their business practices and themselves.

Carnegie sought to incorporate many (but not all) of Spencer's ideas into his own thinking, which he expressed in a stream of articles and books, and in particular, in his book "*Gospel of Wealth*". The *Gospel* was originally a series of Carnegie's articles in which he set out his views on the political and economic systems of the day, sought to explain and justify the creation of great personal fortunes and (crucially) advised how such fortunes could and should be applied for the improvement of human society. Carnegie justified the existence of great fortunes in the hands of the fortunate few by arguing (directly from Spencer) that such men deserved their wealth, that they had rare skills which they were applying for the good of the whole community in accordance with natural laws, and that the alternative would be "universal squalor". However, he also believed that the wealthy were, in effect, simply the trustees of their wealth, and that they were duty bound to apply their wealth to philanthropic projects that would benefit the community as a whole. He disapproved of those who left fortunes to their children, observing that such inheritances were often a burden for the next generation.

International affairs also occupied much of his attention. He had become convinced that Britain and the United States would one day be reunited (in the form of a republic) together with other English-speaking countries such as Canada, New Zealand and Australia, and that this was the best and only hope for Britain if she was to survive in the world. He expressed these, and other similar ideas, in his book entitled *Triumphant Democracy*, which attracted a great deal of attention (albeit not all favourable). He was vocal in his opinion that the best way to deal with international disputes was by way of arbitration, and considered his views vindicated in 1899 when a border dispute between Venezuela and the British colony of British Guiana (in which the United States had become embroiled as a result of the US Government's assertion that the dispute involved the Monroe Doctrine) was finally and peaceably resolved by adopting this approach. And he was a firm anti-imperialist, objecting to America's imperial adventures (such as the Spanish-American War of 1898[43]) as much as he objected to the colonial empires of the European nations.

The Departure of Frick

In the meantime, another dispute with Frick was looming. In 1898, Andrew began to contemplate the possibility of selling his shares in Carnegie Steel if a suitable buyer could be found. In response, Frick suggested that H C Frick & Co and Carnegie Steel should be formally merged, and then sold together, either to the other shareholders or to an outside purchaser if one could be found. Carnegie originally expressed interest in the proposal, but after thinking about it further, he eventually vetoed the idea, to Frick's irritation. Then, a few months later, in March 1899, Frick was approached by William H Moore, a Chicago industrialist acting on behalf of a syndicate of mid-West businessmen who specialized in merging industrial companies. Moore and the syndicate wanted to buy Carnegie Steel (for $250 million) and H C Frick & Co (for $70 million). Carnegie agreed to allow Frick and Harry Phipps to act as his intermediaries in the resulting negotiations, but insisted that the syndicate pay him a non-refundable option price, eventually agreed at $1.17 million, which Carnegie could retain if the deal was not finalized within a specified period. The syndicate itself could only raise $1 million, and Frick and Phipps themselves provided the additional $170,000. Frick and Phipps had their own reasons for being so helpful; unbeknownst to Carnegie, they had been promised a bonus of $5 million by the syndicate if the sale completed satisfactorily.

Unfortunately for Frick and Phipps, one of the syndicate members died suddenly, meaning the deal could not proceed as planned. Carnegie refused to extend the option period despite Frick's request that he do so and furthermore, made it clear that he had no intention of refunding the $170,000 provided by Frick and Phipps, much to their dismay and anger. Carnegie's refusal to refund the $170,000 may have been due to his discovery of the $5 million bonus payment which Frick and Phipps had negotiated for themselves, which did nothing to improve the relationship between Carnegie and his fellow shareholders.

---

[43] As a result of which the United States belatedly but enthusiastically acquired colonies of her own.

Matters became even more tense when yet another dispute erupted in October 1899 over the price at which H C Frick & Co was willing to provide coke to Carnegie Steel. Considering that Andrew Carnegie was the largest shareholder in Carnegie Steel, and that Carnegie Steel controlled a majority of the shares in H C Frick & Co, this was a fight that Frick could not realistically, in the long run, hope to win. Nevertheless, the disagreement continued to fester over the next few months, further poisoning the relationship between Frick and Carnegie, and threatening to embroil the other shareholders. By early December, it was clear that Carnegie and Frick could no longer work together, and on 5th December 1899, Frick finally resigned from the board of Carnegie Steel.

This did not resolve the dispute over the price of coke. Carnegie was convinced that he had reached an agreement with Frick that coke would be supplied at the rate of $1.35 a ton for a five year period, a price which was well below the price of coke in the open market. That agreement, however, had never been set down on paper, and Frick argued that it did not constitute a binding contract. Carnegie now set out to use the power arising from the fact that Carnegie Steel controlled a majority of the shares in H C Frick & Co, arranging for the coke company's board to be reorganized, with the result that following the reorganization, Carnegie controlled five of its seven seats. In early January 1900, the newly constituted board of H C Frick & Co voted five to two to supply coke to Carnegie Steel at the rate of $1.35 per ton.

At the same time, Carnegie was also taking steps to remove Frick as a shareholder in Carnegie Steel. In order to achieve this, Carnegie sought to make use of an agreement – the "Ironclad Agreement" – that the shareholders (or "partners" as Carnegie often referred to them) in Carnegie Steel had entered into several years earlier, whereby any shareholder could be forced to sell his shares back to the company at their book value (that is, at a fraction of their true market value) with the consent of three quarters of the shareholders controlling three quarters of the shares.[44] There was some doubt as to whether the latest version of the Ironclad Agreement was legally effective as not every shareholder had signed it; nevertheless, after one more fruitless meeting with Carnegie

---

[44] Carnegie, as the largest shareholder, was alone immune from any danger of being expelled from the company under the Ironclad Agreement.

(during which Frick became so angry that he came close to physically assaulting Carnegie), an emergency meeting of the board of Carnegie Steel passed a resolution which purportedly transferred Frick's shares to the company, valuing those shares at a book value of approximately $6 million.

Frick unsurprisingly protested vigorously and he was not without his supporters amongst the other shareholders. Quite apart from the possibility that if Carnegie were to be allowed to expel Frick in this fashion, they might well find themselves the next to be ousted, the valuation of Frick's shares was manifestly unfair. Any independent valuation of the company would have valued Carnegie Steel as being worth at least $250 million (and possibly much more), meaning that Frick's 6 per cent shareholding was worth at least $15 million (and Frick publicly claimed his shareholding was worth in excess $16 million). Harry Phipps in particular felt that Frick was being ill-treated, and made no secret of his views.

Carnegie was in no mood to compromise, and so Frick sought a legal injunction in the courts preventing Carnegie Steel from expelling him from the company. Moreover, he did so in the full blaze of publicity, something that Andrew Carnegie may not have anticipated. The press gleefully published details of Carnegie Steel's profitability, details that were not appreciated by the workers working twelve-hour shifts in Carnegie's steel plants. Nor were Carnegie's fellow industrialists happy at the spotlight being shone onto the financial operations of American industry generally. Such was the adverse publicity that Carnegie was eventually obliged to agree in March 1900 to a proposal to consolidate Carnegie Steel and H C Frick & Co's steel and coke businesses under a single holding company, the Carnegie Company, capitalized at $320 million. Frick's interests in the steel and coke businesses were recognized, and valued in excess of $31 million, in exchange for which Frick agreed to drop his legal suit. Carnegie's share of the consolidated business was valued at more than $175 million.[45]

With the settlement of the legal dispute, Frick and Carnegie ceased to have any dealings with one another and they never spoke again. Frick left Pittsburgh and settled in Massachusetts and New York, where he

---

[45] Harry Phipps now almost completely retired from the business. His share of the combined business was valued at approximately $35 million.

assembled the art collection now known as the Frick Collection. He died from heart disease in 1919.

Andrew Carnegie was 65 in 1900, but despite all his musings two years earlier about selling his shares, he initially showed little sign of retiring from the steel business following Frick's departure. On the contrary, the arrival in the late 1890s of new giant competitor firms such as American Steel & Wire, and the Federal Steel Company, the latter having been organized by Wall Street banker J Pierpoint Morgan, the son of Junius Morgan with whom Carnegie had carried out so many profitable bond trades back in the late 1860s and early 1870s, heightened Carnegie's sense of competition. He made it clear that he was prepared to cut costs and prices and do whatever else was necessary to maintain his market share, and aggressively sought to stamp his influence on all areas of the steel industry. J P Morgan heard of Carnegie's activities with mounting displeasure, for he was a firm advocate of introducing consolidation and order into America's steel industry and the elimination of wasteful competition.

Morgan knew that it would be very expensive, and possibly quite futile, to attempt to compete directly with Carnegie, but hoped that Carnegie might be amenable to selling his shares if he received the right offer. He also learned that Charles Schwab believed that consolidation of the steel industry would help it to avoid dangers such as overproduction and enable it to compete more effectively with foreign rivals, views that were very similar to Morgan's own. Morgan therefore initiated informal talks with Schwab to discuss how the consolidation of the steel industry might be achieved, talks of which Carnegie was initially unaware.

The Carnegie Company was key to Morgan's plans for consolidation, but Schwab could not confirm that Carnegie would be willing to sell to Morgan. Morgan told Schwab to go to Carnegie and find out, but before he did so, Schwab asked Louise Carnegie for her advice. Louise had wanted Andrew to retire for several years and she urged Schwab to raise the matter with him, but only after they had played a round of golf, now one of Andrew Carnegie's favoured pastimes. Schwab carefully let Andrew win the round, and then raised the matter with him over lunch, telling him that Morgan had asked that Andrew name his own price. Carnegie considered the matter, and told Schwab his price: $400 million (later increased to $480 million). Carnegie's share would be worth more than $225 million, and he insisted that it be paid to him in the form of 5% gold bonds.

Morgan accepted the price and terms without quibbling, and the two men met in late February 1901 to finalize the details of the deal. The meeting lasted only a few minutes, and as it ended, Morgan shook Carnegie's hand and congratulated him on becoming the richest man in the world.

Morgan's consolidation plans proceeded rapidly after that, and in early March, he was able to announce the formation of the United States Steel Corporation, the world's first billion-dollar company. And with that, Andrew Carnegie's steel empire vanished into history.

The Years of Philanthropy

His steel empire may have gone, but Andrew Carnegie was still alive and as energetic as ever. Considering that he had dedicated much of his boyhood and all of his adult life up to that point to his business interests and the creation of wealth, he adapted remarkably well to the change in his life engendered by the creation of US Steel. Now was the time when he would be free at last to fulfill his true dreams, to demonstrate in practice the truth of the philosophical principles that he had been writing about for more than twenty years. Now was the time for him to dedicate himself to philanthropy in earnest.

Andrew had been involved in philanthropic enterprises prior to 1901. As early as 1874, for example, he had donated £5,000 in order to build public baths in Dunfermline, and two years later offered the town a further £5,000 to help to fund a public library. In 1881 he had established a small library for workers at the ET plant, which was later extended to include public baths, a gymnasium and an art gallery, and in due course he established "reading rooms" for workers at his other steel plants. In 1890, he had funded Carnegie Hall in New York. And in the years leading to the close of the nineteenth century, as his profits from Carnegie Steel rose dramatically (and particularly after the Homestead Strike), he had paid for the construction of a number of free libraries in towns and cities in both America and Britain.

Yet, no matter how generous Carnegie seemed to be, the reality is that prior to the creation of US Steel, he donated only a small percentage of the profits generated by his various businesses. This was largely due to his strict rule that the bulk of those profits should be reinvested rather than paid out as dividends; a rule that many of his fellow shareholders had sought to persuade him to modify, but with only limited success. Prior to 1901, Andrew Carnegie simply did not have large amounts of money that he could apply to philanthropic purposes, and this meant that on occasion he was forced to turn down requests for charitable assistance. This changed following the sale of Carnegie Steel. Now he had the resources to apply to philanthropic causes on a grand scale.

He began by allocating $1 million to maintain the libraries he had established at his former steel works. At the same time, he established a relief fund (worth $4 million) intended to provide support for injured steel workers, and for the families of steel workers who were killed during the course of their duties, and to provide pensions for (worthy) long serving workers after their retirements. He further donated over $5 million to New York City to build 65 branches of the New York Public Library[46], so many in fact that some were still being built in the 1920s. The donations were announced shortly before the Carnegies departed on their annual pilgrimage to Scotland in 1901, attracting favourable comments in the newspapers, and articles which contrasted Andrew's generosity with that of many of his fellow millionaires, much to Andrew's satisfaction. The press coverage also led to a deluge of begging letters, a problem that would plague him for the rest of his life.

He had only just begun. The next few years saw a staggering number of charitable bequests. In 1902, for example, he established a trust (to which he ultimately contributed $10 million) to improve the facilities at several Scottish universities, and to provide financial assistance for poor students. The same year, he agreed to establish the Carnegie Institution of Washington, intended to encourage "pure" scientific research for the betterment of mankind by providing funding for scientists, to which he eventually donated over $22 million. The Institution would go on to fund a wide range of scientific projects and institutions throughout America and the world, including the establishment of the astronomical observatory on Mount Wilson in California, in Carnegie's day home to the world's largest telescope, and still one of the most important observatories in the world today. In 1904, he established his "Hero Fund" (with an initial endowment of $5 million), intended to provide financial support (and a medal bearing his likeness) for civilian heroes (and their families) who demonstrated bravery in seeking to help their

---

[46] 67 were eventually built, many of which are still in existence today.

fellow citizens in life-and-death situations. The following year, he donated $10 million to establish the Carnegie Foundation for the Advancement of Teaching to provide pensions for teachers. And there were many, many other bequests and donations.

However, it was the Carnegie free libraries that most caught the attention of the public, not least because it was the aspect of Andrew Carnegie's generosity that they were most likely to encounter personally. During his lifetime, he funded the building and maintenance of over 2,500 free libraries throughout the English-speaking world, at a cost of over $50 million.[47] Nearly 1,700 libraries were built in the United States, and 660 in Britain and Ireland. Over 100 were built in Canada, 17 in New Zealand and others in Australia, South Africa and the West Indies. With some exceptions, Carnegie usually paid for the building of the libraries themselves, but insisted that the local authorities provide the funds needed to purchase the books, pay the library staff and meet the costs of maintenance, for he believed that subsequent support from the community was as important as the initial bequest. (Occasionally, the local authorities did not agree to these terms. In 1881, for example, Andrew offered to contribute $250,000 to Pittsburgh to help to fund a public library there, but the city's authorities turned the offer down because they doubted they had the legal power to raise the funds necessary to maintain the library once it had been built. Carnegie did not hold a grudge against the city for this refusal; in due course, he would establish the magnificent Carnegie Institute of Pittsburgh.) As might be expected, Andrew Carnegie received much praise for his libraries (public resentment over the Homestead Strike was now fading rapidly, but it would never be completely forgotten) but also a surprising degree of criticism. Some criticised him for a lack of generosity in only paying for the actual construction of the libraries, whilst others objected that his philanthropy was really only an (expensive) exercise in vanity and self-publicity. Such allegations are unfair. Certainly, Andrew Carnegie was a man who enjoyed praise, and certainly he was not averse to the coupling of his name with his charitable endeavours. Throughout his life, however, he saw it as his duty to proclaim and demonstrate the principles of the

---

[47] He also enthusiastically donated organs to churches; a generosity that reflects his early love for church music. Eventually, he donated 7,689 organs, at a cost of over $6 million. He also ensured that a magnificent organ was built at Skibo Castle, where it was played regularly.

responsible disposal of wealth by the wealthy that he had espoused in the *Gospel* and elsewhere, and he saw the use of his name as a means of furthering this end. Furthermore, many communities were proud to be chosen as recipients of Carnegie's largesse, and wanted their free libraries (and concert halls and schools and so on) to bear his name.

Such was the scale of Andrew Carnegie's charitable donations that he could not possibly have dealt personally with all the details of the bequests, or the torrent of requests for assistance which now pursued him wherever he went. Fortunately, he did not have to. Although at first he did not organize his philanthropic interests in the regimented and structured way adopted by John D Rockefeller when he began to give away his fortune, Carnegie nevertheless found it necessary to maintain a team of secretaries and assistants, lead by his personal secretary James Bertram in order to deal with the minutiae of his philanthropy. Between them, Carnegie and Bertram devised a system to help them to screen out all but the most deserving appeals for assistance, and in practice, Carnegie trusted Bertram to deal with the day-to-day matters whilst only concerning himself with the larger issues, or projects which were particularly close to his heart. He still managed to deal with most of his work in the morning, leaving the rest of his day free for other activities.

However, such was the magnitude of his wealth that he found it increasingly difficult to give away his fortune faster than it multiplied. Indeed, by one estimate in 1912, after a decade of continuous philanthropy, his net worth was still well over $200 million. Eventually, he was forced to concede that he was unlikely to be able personally to dispose of all his fortune in a sensible and effective manner before he died, and so in 1911, he organized the Carnegie Corporation of New York, which he eventually endowed with $125 million, whose purpose it would be to continue his philanthropy after his death. It continues to do so to this day.

The Advocate of Peace

Philanthropy was not the only matter that occupied Andrew Carnegie's days in the years following 1901. In 1903, he became the Laird of Pittencrieff, a feudal estate bordering Dunfermline. Pittencrieff was important to Carnegie, for his mother's family (and all descendants, including Andrew himself) had been banned from entering it some fifty years earlier owing to a dispute between the Morrisons and the owners of the estate at that time, the Hunt family. Now the Hunt family had fallen into debt and Carnegie took great delight in buying the estate from them. He had no intention of living there – Skibo Castle was and would forever remain his Scottish home – but he revelled in the title of Laird. In due course, he would donate most of the park to Dunfermline for the benefit of its citizens, but retained a lifetime interest sufficient so he could continue to enjoy his title. He remained the Laird until he died.

He also maintained his interest in public affairs, having supported President McKinley's bid for re-election in 1900, notwithstanding his frequently expressed opinion that much of William McKinley's foreign policy represented the naked imperialism to which he was firmly opposed. To Carnegie's eyes, McKinley might be bad but his Democratic opponent, William Jennings Bryan, whom Carnegie had initially been inclined to support because of Bryan's anti-imperialist views but whose economic policies Carnegie feared might lead to class warfare, was far worse. Following McKinley's assassination in 1901, he transferred his support to McKinley's successor Theodore Roosevelt, at first cautiously, and then with growing enthusiasm as Roosevelt demonstrated a willingness to use the power and influence of the United States to promote international peace.[48] Roosevelt, for his part, found Carnegie's habit of rendering unwanted advice irritating, but recognized the value of the support of a man who was increasingly being hailed as a great philanthropist, and moreover, was still one of the richest men in America.

Carnegie continued to support arbitration as the means of solving international disputes, and after an initial period of hesitation, agreed to help to fund a peace palace at The Hague in the Netherlands, where an international court of arbitration had been established in 1899. He firmly believed that he had a personal role to play in securing world peace, and sponsored and spoke at a series of world peace conferences. In 1905, he gave a speech to students at St Andrews University (of which he had been appointed Rector in 1901) in which he proposed a League of Peace,

---

[48] Andrew Carnegie's approval of President Roosevelt was not, however, unqualified. In particular, he did not support Roosevelt's actions in 1903 when in breach of international law, he sent US warships to blockade Panama, then part of Columbia, in support of rebels in their bid for independence on the understanding that the newly created Republic of Panama would then sign a treaty permitting the construction of the Panama Canal on terms that were extremely favourable to the United States. Andrew Carnegie approved of the construction of the Canal itself though.

under which the world's major powers (and particularly France, Germany, Great Britain, Russia and the United States) would agree to renounce war as a means of solving international disputes. Carnegie's speech was widely reported, and his concept of a League of Peace was a forerunner of President Wilson's League of Nations that would come into existence at the end of the First World War, and the United Nations, which would replace it at the end of the Second. For the time being, though, the world was not ready for Carnegie's League, and the idea languished.

He also strongly supported world disarmament, and particularly naval disarmament. This was a time when dreadnought battleships were deemed to be vital to the security of any country with military pretensions and it was British policy to maintain a fleet that was twice as large as any other two navies in the world. However, Germany was rapidly expanding its naval capability, and this led to political fervour in Britain, as politicians argued about an expansion of the Royal Navy, and who was going to pay for it. Carnegie was keen to promote a plan that would limit the size of battleships that could be built, a plan for which President Roosevelt had shown a degree of lukewarm interest. He tried hard to interest his friends in Britain's Liberal Government in the plan but failed to do so (although to be fair to the British, they had made their own repeated proposals to the Germans about limiting naval construction, all of which had been firmly dismissed). This lack of interest was mirrored by all the other major powers in the world; at an international peace conference held at The Hague in 1907 (of which Carnegie had high hopes) the delegates signally failed to reach any agreement about naval disarmament.

In the years that followed, Andrew Carnegie came to the conclusion that the German Kaiser was the key to world peace. In the summer of 1907, during the course of the Hague peace conference, he had met the Kaiser at Kiel, where the Kaiser was carrying out his annual review of the German fleet, and Andrew convinced himself that the Kaiser was a man of peace. He retained this belief throughout the next few years, repeating it in articles and speeches and he flattered himself that the Kaiser was willing to listen to his views and advice. Sadly, the Kaiser showed no evidence of ever doing so.

The First World War and After

The next few years passed peacefully for Andrew Carnegie. He continued to attend to his philanthropic interests and his writing, and to take an interest in public affairs. He promoted world peace at every opportunity and for a few years managed to convince himself that it was imminent. He supported the election of President Taft after Roosevelt declined to run for a third term (although subsequently became somewhat disillusioned with him, as indeed did Theodore Roosevelt). In 1912, he appeared as a witness before a congressional committee investigating possible breaches of the anti-trust laws by US Steel, an experience that he would appear on the whole to have enjoyed. (But then, he was not the target of the investigation.) He continued to play golf and indulged an interest in yachting. And he continued to enjoy the company of his wife Louise and his daughter Margaret whenever possible.[49] The family travelled widely, but maintained the tradition of visiting Scotland every summer.

Consequently, the summer of 1914 found Andrew, Louise and Margaret in Scotland, first at Skibo Castle, and then in a nearby shooting lodge that the Carnegies had acquired a few years earlier as a country retreat. Andrew, not quite as spry as he was but still surprisingly active for a man in his seventy-ninth year, was busy working on his *Autobiography* when he heard the news on 4th August that German troops had invaded neutral Belgium, following the assassination of Austrian Archduke Franz Ferdinand in Sarajevo and that as a consequence, Britain had declared war on Germany in accordance with her treaty obligations. Carnegie's anguish at the thought that the world peace that he had worked so hard and so long to gain had slipped away as a consequence of the murder in Serbia of the Archduke can only be imagined. He ceased work on his *Autobiography* at once, and in fact never completed it. His horror at the news of war was compounded by the knowledge that a peace conference that he had sponsored had just commenced in Berlin, and that amongst the delegates were a number of British and American citizens. Fortunately, the German Government allowed the peace delegates to

---

[49] Margaret's health had been a cause for concern a few years earlier, for she had suffered from an ailment in one of her legs that had required careful medical care, and her leg had been almost entirely encased in plaster casts for over two years. Fortunately, by 1908, the doctors were able to declare her cured.

leave safely, and upon their arrival in London, Andrew took steps to ensure that they had sufficient funds to return safely to their homes.

At the outbreak of the war, the Carnegies had immediately returned to Skibo Castle, but it was swiftly obvious that they could not remain there – the army requisitioned the horses on the estate, and many of the men who worked on it were liable to be called to serve in the armed services at any moment – if indeed they had not already volunteered to fight. Grimly, the Carnegies decided to return to America, and managed to secure berths on board the Mauretania, which was scheduled to sail from Liverpool to New York in mid-September, notwithstanding the threat now presented by German U-boats. As the Carnegies left Skibo Castle on their journey to Liverpool, they did not know that Andrew would not set eyes on Skibo Castle again.

The Mauretania reached America without incident, and once safely settled in New York, Andrew continued to call for peace, hoping that America could use its influence to halt the carnage that was now unfolding on the European battlefields. But nobody in Europe with the power to halt the war was listening, President Wilson declared America to be neutral in the conflict and slowly Andrew's hope of a swift end to the fighting drained away.

His disappointment took a toll on his health and he began to look and act like an old man. He retreated in on himself, ceased public appearances and pronouncements, and abandoned virtually all contact with his friends, in marked contrast to his exuberant approach to life only a few months before and it has been suggested that he may have suffered some form of nervous breakdown. By 1917, his health had deteriorated sufficiently for him to require the attendance of nurses. Now unable to visit Skibo Castle, the Carnegies acquired a country estate, called Shadowbrook, near Lennox, Massachusetts, which became their primary home in America. He viewed the entry of America into the war on 6th April 1917 as a grim necessity; he no longer had any illusions about the dangers posed by German militarism.

The ending of the war on 11th November 1918 also brought a change to his personal life. His daughter Margaret became engaged to a former college classmate, Roswell Miller, and the wedding took place on 22nd

April 1919.[50] He attended the wedding, though it tired him, and it was clear that it would be unwise for him to attempt to travel to Skibo Castle for the summer. Instead, he and Louise elected to spend the next few months at Shadowbrook.

And so it was there that he died, on 11th August 1919, in his 84th year. He was buried in Sleepy Hollow in Westchester County, New York.

Inevitably, Andrew Carnegie's death attracted a great deal of interest from the newspapers, and the question that most fascinated the reporters was how much money had he left? Some press reports speculated that his personal fortune remained as high as several hundred million dollars, but they were wrong. When details of his estate were released for probate purposes, it was discovered that he had nearly achieved his objective of giving away all of his money; he left an estate of nearly $26 million.

Under his will, Louise received all of his real estate, cars, paintings, books and other forms of personal property; he had of course, already taken steps to ensure that Louise would have a suitable income for the rest of her life. He left no money to Margaret, making clear in his will that he did not wish to burden her with a fortune, and that he trusted Louise to do whatever she thought appropriate when she died.[51]

He left generous bequests to other members of his family, and friends and to his servants on both sides of the Atlantic, but the bulk of his estate was left to the Carnegie Corporation. So his last act from beyond the grave was philanthropic.

Of all the tycoons that America has produced, there can be few who have shown a more interesting study in contrasts than Andrew Carnegie. He was not a cruel man and by all accounts, until the last sad years of the First World War, he was a cheerful, energetic and generous companion to his many friends and to his family. His actions helped to create America's great steel industry, upon which so much of America's economic growth in the twentieth century depended, and upon which it still depends. It cannot however be denied that he was a tough businessman, occasionally a ruthless one. He had no hesitation in exploiting his workers at the lowest possible cost, and thanks to his actions, many thousands led hard

---

[50] That day was also his and Louise's 32nd wedding anniversary.
[51] Louise died on 24th June 1946, having devoted much of her life after Andrew's death to his philanthropic enterprises.

and narrow lives of unremitting labour and some suffered serious injury, and even death. Despite his constructions of baths and reading rooms and libraries at his steel plants, his workers enjoyed little of the fruits of their hard work.

But then this was true of many of the industrial workers of his age. Unlike many of his fellow millionaires, Andrew Carnegie took seriously his principles that he held his wealth, the wealth that his workers had provided for him, for the benefit of the wider community, and ultimately he dispensed over $350 million in accordance with those principles. Moreover, in Andrew's eyes, that community was not simply restricted to the United States, but encompassed much more, particularly of course Britain and the other parts of the English-speaking world. And the benefits of his philanthropy are still being enjoyed by many people today all around the world. Few men have achieved more, or are likely to.

John D Rockefeller

"Do you know the only thing that gives me pleasure? It's to see my dividends coming in."

John D Rockefeller (1839 – 1937)

The Young Rockefeller

Of all the millionaires who flourished during America's Gilded Age, none attracted – or continues to attract – more attention than John D Rockefeller. More than any other man, by creating the corporate giant known as Standard Oil, Rockefeller was responsible for the rationalization of America's hitherto disorganized oil industry, just in time for America's explosion onto the world stage as an industrial superpower and in the process of doing so, he acquired for himself and his family a billion dollar fortune. He also, rightly or wrongly, attracted the opprobrium of the press, public and politicians, who so criticized his business successes, his "tainted money", his ethics and his approach to religion that by the turn of the twentieth century, he was probably the most hated of all of America's tycoons.

And yet, by the time Rockefeller died in 1937, much of that hatred had dissipated, he was being hailed as one of the benefactors of mankind and the very name of Rockefeller would continue to symbolize the twin concepts of wealth and dedication to public service for much of the rest of the twentieth century.

John D Rockefeller – the "D" stood for Davison, his mother's maiden name - was born on 8th July 1839 on a 160 acre farm just outside the town of Richford in New York State. He was the second child (and eldest son) of William Avery Rockefeller and his wife Eliza, who ultimately produced five children who survived to adulthood: Lucy, John D, William, Mary Ann, and Frank.

Rockefeller's father, William Avery – or "Big Bill" as he was often called – may have owned the farm but he was certainly no farmer. He was a curious mixture of showman and con artist, not above committing petty larcenies and often wandering far from home peddling cheap novelties and patent medicines, gaining yet another nickname of "Doc" Rockefeller in the process. He was also suspected of more serious criminal offences, including horse rustling and in 1849 he was indicted (though never arrested) for rape. Unsurprisingly, during Rockefeller's childhood, Big Bill was often absent from home for long periods of time, returning for infrequent visits with his pockets bulging with ready cash, the origins of which were never fully explained. The family moved home several times during this period at Big Bill's behest, ultimately settling in Cleveland in 1853.

Rockefeller's father retained this pattern of itinerant behaviour all his life. In later years, when Rockefeller's fortune had been made, Big Bill would periodically arrive apparently from out of nowhere at his son's home, with presents for his grandchildren and then just as suddenly mysteriously disappear again a few days later, often having borrowed money from his son. John D Rockefeller showed few signs during his life of being close to his father and the Rockefeller family tried to discourage all discussion of Big Bill; inevitably, as Rockefeller's fame and fortune grew, the whereabouts of his father became a public mystery. In 1900, the publisher Joseph Pulitzer set off a nationwide manhunt when he offered a prize of $8,000 for information about Big Bill. It took a number of years for news reporters to uncover the truth, but in 1908 it was revealed that Big Bill had died two years previously at the age of 96 and that he had been living a double life in South Dakota, having bigamously married and adopted the name of Dr William Levingston. John D Rockefeller never publicly commented on the story.

In view of Big Bill's frequent absences, Eliza had little choice but to bear the brunt of raising their children. Eliza was very different from her husband in many ways and, over the years, she must have grown accustomed to (and probably even grateful for) her husband's frequent and prolonged absences. Unlike her husband, she was hardworking, disciplined and religious, with a Calvinistic strictness which she succeeded in passing on to her eldest son, together with little financial and moral maxims such as "wilful waste makes woeful want", which he would delight to repeat in later life.

Rockefeller would as an adult deny that he had yearned to be wealthy when he was a child. However, there are many stories that contradict this. Rockefeller himself once told reporters that at the age of seven, he had taken wild turkey chicks from a nest, raised the brood and then sold them for a profit. A little later, he is said to have lent a local farmer $50 for a year at 7 per cent interest. At the end of the year, he received back the principal and $3.50 in interest and this made a major impression on him. "I determined to make money work for me" he later declared.

His family and friends noted his financial determination too. One day a school friend asked him: "John, what do you want to be when you grow up?" "I want to be worth a hundred thousand dollars", Rockefeller replied, "And I'm going to be, too." With the benefit of close observation, his sister Lucy once commented: "When it's raining porridge, you'll always find John's bowl right side up."

Notwithstanding her domestic troubles, Eliza insisted that her children receive at least some education. By all accounts, John D Rockefeller was not an outstanding student, although he was a hard worker. On leaving school in 1855 (the year of Big Bill's bigamous second marriage), Rockefeller determined to go into business rather than pursue a college education. In later life, his tale of how he set out into the streets of Cleveland to track down the "right" job would take on an almost mythic character and Rockefeller himself considered it one of the most important events of his life. As he explained it, "I went to the railroads, to the banks, to the wholesale merchants. I did not go to any small establishments. I did not guess what it would be, but I was after something big."

It took him some time to find the right job. "No one wanted a boy, and very few showed any overwhelming anxiety to talk with me on the subject" he later recalled. Nevertheless, day after day he approached potential employers and finally, on 26th September his persistence paid off, for he was hired as an office clerk and bookkeeper by the firm of Hewitt & Tuttle, commission merchants and produce shippers. For the rest of his life, he remembered and celebrated 26th September as his "Job Day".

Rockefeller plunged himself into his new duties of keeping the firm's books, chasing payments and writing business letters, commencing work each day at 6.30 am and remaining at his desk well into the evening. He soon impressed his employers by his dedication to business, which seemed almost religious in nature. At the same time, he began to preach at the Erie Street Baptist Church Mission – except for his religious activities, he had little or no other interests outside work - and soon he became involved in the finances of the Church, encouraging fellow parishioners to raise $2,000 needed to ensure the Church's solvency.

Religion played an important role in Rockefeller's life. He never doubted that God favoured his business activities, and his approach to religion reflected this strongly held belief. "God gave me my money" he would declare in later years. He believed firmly that order and discipline, economy, hard work and attention to detail reflected God's will, and these were traits which manifested themselves whilst he was working for Hewitt & Tuttle, and which he would display for the rest of his life.

He also believed in the necessity of regular charitable donations – primarily to his Church and related bodies. It was about this time that he purchased a simple notebook – Ledger A – in which he began to record exact details of all items of his personal income and expenditure. Ledger A disproves accusations that were later thrown at Rockefeller to the effect that his charitable giving only commenced as a cynical attempt to escape the criticisms which were later made against him, for it is apparent from the ledger that Rockefeller was a consistent charitable donor from the earliest days of his working life. Ledger A became very important to Rockefeller – he never kept a diary and the ledger was for him the equivalent – and in later years he kept it in a safety deposit vault.

Rockefeller worked for three months at Hewitt & Tuttle without receiving any payment; on the last day of 1855 he was paid $50, and informed that his salary for the forthcoming year would be $300. By 1858, his annual salary had doubled to $600 and he had managed to save $800. By now however, he had come to feel undervalued by his employer, not least because in the interim, Tuttle had resigned from the firm, and Rockefeller had effectively taken over all Tuttle's duties without a corresponding increase in salary. Rockefeller therefore asked Hewitt for a raise in salary. When it became apparent that Hewitt couldn't or wouldn't meet this demand, Rockefeller began to look for opportunities elsewhere.

An opportunity soon presented itself in the form of an Englishman called Maurice B Clark. Clark was 28, worked as a commission clerk for another produce shipping firm and had met Rockefeller several years earlier. Rockefeller's reputation as an unusually dedicated and talented bookkeeper impressed Clark, and even though Rockefeller was only aged eighteen, Clark proposed that they should go into partnership together, with each partner contributing $2,000 to the new business. In order to be able to make the contribution, Rockefeller had to ask his father to lend him $1,000. Big Bill lent him the money, but required that Rockefeller pay him interest at ten percent until he became 21. Rockefeller had to ask his father for money on several further occasions over the next few years, as he struggled to expand the fledgling business, and each time Big Bill produced the money but only on rigorous terms, arguing that in doing so, he was honing his son's financial education. Big Bill also delighted in calling in his loans just at the times when Rockefeller found it most difficult to redeem them and yet somehow they were always repaid. Rockefeller never complained, but later in life he wrote: "I confess that this little discipline should have done me good and perhaps it did, but while I concealed it from him, the truth is I was not particularly pleased with his application of tests to discover if my financial ability was equal to such shocks".

In any event, the new firm of Clark & Rockefeller was established in 1858 and was soon a success, benefiting from an upwards swing in the business cycle and netting a profit of $4,400 in its first year, with profits rising even further in the next year. In 1859 a new partner – George W Gardner joined the firm, which was renamed Clark, Gardner & Company. Rockefeller was not particularly pleased that his name was dropped from the firm's title and later admitted "I considered this a great injustice as I was an equal partner". Nevertheless, he concluded that for the moment, it was wiser for him to agree to the change without complaining. Tensions grew however, between Rockefeller and his partners, as Clark and most especially Gardner were too fun-loving, too casual and (to Rockefeller's eyes) too extravagant to be comfortable business partners of the serious-minded Rockefeller. By 1862, Rockefeller had contrived to oust Gardner from the partnership and the firm was once more known as Clark & Rockefeller.

The firm by this time had expanded considerably, profiting in particular from the flood of business triggered by the outbreak of the American Civil War in April 1861. Rockefeller's youngest brother, Frank, enlisted in the Union army (lying about his age in the process) and saw active service, suffering two wounds during the course of the war. In contrast, John D, although a staunch supporter of Abraham Lincoln and a fervent opponent of the evils of slavery, remained a civilian businessman in Cleveland. "I wanted to go in the army and do my part" he later claimed, "But it was simply out of the question. We were in a new business and if I had not stayed it must have stopped – and with so many dependent on it." Rather than joining up, Rockefeller donated money to the Union cause and he purchased two large maps which he placed in his office to allow him to follow the war's progress.

By 1862, the firm's annual profits had risen to $17,000, and Rockefeller had come to be regarded as a wealthy young man. He now had spare funds to invest into other business ventures and his attention turned to a new industry which was just arising in and around western Pennsylvania. The crude oil business was in the process of being born.

The Oil Regions

Until the middle of the nineteenth century, whale oil had provided the primary source of illumination for the American pioneers as they pushed ever westwards across the North American continent. Whale oil was also of increasing importance as a lubricant for the rapidly expanding industries. Vast whaling fleets operated out of the ports of New England such as New Bedford and Nantucket, but as the century progressed, the whalers were experiencing increasing difficulties in meeting the rising demand. By the 1850s, finding alternative supplies of oil was becoming of vital importance.

It had long been known that there was oil to be found under the rocks of western Pennsylvania. There, along a tributary of the Allegheny River known as Oil Creek, it oozed out of the ground contaminating the local streams to the disgust of local settlers and the delight of local druggists who followed the example of the local Indians by collecting the "rock oil" and selling it as a patent medicine. In the 1850s, it was recognized that rock oil could be distilled to provide a new form of illuminant, together with other useful substances, and a local businessman known as George Bissell established the Pennsylvania Rock-Oil Company to explore the possibility of finding commercially viable deposits of oil along the banks of Oil Creek. In 1857, the Pennsylvania Oil-Creek Company dispatched former railroad conductor Edwin L Drake to Titusville, a town near to Oil Creek to spearhead the search. In order to impress the locals, the company addressed letters to him as "Colonel Drake" (a title to which he was most emphatically not entitled) and it is as Colonel Drake that he has entered the history books.

Initially the search did not go well, and Drake found it difficult to locate viable oil deposits. Moreover, whenever he tried to dig for oil with pickaxes and shovels, the sides of his excavations would crumble. By 1859, the finances of the company were precarious, and Drake, recalling a technique used in salt mines, and in the face of much derision, decided he would try to drill a well rather than simply dig a hole. Somehow, he assembled the materials and equipment he needed to build an oil derrick (swiftly dubbed "Drake's Folly") and began to drill. One month and then another went by without result and then (just as the directors of the Pennsylvania Rock-Oil Company were concluding that they should write off the entire project) Drake struck oil on 28th August 1859. Drake had drilled America's (and the world's) first oil well.

News of the discovery swiftly spread, and prospectors and speculators poured into western Pennsylvania – an area soon to be known as the Oil Regions. It was almost like a re-run of the California Gold Rush of 1849. New oil derricks and ramshackle oil refineries sprang up almost overnight as newcomers and locals alike struggled with one another to gain advantage from the new bonanza, and the price of oil leases in the area soared. Such chaotic yet potentially profitable activity inevitably attracted the attention of businessmen in Cleveland (one day's travel from Titusville) and within a few short years, refineries were established in the city, which (after 1863) had the advantage of good railroad links to New York.

Rockefeller was too good a businessman not to be aware of the potential implications of the new oil strikes. However, although he may have dabbled a little in the oil business as early as 1860, he did not initially rush to become involved to any major degree. The oil business was still too new, too unpredictable, and there were major challenges involving the transport, refining and storage of commercially viable quantities of oil that would have to be addressed. Until those challenges were surmounted, Rockefeller was content to continue to devote most of his time to the produce shipping activities of Clark & Rockefeller.

It was the entry of another Englishman into his life that persuaded Rockefeller to reconsider his involvement in the oil industry. Samuel Andrews was a friend of Maurice Clark, Rockefeller's partner, and worked in a lard-oil refinery business. Andrews was a self-taught chemist, with considerable knowledge of distillation processes and was reputed to have been the first man in Cleveland to have distilled kerosene from crude oil. Perhaps as a consequence, he was somewhat fanatical on the properties of kerosene, believing it to be the ideal illuminant and was determined to leave his employer and set up in the refining business for himself. In 1863, he approached Clark and Rockefeller as potential partners in his new enterprise, and after careful consideration, Rockefeller and Clark agreed to use some of their surplus profits to establish a new refining business with Andrews. The new business was to be known as

Andrews, Clark & Co, with Rockefeller very much playing the role of a silent partner.

By this time, Rockefeller had established himself as a successful Cleveland businessman and had reached a stage in his life when he considered that he could prudently establish a family. In March 1864, he became engaged to Laura Celestia Spelman - commonly known as "Cettie" - a young woman from a prominent Cleveland family whom he had first met in high school. Unlike many of her female contemporaries, Cettie was interested in business matters and encouraged Rockefeller in his efforts to improve his financial standing. She was also deeply religious and had a well-developed social conscience, making her – from Rockefeller's perspective – the ideal companion. He valued her opinions and in later life he declared "Her judgment was always better than mine. Without her keen advice, I would be a poor man."

They married on 8th September 1864, and Rockefeller duly recorded the event in his ledger – Ledger A had by now been filled and he had commenced Ledger B: "Married at 2 o'clock pm to Miss L C Spelman by Reverend D Wolcott assisted by Rev. Paige at the residence of her parents." Typically, Rockefeller worked on the morning of his wedding day. After a month-long honeymoon, he returned to Cleveland and to his business affairs.

Whether he wished it or not, those business affairs were increasingly dominated by oil. More and more oil refineries were being established in Cleveland, and whilst there were concerns that the oil supplies might dry up – no major deposits had yet been discovered outside the Pennsylvania Oil Regions – demand for the products of oil, kerosene most of all, was soaring, both in the United States and abroad. Gradually, Rockefeller found he was devoting more and more of his time to the business of Andrews, Clark & Co, concentrating on financial matters, whilst Andrews tended to focus on the technological problems and Clark liaised with the oil producers and shipping teamsters.

Rockefeller was always keen to eliminate inefficiencies and to ensure as far as possible the independence of his business ventures. The teamsters, those men who transported the barrels of crude oil from the producing wells to the refineries by means of horse-drawn wagons, were notoriously unreliable and difficult to deal with. Before long, Andrews, Clark & Co had established its own fleet of wagons, making the firm effectively independent of the teamsters. Similarly, Rockefeller objected to paying

$2.50 per barrel for barrels made by outside suppliers; he arranged for Andrews, Clark & Co to manufacture its own and was delighted to demonstrate that he could do so at a cost of less than a dollar per barrel. He continued to find ways of marketing the by-products of the kerosene distillation processes and was soon selling products such as petroleum jelly and benzene.

However, by 1865, tensions had developed between the partners, who by now had been joined by two of Clark's brothers. Rockefeller wanted to expand the business and wanted to borrow money to do so; Maurice Clark strongly disagreed. Rockefeller also found it difficult to work with Clark's brothers (not least because they drank, smoked, had little religious interest and tended to look down on him as being little more than an office clerk, something which Rockefeller found increasingly annoying). Rockefeller also feared that working together, the Clark brothers would always be able to outvote Andrews and himself, and thus control the business. Having gained Andrews' agreement (and arranged financing from friendly banks in anticipation), Rockefeller manoeuvred the Clark brothers into agreeing that the firm should be put up for auction, with the business being sold to the highest bidder. The auction was held in February 1865 and Rockefeller later related the events as follows: "Finally it advanced to $60,000 and by slow stages to $70,000 and I almost feared for my ability to buy the business and have the money to pay for it. At last, the other side bid $72,000. Without hesitation, I said '$72,500'. Mr Clark then said 'I'll go no higher. John, the business is yours'." Rockefeller and Andrews resolved to continue the business under the name of Rockefeller & Andrews, and one month later, the old firm of Clark & Rockefeller was dissolved.

Rockefeller was now 26 years old. By eliminating the Clark brothers, he had freed himself from the constraints of unimaginative and (to him) uncongenial partners (Andrews was more of a technical adviser than a partner in any real sense and in due course would find himself eased out of the business). In doing so, Rockefeller had gained control of the largest refinery in Cleveland, with twice the capacity of its nearest rival and he had done so at the height of the oil boom. He immediately set out about further expanding the business, borrowing money from banks in order to secure the necessary funding. Within months, Rockefeller had established another refinery and recruited his brother William into the business, sending him to New York to oversee Rockefeller's oil export business.[52] It was also at this time that Rockefeller made the acquaintance of a man alongside whom he was to work for more than forty years and who would help him to establish the industrial giant that was Standard Oil. That man was Henry M Flagler.

Henry Flagler and the Creation of Standard Oil

Flagler was nine years older than Rockefeller, having been born in Hopewell, New York in 1830, the son of a poor Presbyterian preacher. By all accounts he was a dashing and distinguished looking man, with prominent black moustache and according to the reminiscences of one observer, he possessed "the most beautiful hair I had ever seen". Before meeting Rockefeller, he had moved to Ohio, where he had become involved in the business of a wealthy grain merchant and distiller called Lamon Harkness (the brother of his mother's first husband). Flagler himself married Lamon Harkness' daughter, Mary, in 1853 and invested in a distillery co-owned by his Harkness in-laws. Eventually, he decided to leave the liquor business, claiming that: "I had scruples about the business and gave it up" although he also admitted that he did not do so until he had made $50,000. Alas, he subsequently lost his money in an ill-advised investment in the salt industry (demand for salt had soared during the Civil War, and just as rapidly declined with the return of peace) and after a period of poverty, decided to move to Cleveland and take a job as a grain salesman working for none other than Maurice Clark, Rockefeller's former partner.

Rockefeller, who had previously been acquainted with Flagler in the days of the Clark & Rockefeller partnership, invited Flagler to rent office space from Rockefeller & Andrews. Flagler gradually prospered as a grain merchant and with some help from his still prosperous in-laws, he began to improve his financial position. More importantly, he and Rockefeller struck up a genuine friendship. Rockefeller later wrote that: "It was a friendship founded on business, which Mr Flagler used to say was a good deal better than a business founded on friendship and my experience

---

[52] Interestingly, Rockefeller's other brother, Frank, was never admitted to the "inner circle" and eventually he would become a vocal critic of Rockefeller, publicly criticizing him, testifying against him before Congressional committees and working for Rockefeller's business rivals. This did not however prevent him from borrowing large sums of money from Rockefeller at regular intervals.

leads me to agree with him." It was only a matter of time before Rockefeller invited Flagler to join him in the oil business, which he did in 1867, leading to the creation of yet another new partnership, this one to be called Rockefeller, Andrews and Flagler.

Flagler was the first of many lieutenants who were to join Rockefeller and in due course make their fortunes. All brought skills and experience which complemented and enhanced Rockefeller's own, and frequently allowed him to maintain some degree of distance (and where necessary plausible deniability) from some of the more disreputable aspects of his businesses. In due course, Flagler would become a very wealthy man, demonstrating many of the grandiose tastes of America's richest tycoons, and in later life he devoted much of his time and energy to the development of Florida into a playground for America's elite. In the early days however, Flagler led a life which was far more restrained (and thus more to Rockefeller's own taste), avoiding bars and theatres, assiduously attending the local Presbyterian church and preaching the gospel of self-discipline and the advantages to be gained from a rigorous attention to one's business.

Flagler was a particularly gifted negotiator, with an eye for spotting loopholes and pitfalls in legal documents although when enthused with an idea, he had a tendency to overlook legal niceties. Even Rockefeller himself observed that Flagler had need of "a restraining influence at times when his enthusiasm was aroused", but nevertheless, he allowed Flagler to take the lead in negotiations with the railroad companies over the carriage of oil supplies by rail, a topic which would eventually lead to Rockefeller being pilloried in the press.

The problem of transportation had long been a bottleneck of the oil industry, with the oil wells too distant from the newly constructed oil refineries and the oil refineries themselves facing the problem of how to transport their refined oil products to their customers. Refineries were frequently sited alongside or near the railroads that could thus deliver their products into the major cities, but in the early days, few railroads served the Oil Regions and the transportation of oil from the wells to the refineries was thus dominated by the teamsters who fiercely opposed any attempt to introduce an oil pipeline network which would have largely solved the problem. In due course, the railroads extended their lines into the Oil Regions, which should in theory have assured the refineries of a steady supply of crude oil. In practice, the railroads found that the erratic oil production of the chaotically organized producers of the Oil Regions meant that they were at times overwhelmed with demands for transport, and at other times obliged to run trains that were carrying so little oil that they were rendered unprofitable. From the railroads' perspective, what was needed was a steady, high volume and above all predictable demand for their transport services. What was needed to achieve this was someone who could control all the aspects of the oil business – its production, refinement and distribution to customers - and the person best placed to assume this control was the person who owned the greatest refining capability in Cleveland. That man, of course, was John D Rockefeller.

Rockefeller was not unaware of the need to meet this challenge, and the opportunities awaiting the man who could meet it. Nor were the other refiners who had established themselves in Cleveland (and elsewhere – by now, oil refineries had also been established in New York, Philadelphia, Pittsburgh, and in the Oil Regions themselves) and Rockefeller's competitors sought to reach agreements of their own with the various railroad companies. Rockefeller, however, had the advantage of controlling a greater share of the refining capability of Cleveland than anyone else, and Cleveland in turn possessed the advantage of having access to the Erie Canal, thus allowing the Cleveland refiners (if they so wished) to transport their refined oil products by water, at least in the summer months, doing so at rates which were cheaper than those offered by the railroads. In 1867, Rockefeller dispatched Flagler to negotiate with representatives of various railroad companies, including the Erie and the New York Central. Essentially, Rockefeller and Flagler were seeking to reach a deal with the railroad companies whereby Rockefeller oil would be carried by the railroads at a substantial discount as compared to the prices paid by Rockefeller's rivals, in exchange for Rockefeller agreeing not to use the services of the Erie Canal, and ensuring a constant, substantial and predictable demand for the railroads' services. In order to maintain secrecy, the discounts took the form of "rebates", but they essentially constituted special reduced rates which were not available to Rockefeller's competitors.

It must be said that Rockefeller and Flagler did not invent the concept of the rebate, which had been common practice in the railroad industry for years and was not unique to the transportation of oil. Nevertheless, when news of the rebates leaked out (as inevitably, it did), there was an outcry amongst the other Cleveland oil refiners. The railroads attempted to justify the use of rebates by saying that if the other refiners could offer comparable guarantees to those provided by Rockefeller as to the volume of oil to be transported, they too could have rebates. Other refiners did in fact receive rebates (some actually received more favourable rebates than Rockefeller), but none on the scale of Rockefeller. There were accusations of unfair business practices and the "rebate scandal" was to haunt Rockefeller time and time again in future years. Rebates were eventually declared illegal under the Interstate Commerce Act of 1887.

In the meantime, Rockefeller had the task of ensuring that he could deliver the level of business he had promised to the railroads. The capacity of his refineries, substantial as it was, could not alone ensure that he could meet this promise and nor did he have sufficient control over the oil producers so as to guarantee a constant supply of crude oil to his refineries. However, by the end of the 1860s, the refineries were themselves facing an industry-wide crisis thanks in part to the large number of refineries that had been hastily established, which had led to the field becoming seriously overcrowded. To make matters worse, oil prices were falling in the late 1860s due to overproduction and yet just as oil producers found it impossible to keep from drilling, even when they lost money in doing so, so too did the oil refineries find it difficult to curtail their refining activities, notwithstanding that many of their plants were too antiquated and too small to operate efficiently.

It was clear that it would be necessary to impose some form of order over the oil industry, although Rockefeller preferred to refer to the necessity of introducing "cooperation" in place of "ruinous competition". He began to envisage a cooperative framework within which the refiners would operate, and considered that he was merely following in the footsteps of the oil producers who had established the Petroleum Producers' Association in an attempt to regulate oil production and to maintain stable prices, although with scant success.

Unfortunately, imposition of the control and degree of cooperation Rockefeller sought would be expensive, not least because of the need to buy up unproductive and obsolete refineries and then to close them down. In order to raise the necessary funds, Rockefeller and his associates determined to follow a recommendation first proposed by Flagler, namely to incorporate their business.

Consequently, on 10th January 1870, the existing partnership of Rockefeller, Andrews & Flagler was abolished; in its place, capitalized at

$1 million, with 10,000 issued shares was the Standard Oil Company (Ohio). Rockefeller owned over 25 per cent of the issued share capital; other major shareholders included Flagler, Andrews and Rockefeller's brother William. From the beginning, Rockefeller had grand ambitions for Standard Oil, which at its inception controlled over 10 per cent of America's total refining capacity. He told a Cleveland businessman that Standard Oil would one day "refine all the oil and make all the barrels".

Contemporary opinion in the business world was not initially enthusiastic about the new company and at first Standard Oil found it difficult to attract outside investors. This was partly because the country was going through a period of economic uncertainty (the cause of which was popularly attributed to the collapse of the attempts of Jay Gould and Jim Fisk, opponents of Commodore Vanderbilt in the Erie Railroad Wars[53] which had just ended, to corner the US gold market in September 1869) and partly because the disorganized nature of the oil industry still deterred many of the more conservative businessmen. Nevertheless, Standard Oil did well enough in its first 12 months of operation to pay a dividend of 105%. In 1872, Standard Oil's capitalization was increased to $3.5 million and Rockefeller began to lay his plans to gain control of the rival Cleveland refineries.

In this task, Rockefeller was to receive substantial assistance from the railroad companies. By offering him transportation rebates, the railroad companies now had a substantial vested interest in ensuring that Rockefeller could consolidate his position as the pre-eminent refiner of oil in Cleveland (and later on, further afield). In recognition of this, in 1871 Thomas Scott, the President of the Pennsylvania Railroad[54] (and one-time mentor and occasional informal business partner of Andrew Carnegie) proposed an alliance between the Pennsylvania, Erie and New York Central Railroads and Standard Oil and other large refiners.

Rockefeller was no fan of Tom Scott (he feared an alliance between the Pennsylvania and rival refiners), but nevertheless was willing to hear further details of Scott's plan. In November 1871, Rockefeller and Flagler journeyed to New York to hear details of Scott's proposals presented by Peter Watson, a senior official of the Lake Shore Railroad, part of the New York Central railroad system. Scott's plan entailed the creation of a

---

[53] see page 47
[54] see page 68

new type of corporation – a holding company – that would allow investment both inside and outside the state. (One of the drawbacks of many of the companies established before that time, and this applied to Standard Oil itself, was that they were usually prohibited from investing outside the state in which they were incorporated, a restriction that caused considerable problems for Standard Oil in later years, although none that Standard Oil's lawyers could not overcome by one means or another.) Scott had gone so far as to obtain a special charter for such a company from the Pennsylvania State Legislature. The new company was to be known as the South Improvement Company and was essentially authorized to conduct any type of business anywhere.

Under Scott's plan, the railroads would sharply increase the cost of oil transportation for all oil refiners everywhere; however, those who invested in the South Improvement Company would receive substantial rebates, on far more generous terms than they were presently receiving from the railroads. Moreover, the investors would receive what they called "drawbacks" – that is payments from the railroads for each barrel of oil shipped by non-investing refiners, together with detailed information about the oil being carried by their competitors.The rebates, drawbacks and secret provision of information represented a staggering competitive advantage for Rockefeller and his fellow investors, and by January 1872, Standard Oil had signed up to the plan.

The plan had been conceived in total secrecy, but once the new railroad rates were published, it did not take long for the secret to be uncovered. The refiners in the Oil Regions – who had not been invited to join the plan – were horrified. The drawbacks in particular aroused fierce opposition. "The Oil Region was afire with all sorts of wild stories" Rockefeller later recalled, and there were public demonstrations, meetings and petitions, at which the angry refiners singled out Rockefeller as one of the chief architects of the plan and Standard Oil identified as a corporate anaconda intent on strangling the independent refiners. Standard Oil employees were attacked in their offices and Standard Oil equipment vandalized and defaced. There was no sign, however, that Rockefeller ever paused for thought, or considered the morality of his position. "It was right", he later said. "I knew it as a matter of conscience. It was right between me and my God."

As the public outrage continued, the Oil Region's producers tried to establish their own organization – the Producers' Protection Organisation

– one that was pledged not to sell crude oil to Standard Oil (although the inability of its members to control their production meant that Standard Oil was never seriously threatened). Nevertheless, Rockefeller continued to concentrate on expanding his refining capability in Cleveland, taking advantage of the confusion in the industry to buy up as many of his competitors' refineries as he could. He genuinely considered this to be an act of Christian charity, arguing that if he had not taken over his weaker rivals, they would eventually have gone bankrupt. "The Standard was an angel of mercy" he later told a biographer, "reaching down from the sky and saying 'Get into the ark. Put in your old junk. We will take the risks". He frequently offered shares in Standard Oil as part of the price he was willing to pay for the refineries of his rivals, telling them "take Standard Oil stock and your family will never know want." For those of his competitors who did sell to him and took and retained the stock, this prediction in fact turned out to be true; however, the prices he was willing to pay were not generous (he did indeed consider many of the refineries he was acquiring to be old junk, fit only to be closed down) and many of his vanquished rivals, forced to sell out at rock bottom prices, nursed a bitter hatred for him as the author of their misfortunes. The affair became known as the "Cleveland Massacre".

Eventually, such was the public outcry throughout the oil industry that the politicians were forced to act and the railroads to back down – the Pennsylvania State Legislature repealed the South Improvement Company's charter and the railroads offered new contracts to all refiners. By that time, however, Rockefeller had acquired all but three of Cleveland's refineries; giving him an effective monopoly over Cleveland's refining capacity (representing one-quarter of the refining capacity of the entire country).

He had not given up on the idea of imposing order and control over the oil business as a whole. Together with refiners from Philadelphia and Pittsburgh, he visited the Oil Regions, seeking to establish a new voluntary association of refiners, but made little progress – the prejudice against his name, and that of Standard Oil was too great. He did however, enlist the support of some of the local refiners, including John D Archbold who until this time had been one of the fiercest critics of the South Improvement Company but who would eventually lead Standard Oil itself. Rockefeller became convinced that voluntary associations would not suffice to bring order and restraint into the oil refining arena and concluded that as much of it as possible must be gathered under the control of Standard Oil.

By 1873, Standard Oil was earning over a million dollars a year on its oil shipments alone. Coupled with friendly banks and a close working relationship with the railroads, these earnings gave Rockefeller and his colleagues an immense advantage in the task they set themselves, namely the acquisition of as many of their refinery competitors as possible. Over the next few years, aided by a nationwide economic slump that depressed oil prices and forced his competitors to sell out at rock-bottom prices, Rockefeller steadily increased Standard Oil's grip over the oil refining industry. He achieved this largely in secret (Rockefeller grew increasingly secretive about his business affairs over the years), and often insisted that his newly acquired businesses should not publicly advertise that they were now part of the Standard Oil group. He then used those newly acquired businesses to acquire still more of the independent refineries before their owners became aware of who was really offering to buy them out. And despite Rockefeller's protestations to the contrary, Standard Oil continued to enjoy extremely competitive rebates from the railroads and indulged in price fixing to maintain and enhance its dominant position.

By 1880, the process was nearly complete. Standard Oil refined 95% of the oil produced in the United States, meaning that Rockefeller and his colleagues (they would be dubbed the "Standard Oil Gang") effectively controlled 95% of the world's oil supply. Rockefeller was well on the way to becoming the richest man in the world.

Unlike many of the tycoons of the Gilded Age, Rockefeller and his wife did not succumb to the usual extravagances that tempted many of America's newly created millionaires. They did acquire a dignified townhouse in Euclid Avenue in Cleveland, where so many of Cleveland's financial elite had gathered that it was popularly known as "Millionaire's Row", and subsequently the Rockefellers purchased 75 acres of woodland estate at Forest Hill, four miles from Euclid Avenue. Over time, Rockefeller subsequently expanded Forest Hill into a 700 acre estate and built a mansion there which he originally intended should function as a hotel, but which soon became his primary and much favoured summer residence. Other forms of conspicuous consumption were however rigorously excluded from the daily life of the Rockefeller family, which abhorred any appearance of partaking in the frivolous social life of the rich. As far as Rockefeller was concerned, his growing fortune had been granted to him by the Lord and as such was to be held on trust, although for exactly what purpose was perhaps not immediately clear to him. He was as firm in his view that his wealth was not to be squandered, as he (and his wife) were determined that the family would live lives of Baptist sobriety.

That family had by now expanded to include four children, three girls and a boy. The daughters were called Elizabeth (Bessie), Alta, and Edith; the boy, youngest of the children, born in 1874, was named John Davison after his father, and has become known to history as "Junior". Another daughter, Alice, had died as an infant in 1870. For Rockefeller, family life was all-important – he was a kind and attentive father to his children – and the private man his family saw was increasingly at odds with the image often depicted in the press of Rockefeller as an evil spider sitting at the centre of a web of deceit, or a snake bent on swallowing up an industry painstakingly built by others.

At work, he was the dominant figure in the company, constantly moving from one Standard Oil installation to another, inspecting, questioning and suggesting all manner of things. Some of his actions have passed into folklore as when, for example, he was watching some of his workers construct barrels for the shipment of oil. He found that 40 drops of solder were used to seal each barrel and he asked whether the workmen have ever tried to use 38. The answer was that no, they hadn't, and when they tried, some barrels so constructed showed a tendency to leak. None leaked when 39 drops were used, and from then on, 39 drops became the rule for all Standard Oil barrels. Rockefeller was very pleased with himself for this and other small economies and in later life boasted that such seemingly small acts had save "a fortune".

By the mid-1880s, in order to overcome the legal prohibitions which fettered its abilities to carry out its businesses on an inter-state level, Standard Oil had re-organised itself into a trust based in New York, with subsidiary companies in the various states, such as Standard Oil of New Jersey and Standard Oil of New York. The trust had nine trustees, including John D Rockefeller, his brother William, Flagler and Archbold, and was based at 26 Broadway. From here, Rockefeller and his fellow Standard Oil potentates oversaw a $70 million business that had by now established itself as America's leading force not only in refining, but also in oil transportation and distribution. Standard Oil did not, however, enjoy a dominant position so far as oil production was concerned. There is no clear reason why this should have been so, though until that time, more often than not there had been oil surpluses rather than oil shortages and it may be that Rockefeller had simply found it easiest to buy crude in the open market, where competition between producers helped to keep prices low. It may also be that Rockefeller, who was painfully aware of the public outcries that had accompanied Standard Oil's expansion in the refining and transportation fields, may have feared even further public and political turmoil if he had dived into the production field as well. For whatever reason, as late as the early 1880s, Standard Oil had virtually no oil producing properties of its own.

This changed after 1885. It was in that year that the great oil fields of Ohio were discovered; at about the same time, the Russian oil fields at Baku were coming into production and Americans were having to adjust to the likelihood that non-American oil production would soon outpace that of the USA (as indeed, occurred as early as 1888 with the result that Standard Oil no longer enjoyed a supremely dominant position in the world at large, but remained all-powerful at home.) Rockefeller was intensely interested in the Ohio fields for he, like many other oilmen, had been increasingly concerned that the oil fields of Pennsylvania, which had provided so much of Standard Oil's crude oil to date, were reaching peak production and he worried about a possible shortage of crude in the not too distant future. With such fears in mind he insisted that Standard Oil should invest in the oil fields of Ohio. Many of his colleagues at Standard Oil did not agree; the Ohio oil had been found to have high levels of sulphur impurities, but a relatively low kerosene content (at this time, oil was still primarily valued for its kerosene derivative, although other uses for the distilled oil products were being found on almost a daily basis). The high sulphur content damned the Ohio oil in the eyes of many, since it caused the oil to corrode machinery and emitted such a revolting smell that it was difficult to imagine anyone wishing to use it as an illuminant in the home (one commentator observed that the Ohio oil smelt like a "stack of polecats"). This inevitably had an effect on the price of Ohio crude.

Despite these difficulties, Rockefeller had faith that ways would be found to treat the Ohio oil so as to render it commercially viable. His colleagues took some persuading – John Archbold (who by now was far removed from the anti-Standard Oil man he had been a few years before) publicly promised that he would "drink all the oil" that could be produced in Ohio. Eventually, Rockefeller had to put up $3 million of his own money (selling some of his Standard Oil shares in order to do so) before he could persuade his colleagues to make the investment. It was a huge gamble for Rockefeller and an unusual one for a businessman who did not like surprises and did not like to take unnecessary risks. It was however a gamble which paid off; Standard Oil hired the services of the great German chemist Herman Frasch, who had come to the USA to study the chemical possibilities of the oil industry and by 1888, Frasch had invented a process which succeeded in eliminating the sulphur contaminant from the Ohio crude. The price of Ohio crude rose accordingly and Rockefeller's stance was vindicated. (Standard Oil also owned the patents for Frasch's process, which was widely adopted throughout the oil industry, in due course, significantly boosting worldwide oil production, and those patents also earned handsome returns for Standard Oil. They also demonstrated that the day of the industrial research scientist had at last arrived).

The emergence of Standard Oil as a major oil producer in Ohio led Rockefeller and his colleagues to look at other oil producing regions with covetous eyes and they began to acquire rival oil producers at an astonishing rate. By 1891, Standard Oil, in addition to its dominant position in the refining and transportation fields, also controlled a quarter of America's oil production. In the process, it inevitably attracted more public criticism, both in the press and in the political arena. Standard Oil was now too large, too successful, too efficient; rivals could not compete – could not even begin to compete – and Standard Oil's and Rockefeller's reputations had never been darker.

Inevitably, lawyers, politicians and jealous rivals began to circle, looking for ways to bring down the Standard Oil giant (they had been doing so for quite some time in fact, but now the assaults took on a deadlier edge, aided by the slow but steady development of anti-monopoly sentiments in Congress and before the courts). Other monopolies also suffered in this manner, but none to the degree of Standard Oil.

Standard Oil was assailed with public enquiry after public enquiry, and lawsuit after lawsuit. To begin with, Standard Oil batted these away with almost contemptuous ease, but steadily, over the years, the pressure began to tell. Rockefeller himself became quite adept at avoiding reporters and process servers; when forced to testify or comment, he sometimes adopted an approach of seeking to disassociate himself from colleagues such as Archbold, insisting that if there were problems, they were caused by some of his colleagues acting as free agents and beyond the control of Standard Oil itself. On other occasions, Rockefeller's replies were so vague as to exasperate his interrogators; he frequently asserted an inability to remember crucial facts (such as the organizational structure of Standard Oil) and a reporter once commented that "The art of forgetting is possessed by Mr Rockefeller in its highest degree". None of this helped Rockefeller in the eyes of public opinion, who needed no persuading that he was guilty of many hidden crimes.

In public, he continued to act calmly and coolly, insisting that he had done nothing to warrant such public criticism; in private, the continual attacks and criticism began to take their toll. He began to suffer from sleeplessness and digestive difficulties (when a newspaper reported that such was the state of his stomach that Rockefeller was unable to eat a steak, there was public delight) and as the 1890s began to pass by, he began to age noticeably, suffering from such severe baldness that he was forced to wear a wig. The time was approaching when he would have to consider whether he wished to remain at the helm of Standard Oil indefinitely.

In the meantime though, he was richer than ever before. Not only had Standard Oil continued to generate ever greater dividends, but Rockefeller had become (to use his words) "a regular dumping ground" for colleagues who wished to sell part of their Standard Oil shareholdings for one particular project or another. By the early 1890s, he was worth at least $100 million and his fortune continued to grow.

The question of what he should do with his wealth exercised him more and more. Much of it was earmarked for his children of course, primarily for Junior, to whom he eventually left more than $500 million, but by now the money was growing so rapidly that he found it hard to spare adequate time to invest it properly. (It has been estimated that between 1895 and 1896, Rockefeller's dividends from the Standard Oil trust alone amounted to approximately $40 million). He continued to give money to charity of course – by 1892, his annual charitable giving exceeded $1 million, but as he grew older, he became increasingly convinced that God wanted him to bring his organizational skills to charity as he had once brought them to bear on the oil industry. (He had, of course, long believed that he had been provided with his fortune by the hand of God). Moreover, he had the example of Andrew Carnegie before him. Carnegie, who had built his own multi-million dollar fortune in the iron and steel business, had regularly preached that it was the duty of wealthy men to apply their fortunes for the public good and indeed had already begun to make substantial charitable donations himself (although not on the scale that he would adopt following the sale of Carnegie Steel[55] in 1901) and Rockefeller approved of Carnegie's actions. However, Carnegie was nothing if not flamboyant in his charitable giving; he saw no harm in self-publicity and reveled in the public appreciation he thereby gained. Such an approach did not endear itself to Rockefeller's more sober and retiring nature. In any event, such was Rockefeller's reputation now that on at least one occasion, a donation he offered to a group of missionaries was publicly rejected as "tainted money" and Rockefeller was taunted in the press as a rich but guilty man desperately trying to purchase the salvation of his soul. Clearly, the realm of public philanthropy had to be approached cautiously, and possibly anonymously.

The situation was made yet more complicated by the deluge of begging letters which descended daily on Rockefeller's offices at 26 Broadway, many of them for worthy causes, some of them less so. There was simply no way that Rockefeller could have weeded out the good from the bad, and in any event, he could not possibly have spared the time. He needed assistance.

He found it in the form of Frederick T Gates. In the late 1880s, Rockefeller had allowed himself (somewhat reluctantly) to become involved in the establishment of a Baptist college in Chicago; Gates was a minister who acted as secretary to a group of ministers championing the cause of Baptist education, and who had strongly recommended the establishment of the new college. Rockefeller's limited financial support for the new college had initially disappointed the ministers, but he and Gates got on well together, and at Gates' urging, Rockefeller's financial contributions to the new institution (which evolved into the University of Chicago) slowly rose, until by 1910, it was calculated that he had donated $45 million to the cause. (Later in life, he considered that his support for the new University was one of the best things he had ever done.)

By 1891, Rockefeller had realized that Gates was the man to assist him in his philanthropic endeavours and he hired him to oversee all of his charitable works. Gates set about organizing Rockefeller's donations with relish, intercepting all appeals and only forwarding to Rockefeller those

---

[55] see page 101

which he felt had merit. He also investigated Rockefeller's favoured charities to date and as he himself wrote, "…found not a few … to be worthless and practically fraudulent." Gates prided himself on applying "scientific principles" to philanthropy and before long, he was also advising and assisting Rockefeller on his private investments outside the arena of Standard Oil, which by now had become substantial.

The Dissolution of Standard Oil

The burden of Standard Oil remained, but in 1896, Rockefeller began, gradually to "retire". He stepped back from the business and ceased to attend the offices at 26 Broadway on a daily basis; John Archbold assumed responsibility for day to day business decisions (and in the following year, he would be joined by Junior fresh from college, although for the first few years, Junior had no definitive place in the Standard Oil hierarchy and his original role at 26 Broadway was vague and low-key). Away from the office, Rockefeller began, at long last, to devote himself to other pursuits. In 1893, he had bought a 400 acre estate in the Pocantico Hills overlooking the Hudson River (the estate was later extended to 3000 acres) and he now began to devote more time to it, improving it to such an extent that one Broadway comic later joked that Pocantico was an example "of what God would have done if only He'd had the money". Rockefeller laid out a golf course there and by the 1900s, golf had become one of the greatest pleasures in his life. He played daily, regardless of the weather.

Rockefeller may have stepped back from day-to-day involvement in Standard Oil, he may have begun to reorganize his charitable giving so that in future decades it would amaze the world, but so far as the general public was concerned, he was still identified as "Mr Standard Oil", the epitome of all that was evil in the world of American Big Business. The attacks continued, and in 1902, they reached a climax in the form of a series of articles entitled *"The History of the Standard Oil Company"* which appeared in *McClure's Magazine*. Written by a journalist named Ida Tarbell (who had grown up in the Oil Regions and had witnessed first hand the effect of Standard Oil's business activities on its competitors), they were vicious no-holds barred denunciations of Rockefeller's career, and drew particular attention to Rockefeller's success at obtaining favourable transportation rebates, which she and many of her readers considered to be unfair. Standard Oil was attacked as a monopoly (which in effect it was) and one that did untold harm to myriads of small businesses (which was perhaps more open to debate. Certainly Rockefeller himself continued to insist that Standard Oil was a "beneficial organization to the public".) Such attacks whipped the public's antagonism against Rockefeller to new heights, although by now, Standard Oil was not the only monopoly-like trust; it has been estimated that between 1898 and 1902, nearly 200 other trusts were created, specializing in areas as diverse as sugar, rubber, tobacco, coal and steel. Nevertheless, Standard Oil remained the prime target for public anger. Rockefeller himself received death threats, and was obliged to hire private detectives to escort him when he went to Church.

To date, although he had suffered long and sustained attacks in the popular press, Rockefeller and Standard Oil had generally managed to avoid serious trouble at the hands of politicians, not least because as a general rule, he enjoyed good relations with the US Government. Standard Oil was also not above buying favours from politicians when this was felt necessary. This is not to say politicians didn't attack him when it suited them; William Jennings Bryan, the Democratic candidate for President in 1896 launched a series of scathing attacks during his presidential campaign but failed in his bid for the White House, which was won by business-friendly William McKinley. McKinley, all too conscious of the extent to which big business had funded his presidential campaign (Standard Oil alone had contributed a quarter of a million dollars to his campaign war chest), declared himself opposed to anti-trust legislation, much to the satisfaction of his business supporters. So long as new anti-trust legislation could be kept off the statute books and the existing statutes not enforced (the Sherman Antitrust Act had been in force since 1890, but the McKinley administration largely ignored it), the financial resources of the trusts generally (and Standard Oil in particular) meant that they could deal with the myriad of law suits which were launched against them through the courts and could afford to ignore popular opinion.

Such satisfaction was short-lived. On 6th September 1901, six months after he had been inaugurated for his second term, McKinley was shot by an anarchist named Leon Czolgosz in Buffalo, New York (the third President to be killed in office), and succumbed to his wounds eight days later. His Vice President, Theodore Roosevelt, was subsequently sworn in as the 26th President of the United States.

Roosevelt was not vehemently opposed to the trusts but was well aware of the depths of public resentment towards them. In addition, although he was a Republican, he was not automatically on the side of big business and great wealth; he saw himself (and was frequently seen) as a "man of the people" and he recognised the need for legislation designed to discourage the worse excesses of unbridled competition. "We draw the line against misconduct, not against wealth", he declared. He increased the powers of the Interstate Commerce Commission and encouraged it to turn its attention to Standard Oil.

By 1907 (half way through Roosevelt's second term), the US Government and various states had filed a multitude of suits against Standard Oil alleging breaches of various Acts of Congress, including the Elkins Act, which was designed to discourage the ongoing problem of railroad rebates. That year, a court in Chicago presided over by Judge Kennesaw Mountain Landis held that Standard Oil of Indiana was guilty of receiving illegal rebates and price fixing and (after a withering attack on Standard Oil and its lawyers) issued a fine for $29.24 million, the largest corporate fine in history until that time. The news of the fine caused public delight (when asked to comment, Mark Twain is reported to have declared that it reminded him of the bride's words after her wedding night: "I expected it but didn't suppose it would be so big"); however, the public's delight was somewhat premature. When told of the fine whilst playing a round of golf in New York, Rockefeller simply pocketed the yellow telegram bearing the news and observed "Judge Landis will be dead a long time before this fine is paid" and continued with the game. (By all accounts, he played a very good game that day). Rockefeller was right; the Landis decision was overturned on appeal.

But whilst Standard Oil may have succeeded against Landis, it still faced an avalanche of lawsuits. Finally, the Department of Justice petitioned the courts for a dissolution of the Standard Oil trust, requiring that it be broken up into its various constituent parts. Standard Oil fought the case through to the Supreme Court but finally in May 1911, the Supreme Court ordered that Standard Oil's dissolution must occur within a period of six months. On hearing the news, Rockefeller sent a message to his partners: "Dearly Beloved, we must obey the Supreme Court. Our splendid happy family must scatter."

It indeed seemed as though Rockefeller's critics – and the US Government - had won. However, upon the dissolution of the trust into its constituent parts (there were 34 of them), the various stockholders received shares in the underlying subsidiary companies. Effectively therefore, the stockholders together still owned the underlying companies and all of their assets.

Moreover, by 1911 the age of the automobile had arrived and oil companies were reaping spectacular profits from the motor industry. These profits manifested themselves dramatically when the various Standard Oil companies were traded on Wall Street for the first time – their share prices shot up, driven high by popular demand (Standard Oil of New York alone went up from $260 to $580 between January and October of 1912). As the major shareholder in the various companies, Rockefeller's wealth soared as well until by 1913, his net worth was estimated at $900 million, far greater than it had been in the days of the Standard Oil trust and making him the richest man in America.

The fact that Rockefeller and the rest of the Standard Oil Gang remained substantial shareholders in all of the newly liberated Standard Oil companies caused some people to question whether the US Government's actions had in fact solved the problem of the oil monopoly. J.P. Morgan, the great Wall Street banker (and himself responsible for assembling US Steel, one of the greatest trusts of all) asked: "How the hell is any court going to compel a man to compete with himself?" Teddy Roosevelt (no longer President, but seeking re-election as a third party candidate in the 1912 presidential elections having fallen out with his successor and former protégé, President William Taft) also was not amused. "All the companies", he said "are still under the same control, or at least working in such close alliance that the effect is precisely the same." Roosevelt also commented on the dramatic increase in Rockefeller's wealth: "The price of stock has gone up over one hundred per cent so that Mr Rockefeller and his associates have actually seen their fortunes doubled. No wonder that Wall Street's prayer is now: 'Oh Merciful Providence, give us another dissolution.'"

Rockefeller's Philanthropies

In the meantime, Rockefeller and Gates had continued to concentrate on their charitable work. Rockefeller was supremely conscious that his fortune would allow him to tackle philanthropic causes on a scale that had not been seen before; he insisted however that his charitable endeavours should reflect the approach he had adopted when seeking to rationalize the oil business. This meant a focused well-organized large scale approach rather than haphazard and indiscriminate donations. Gates meanwhile, saw the opportunity of using Rockefeller's millions to forward Christian (specifically Baptist) causes, envisaging a great series of "corporate philanthropies". It was a dream that harmonized well with Rockefeller's wishes and promised a solution that had haunted both of them – the problem of doing nothing with the fortune. Gates went so far as to warn Rockefeller of the dangers of charitable inactivity. "Your fortune is rolling up, rolling up like an avalanche" he wrote to Rockefeller. "You must distribute it faster than it grows! If you do not, it will crush you and your children and your children's children!"

They first concentrated their attentions on the fields of medicine and public health, correctly identifying that this was an area where Rockefeller's fortune could be applied to spectacular effect. The Rockefeller Institute for Medical Research was established in 1901, with a staff of brilliant doctors and public health experts lead by Dr Simon Flexner. Steadily (but initially not over-generously) funded, within a few short years, the RIMR had established a formidable reputation for medical research and development. In 1905, for example, Flexner developed a serum to treat cerebrospinal meningitis, which the RIMR distributed free as a public service. Important work was also carried out by the RIMR in areas such as heart disease, polio and syphilis and by 1910, the RIMR had established a hospital which provided free treatment for such diseases. In 1912, a doctor employed by the RIMR, Dr Alexis Carrel, won the Nobel Prize for Medicine and Physiology for ground-breaking work in the field of organ transplantation and public approval of the work being carried out by the RIMR provided a welcome respite from the continuing public relations difficulties suffered by Rockefeller as a result of the anti-trust crusade. Nevertheless, the irony is that Rockefeller, now funding groundbreaking medical advances, himself remained extremely sceptical of doctors and modern medicine. All his life he remained beguiled by the dubious talents of homeopaths and quasi-faith healers, to the increasing frustration of his doctors.

Having established the RIMR, Rockefeller and Gates then turned their attentions to the field of education and in particular the plight of poorly educated blacks in the South, a cause which had fired Rockefeller's Baptist conscience (and had long been an area of concern for his wife Cettie and members of her family). Junior too was passionately interested in the cause and when Rockefeller procured the establishment of the General Education Board in 1903, it was Junior who took on primary responsibility for liaising with the GEB's board of directors. Rockefeller donated $1 million to the GEB at its inception, $10 million in 1905 and a further $30 million in 1907, and the GEB was granted corporate status by Congress (the bill granting such status being guided through Congress by Senator Nelson Aldrich, Junior's father-in-law).

Initially, the GEB focused its attentions on the creation of high schools, largely but not exclusively in the South; later it broadened its scope of operations to include higher education, including the newly formed University of Chicago. However, the GEB's aspirations in the field of black education suffered continued setbacks as a result of pernicious racism and in the end, the overwhelming majority of the GEB's funds were applied in favour of white schools or medical training. Nevertheless, during its thirty years of operation, the GEB distributed over $130 million in support of educational causes.

The Rockefeller Sanitary Commission followed in 1909. It had its origins in a challenge Rockefeller presented to a small group of medical researchers, when he asked if they could identify any disease "affecting large numbers of people, of which you can say 'I know all about this and I can cure it, not in fifty or even eighty percent of cases but in one hundred percent.'" The answer to Rockefeller's question was hookworm, a condition that was widespread amongst the poor of the South, causing extreme lethargy in millions of people and contributing to the widespread belief that the poor of the South were indolent idiots. A few years earlier, it had been discovered that hookworm could easily be cured with 50 cents' worth of Epsom salts and thymol and yet so widespread was the problem that the US Government had neither the resources nor the will to seek its eradication.

The US Government perhaps could not launch an anti-hookworm campaign, but Rockefeller and Gates could in the form of the Rockefeller Sanitary Commission. The Commission set about a widespread campaign of public health education and treatment and the results were nothing less than amazing. Within five years, over half a million people had been identified as suffering from hookworm and cured and the Southern states had introduced measures designed to limit the risk of re-infection. It was philanthropy on a scale and with a simplicity which very much appealed to Rockefeller and again generated a measure of public goodwill towards the Rockefeller name.

By 1910, the RIMR, the GEB and the Rockefeller Sanitary Commission had all been established and were operating successfully. Nevertheless, for Gates at least, there was still more philanthropic work to do. He had been urging Rockefeller to make further donations out of his fortune "for the good of mankind" and in 1910 Rockefeller agreed to establish the Rockefeller Foundation, which was to be endowed on a scale that dwarfed Rockefeller's previous donations. Rockefeller's first gift to the Foundation was to consist of $50 million dollars' worth of shares, the first tranche of an initial endowment of $100 million. Over the years to come, further hundreds of millions of dollars would be donated by Rockefeller and his family.

The aims of the Foundation were wide: to promote the wellbeing of mankind throughout the world. Initially, Rockefeller had attempted to obtain a federal charter for the Institute but Congress failed to pass the necessary legislation; public hostility to the name of Rockefeller was still too strong. Finally, Rockefeller gave up the attempt and instead obtained a charter from the state of New York. The Foundation, under the leadership of Gates, was then in business, concentrating on public health and medical education in both the United States and overseas. It became a truly global operation extending the Sanitary Commission's anti-hookworm program to over 50 countries and tackling problems such as yellow fever, typhus and malaria worldwide. Substantial donations were made to medical schools both at home and abroad (with a particular emphasis on China) and millions were spent to encourage University-level medical training. Many of the triumphs of twentieth century medicine were achieved thanks to support provided, directly or indirectly, by the Foundation. Ultimately, it would prove to be Rockefeller's greatest legacy to the world, greater even than the rationalization of the oil industry.

Both Rockefeller and Gates knew this. When Gates finally stepped down from the Foundation's trustee board, at the age of 73, he asked his colleagues: "When you die and come to approach the judgment of Almighty God, what do you think He will demand of you? Do you for an instant presume that He will enquire into your petty failures or trivial virtues? No. He will ask just one question. What did you do as a trustee of the Rockefeller Foundation?"

Meanwhile, Rockefeller's life of semi-retirement continued. Public criticism of him had reached its peak at the time of the dissolution of

Standard Oil; Rockefeller's philanthropic activities had gone some way to assuage this, but not far enough; there were still many who saw Rockefeller's charitable works as the attempt of a rich man to escape the consequences of past sins. Rockefeller was aware of this but continued to maintain his general policy of silence in the face of criticism. In contrast, Junior felt strongly that his father was being misjudged (he hero-worshipped his father) and was determined something must be done to address the problem. A preliminary step had been taken in 1907, when Standard Oil hired a publicity agent (one of the first such appointments by a US business) whose function was to engage with critics of the trust and challenge inconsistencies and errors in reporting. As Standard Oil's views began to percolate out into the media as a consequence of this policy, Rockefeller himself began to be seen in a new light. Having seen how useful a publicity agent could be to Standard Oil, Rockefeller procured the services of Ivy Lee, perhaps the best publicity agent in the United States at that time, and under Lee's guidance, as the years passed, Rockefeller began to be seen less as an industrial tyrant and more as a philanthropic grandfatherly gentleman, playing golf and dispensing dimes to children. This process was of course aided by the simple fact that Rockefeller lived so long – many of the people who had played a role in the creation of Standard Oil predeceased him as did many of his critics, while he lived on and on, traveling between his various homes scattered throughout the country. By the mid-twenties, newspapers and magazines were presenting him as a man who had met and overcome all the challenges that life could give him and he became known for dispensing short pieces of homely financial wisdom, generally emphasizing the advantages of sensible saving and frugal living. He had become an elder statesman of finance.

More and more the affairs of the Standard Oil companies and the philanthropic institutions were in the hands of others, Junior in particular. Cettie, Rockefeller's wife, died in 1915. All of his children married (some well, some disastrously) and Rockefeller made substantial donations to them and their families before his death. The bulk of his remaining fortune however, amounting perhaps to as much as half a billion dollars, was gradually passed to Junior who grappled with the problems it posed earnestly but with a considerable degree of self-doubt. Ultimately, Rockefeller retained a "mere" $25 million for himself.

One of Rockefeller's last forays into public life followed the Wall Street Crash in 1929. In an effort to restore public confidence in an economy which was collapsing into the Great Depression, Rockefeller was persuaded to read a press statement, in which he declared: "These are days in which many are discouraged. In the ninety years of my life, depressions have come and gone. Prosperity has always returned and will again. Believing that the fundamental conditions of the country are sound, my son and I have been purchasing sound common stock for some days." (To which the comedian Eddie Cantor is said to have replied: "Sure. Who else has any money left?")

Rockefeller's press statement did not restore public confidence; Americans and the world faced more than a decade of economic stagnation and misery. Nevertheless although serious losses were sustained as a result of the Depression, the Rockefeller fortune remained fundamentally intact as did the funds he had allocated to his charitable institutions. He himself however saw his remaining personal fortune reduced to $7 million, prompting one of his grandchildren later to comment: "For Grandfather, that was practically broke!"

Rockefeller by now was in his mid-nineties. His body was weak but his mind was still alert. In a conversation with one of his grandchildren, he likened himself to a bicycle coasting down a hill and was determined to live until the age of one hundred. He was delighted when he reached his 95th birthday – he had insured his life and on reaching this goalpost, the insurance company was obliged to pay out $5 million. Physical weakness had by now forced him to give up golf, instead he spent his time sitting in the sun or watching movies at The Casements, a winter home he had bought for himself in Florida and where he now spent most of his time. Religion still dominated his life; he remained serenely confident that he was guaranteed a place in the hereafter.

Celebrating his 100th birthday was however, one goal that he was not destined to achieve. On 23rd May 1937, just a few weeks before his 98th birthday he suffered a heart attack and died a few hours later in his sleep.

Public attention to his death was gentle – far gentler than would have been predicted 25 years before. His obituaries praised his philanthropy; there was little mention of his role as the tyrant of Standard Oil. On his death, he left a little over $26 million (his fortune having apparently recovered somewhat since the darkest Depression days). The Rockefeller Foundation, the Rockefeller Institute for Medical Research, the General Education Board – all were functioning better than ever under the careful guidance of boards of trustees chaired by Junior, carrying out their mandates to improve the lot of mankind in a myriad of fields.

John D Rockefeller's legacies were and remain substantial. He set a standard for philanthropic giving that has seldom (if ever) been matched since. Moreover, it was Rockefeller who, in the form of Standard Oil, by promoting harmonization and cooperation in the oil industry, prepared it for the demands that the twentieth century would make upon it, not least during the course of the First and Second World Wars, when the Standard Oil companies played leading roles in ensuring adequate oil supplies for the Allies. As regards those companies, many of them survive to this day in one form or another. ExxonMobil, Amoco, Chevron, all can trace their ancestries back to, or were otherwise associated with, the original Standard Oil trust and its subsidiaries (albeit that some of them have now merged or otherwise been acquired by other oil companies).

Against those achievements however, must be weighed the crushing effects of the monopolistic policies pursued by Standard Oil at the behest of Rockefeller (and, it must not be forgotten, the other members of the Standard Oil Gang), the elimination of smaller and ultimately unsuccessful competitors, the use of illegal rebates and price fixing, the political corruption and (on occasion) the intimidation by which Standard Oil secured its monopoly and the Rockefeller family gained its fortune. Was Rockefeller therefore primarily a sinner or a saint? He himself would unquestionably incline towards the latter interpretation. The reality however is more prosaic. Like most people, he was a little of both.

Henry Ford

"There is one rule for industrialists and that is: make the best quality of goods possible at the lowest cost possible, paying the highest wages possible."

Henry Ford (1863 – 1947)

The Young Mechanic

Henry Ford, founder of the Ford Motor Company and perhaps more than any other man responsible for the introduction of modern mass production techniques into the automobile industry, was born on his father's farm in Dearborn, Michigan on 30 July 1863. His father, William, had been born in County Cork, Ireland, where he had worked as a tenant farmer before emigrating to the United States in 1847 with his parents, two brothers and three sisters in order to escape the effects of the Irish potato famine.

In many respects, William and his family were luckier than many of their fellow countrymen who were forced to seek a new future across the Atlantic Ocean. They were Protestant, and thus did not suffer from the anti-Catholic prejudice that was to be found in many parts of the United States at that time. They were not financially destitute. Nor were they the first Fords to move from Ireland to America; two of William's uncles, Samuel and George Ford, had emigrated in the early 1830s and had settled in Michigan, where they had prospered and were now raising families of their own. William and his family travelled to join their Ford relatives in the Dearborn area of Michigan where, with the help of Samuel and George, they sought to build new lives for themselves.

William's father acquired 80 acres of land near Dearborn and William helped to clear it and to establish a small farm. He also hired himself out as a carpenter, partly to earn money to pay off the mortgage on his father's farm, and partly so he could save enough money to buy land of his own. It was whilst he was working as a carpenter and general handyman for a neighbour, Patrick O'Hern, another Irish immigrant, that William met the woman who was to become his wife and Henry's mother. Mary Litogot was the daughter of a Belgian immigrant who had died in an accident, and she had been adopted by O'Hern and his wife.

Mary was fourteen years younger than William and still at school when they met. They married in 1861 and William bought 91 acres of land from his new father-in-law, on the understanding that O'Hern and his wife would live with the newly-weds.

Mary gave birth to a son in 1862, but he died at birth and so Henry, who was born in July of the following year, was William's eldest surviving child. Other children followed in swift succession, five surviving into adulthood, and before long, William's farm became a crowded but happy family home. The family prospered, and William became a figure of some standing in the Dearborn community, becoming a Justice of the Peace and Churchwarden. Henry, for his part, did not enjoy a particularly warm relationship with his father, but was close to his mother, whom he praised in later life for making the farm "a good place to be". She was something of a disciplinarian, anxious that her children accept the responsibilities that life would place on their shoulders and carry out their duties, no matter how unpleasant, without self-pity. The result of the constant repetition of precepts such as these was that Henry grew up to be a quiet and introspective young man, yet with a steely determination to satisfy his own wishes and aspirations, whatever they may have been.

Henry disliked the farm chores that he was assigned and was frequently distracted by other interests, especially anything involving mechanical tools and devices. When not at the local school (which he began to attend at the age of seven and where according to all accounts, he was an average, if somewhat inattentive pupil), he would often be found tinkering with any gadget that caught his attention and he became fascinated by watch mechanisms. He is reputed to have devised watchmaker tools out of his mother's knitting needles; what his mother thought of this is not entirely clear, but since she frequently referred to him with pride as a "born mechanic", it seems likely that she approved.

He also grew interested in steam engines and devised his own experiments with kettles and steam boilers. One of these nearly ended in disaster; he decided one day to investigate a steam engine which powered a threshing machine used on the farm (the powered mechanization of agriculture had just begun, and prosperous and imaginative farmers such as William Ford were anxious to invest in the new machinery that was becoming available in the hope of increasing productivity whilst at the same time reducing the amount of often back-breaking labour that farming demanded). Something went wrong and the engine blew up, knocking Henry over and damaging a nearby fence. He was lucky to escape serious injury.

William approved of such experiments to the extent that they had practical applications on the farm; indeed he himself had a considerable interest in mechanical devices, but he was more cautious about Henry's activities when they appeared to have no value in the real world. Notwithstanding this, he did permit Henry to set up a small workbench in his room. Henry, who in later life was not above embellishing and on occasions rewriting his memories to better suit his image of himself, later claimed that his father had been so eager for him to become a farmer that he had been obliged to set the workbench up in secret in order to avoid his father's hostility, but this account was disputed by other members of the family. It seems unlikely that Henry could have kept the existence of his workbench a secret from his father; certainly his younger brothers and sisters were aware of it and in later life, Henry's sister Margaret claimed that William was very tolerant of Henry's constant demands for new tools. Moreover, William had a well-equipped workshop of his own, where Henry sometimes worked.[56]

The Ford family suffered a cruel blow in March 1876, when Henry's mother, aged only 37, lost first a baby, her ninth child, in childbirth and then, twelve days later, her own life as a result of a fever. Henry never forgot his shock and grief at the loss of his mother. He reacted by becoming even more insular and taciturn and still more determined to escape what he saw as the drudgery of farm life for the more exciting world of machines and engineering.

According to his own account, Henry's fascination for steam-powered machinery received a powerful boost several months after the death of his mother. Riding with his father in a horse-drawn wagon, he saw trundling along the road towards them a steam powered engine. Henry had certainly encountered steam engines before, both on his father's farm

---

[56] In later life, Henry was noticeably reluctant to admit that his mechanical aptitude, or indeed ultimate financial success, owed anything to the influence of his father. This attitude contrasts strongly with his view of his mother, to whom he gave extensive credit for his success in life. This seems to have been a result of a quirk of Henry's personality, and was unfair to William who, whilst trying run a farm and raise a family, provided at least some measure of support for the mechanical tastes of his eldest son.

and elsewhere, but this was the first steam engine he had seen moving under its own power down a road rather than along railroad tracks. The steam engine pulled to the side of the road to allow William Ford's wagon to pass, and Henry (possibly to his father's irritation) leapt out of the wagon to ply the engine driver with questions, which the driver did his best to answer. Henry remembered this encounter for the rest of his life, and when he returned home he began to apply himself more and more to his mechanical studies and less and less to his obligations on the farm.

After three more years, it was obvious, at least to Henry that his future lay elsewhere than on the family farm. In December 1879, he left the farm and sought work in nearby Detroit in a machine shop. He later claimed that his father had been trying to force him to stay and work on the farm and so he had simply left home, without saying a word to anyone and without his father's permission. According to Henry, by the time his father found him, a week later, he had already found employment, so that his father had little choice but to agree that Henry need not return with him. Other reports however suggest that far from not supporting his son in his ambitions, and seeking to force him into a farming life that he hated, William actively helped his son by accompanying him on his journey to Detroit, introducing him to friends who were able to help Henry find a job. From what we know of William and Henry, and in particular, Henry's peculiar reluctance to acknowledge that his father deserved any form of credit for Henry's achievements, the latter story seems the more likely to be true.

In any event, the winter of 1879 found Henry Ford working in Detroit, a city then in the throes of rapid industrial expansion. This was partly due to the city's location, situated as it was on the Detroit River, in close proximity to the Great Lakes and particularly Lake Erie which thanks to the opening of the Erie Canal in 1825, allowed easy access by boat between Detroit and New York. This led to Detroit rapidly becoming a major terminus for the hordes of settlers who were pushing west, particularly after Michigan achieved statehood in 1837. The establishment of a railroad link to Chicago in 1852 meant that Detroit was soon one of the primary shipping and transfer centres in the country, whilst the exploitation of Michigan's natural resources, ranging from the rich fishing grounds of the Great Lakes to vast forests which could supply apparently unlimited amounts of timber, and great deposits of copper and other mineral ores meant that by the time Henry Ford moved to the city, Detroit was also rapidly developing into one of the most important manufacturing centres of the United States. Unsurprisingly, in light of all of this industrial activity, demand for mechanics of all types was acute, and Henry (either with or without his father's help) soon found himself employed as an apprentice at the James Flowers and Brothers Machine Shop. However, he stayed there for only a few months and then, dissatisfied with the low pay, he moved to join the Detroit Dry Dock Company, a large shipbuilding concern, where he worked as a mechanic by day. By night, he worked for a local jeweller, repairing watches, in order to supplement his meagre daytime wages that, alone, were insufficient to enable him to meet the costs of food and lodgings. He gained valuable experience, but decided that he wanted to be a manager rather than an employee. He dreamt of going into business for himself, possibly as a watchmaker, but could not imagine making and selling enough watches to make it pay.

After working for two years in Detroit, Henry decided to return to the family farm, but decidedly not to the farming life. He had continued his mechanical experiments whenever he could during his time away from home, and was now regarded (and regarded himself) as an expert steam engineer. He earned money by selling his engineering skills to his neighbours, and worked part-time for the Westinghouse Engineering Company, which rented steam engines to local farmers. Henry was appointed by Westinghouse to travel around the district, driving the engines to where they had to go and ensuring they remained in working order. Henry loved this job, and in later life frequently referred to this period as a "happy time". He also attended a business college in Detroit, studying typing, shorthand and accountancy, skills that he believed would help him when he eventually set up a business of his own.

Henry by now was entering his twenties, and (perhaps somewhat belatedly) began to realise that there were other interests in life apart from steam engines and machine tools. He decided to take dancing lessons in order to increase his social skills (and indeed eventually became known as a good dancer[57]), a decision which reaped rewards in late 1884 when at a local dance, he met a young woman named Clara Jane Bryant who would become his wife. She was the daughter of a local farmer, three years

---

[57] In later years, he would become an enthusiastic advocate of square-dancing, forcing his reluctant staff to participate whether they wished to do so or not. Allegedly, one of the reasons for this enthusiasm was his objection to "excessive touching" during the course of more traditional dancing.

Henry and his friends continued to work on the Quadricycle over the next few months, making minor improvements to the steering mechanism and strengthening its metal frame. He was encouraged in his endeavours by no less a person than Thomas Edison, whom Henry met in August of 1896 at a company function in New York, and with whom he discussed the merits of petrol-powered cars as compared to electric cars. After meeting Edison, Henry decided to sell the Quadricycle (for $200) and set about building a new and improved automobile on which he worked whenever he could escape from his duties at the Edison plant.

Henry's work began to attract interest amongst the more entrepreneurially minded of Detroit's leading citizens, a process which culminated in August 1899 when William Maybury, the Mayor of Detroit (and an old friend of William's father) and some friends decided to set up the Detroit Automobile Company. The new venture was the first automobile manufacturing company to be established in Detroit, and they invited Henry to join them as chief engineer. Henry accepted the invitation, and resigned from the Edison Illuminating Company.

Rather than manufacture the car that Henry had designed and built after selling the Quadricycle (and which had successfully been driven for more 60 miles without suffering a breakdown), it was decided that the new company should produce a petrol-powered delivery wagon, which was unveiled to the local press in August 1900 to considerable acclaim. Over the next few months, several were manufactured and sold to local businesses, but Henry grew dissatisfied with the manufacturing process – each vehicle was custom built in a time-consuming process - and his partners in the business seemed only interested in making immediate sales. This approach left Henry with little time for experimentation into ways in which both the automobiles and the manufacturing process might be improved, which in turn would enable costs to be lowered and thus encourage wider car ownership, something that he was keen to do. In November 1900, having grown contemptuous of the "millionaire parasites" (as he called them behind their backs) he decided to resign, and the company ceased to trade.[59]

---

[59] To be fair, it should be noted that Henry's partners were also growing dissatisfied with *him*. They complained that whilst they had hired mechanics, and paid for machine tools and for the workshop which housed them, Henry had failed to deliver final sets of blueprints which would enable car production to be

Other automobile companies were being established at this time, but rather than seek employment with one of them, Henry decided to strike out in a new direction. He concluded that the best way to develop his ideas would be to build a racing car which could compete in the auto races that were then capturing the imagination of the American public and helping to drive forward innovation in the fledgling automobile industry. Over the next few months, Henry worked hard to build a new racing machine based on the principles of his Quadricycle. Money was tight, and he, Clara and Edsel were forced for a time to move in with his father, who had at last retired from his farm and moved to Detroit.[60] Nevertheless, the new racer was completed and Henry decided to enter it in a motor race to be held at Grosse Point, just outside Detroit, on 10 October 1901. First prize was to be $1,000 and a crystal punchbowl, and other competitors included famous pioneer motorists Henri Fournier, Alexander Winton and William K Vanderbilt Jr., each of whom had entered machines that were considerably more powerful than Henry Ford's new racer. By way of example, Fournier's car was said to be capable of producing 60 horsepower, and Alexander Winton's was rated at 40, whilst Henry's racer produced a mere 26.

The first race of the day was for steam-powered cars, and was followed by one for electric cars. By the time the call went out for the petrol-powered cars to assemble on the track, the number of competitors had diminished considerably due to technical difficulties. Only three cars actually appeared at the starting line, and one of those had to be promptly withdrawn thanks to a leaking cylinder. The race was to be between just two competitors – Henry Ford and Alexander Winton.

When the starting gun fired, Winton immediately roared into the lead and held it for the first few laps, seemingly a far better driver than Henry, who merely drove doggedly onwards. But then, slowly Henry began to gain on Winton, whose car was seen to be emitting smoke from its rear and seemed to be slowly losing power. On the seventh lap, Henry

---

set up in earnest. Moreover, he had a tendency to absent himself from the workshop for hours at a time, ostensibly so he could "design", seriously delaying progress. By the time Henry resigned, his partners were not sorry to see him go, notwithstanding that they lost much of the money they had invested in the company.

[60] William died in 1905.

managed to draw level with Winton and then pulled past him into the lead, which he maintained until the finishing flag came down.

Henry's victory made his name known in motoring circles all over the United States, with many commentators contrasting the reliability of Henry's racer with that of Winton's more powerful but mechanically less robust machine. This was a golden opportunity for Henry, who decided that the time had come to establish another automobile company. His success in the race attracted a small syndicate of wealthy men, including several who had previously invested (and lost money) in the Detroit Automobile Company but who, having watched the race, were willing to take another chance on Henry. On 30 November 1901, the Henry Ford Company was incorporated, and Henry was awarded 1,000 of the 6,000 shares available, and appointed chief engineer.

The investors were willing to gamble that Henry's mechanical talents would make them money, but they were certainly not willing to run the risk of another debacle like the Detroit Automobile Company. Led by William Murphy, the unofficial leader of the syndicate, they kept a close eye on Henry and before long they were dismayed to learn that rather than concentrating on designing a simple car which could be marketed and sold to the (wealthy) public (as he had promised to do), Henry was secretly working on a new racing car. Fortunately, Murphy was friendly with Henry M Leland, a famous engineer and designer who was willing to join the company and take charge of the shop floor. Unsurprisingly, Henry vigorously protested this apparent usurpation of his authority (particularly as Leland did not mince his words when explaining that he considered that he reported to William Murphy rather than Henry Ford), but to no avail, for the investors backed Leland. In a fury, Henry resigned from the company in March 1902, a mere four months after it had been formed, agreeing by way of settlement to accept $900 in cash, the blueprints for his new racing car and an undertaking that the company should no longer bear his name. The company was renamed the Cadillac Automobile Company and under the technical guidance of Henry Leland, it rapidly established an enviable reputation as one of the finest automobile manufacturers in the country. It eventually became part of the General Motors Corporation. Henry, for his part, was approaching 40, unemployed again and had the unenviable reputation of having failed in two commercial automobile ventures in less than two years.

Henry remained apparently undaunted by his business failures, and continued to focus his attention on the racing arena. Needing financial backing, he teamed up with Tom Cooper, a wealthy cycling champion who was keen to become involved in the world of motor racing. Together, with the help of a young draughtsman called C. Harold Wills, they constructed two new racers, which they named after famous trains of the time: the "Arrow" and the "999". The 999 was the more powerful machine (capable of producing 70 horsepower), and Henry and Cooper decided to enter it in a motor race scheduled to be held at Grosse Point on 25th October 1902, in which one of their competitors was again to be Alexander Winton.

The 999 was not an easy car to drive and (partly as a result of Clara's entreaties) Henry and Cooper decided to ask a cycling friend of Cooper's called Barney Oldfield to act as the driver in the race. Oldfield, who had a reputation for being fearless, promptly accepted, notwithstanding the fact that he had never driven a car before. He had one week to learn, which he duly did.

Oldfield dominated the race from the fall of the starter's flag and the other competitors never really stood a chance. He completed the five mile course in 5 minutes and 28 seconds, setting a new record, and Henry Ford's name was again quoted with approval throughout the motoring world. Oldfield went on to have a successful racing career, but Henry's attention, now that he had re-established his reputation, was beginning to veer away from racing and back to the manufacture of everyday passenger cars. He still had not forgotten his dream of producing a small reliable car that could be produced in bulk and marketed to the general public at an affordable price.

The Ford Motor Company and the Model T

Shortly after the race Henry parted company with Cooper following a disagreement (much to Clara's relief, for she did not trust him), but even before that had happened, during the summer of 1902, Henry had entered into talks about a joint business venture with Alexander Malcomson, a prosperous coal merchant of Scottish descent whom Henry had met during his days working for the Edison Illuminating Company, and who was keen to invest in the fledgling automobile industry.[61] Malcomson was not afraid to take risks in business and he and Henry, together with several other businessmen who Malcomson persuaded to join them, set up a new business that was soon to be reorganized and incorporated on 16th June 1903 as the Ford Motor Company.

Between themselves, Henry Ford and Alexander Malcomson owned just over half the shares of the new company and it was their intention that the new business should produce a small two cylinder passenger car, to be known as the Model A, generating eight horsepower and capable of perhaps 45 miles an hour. To this end, the company acquired a small factory plant on Detroit's Mack Avenue, and began to hire employees, two of whom in particular were to make substantial contributions to Henry's ultimate success.

The first was C. Harold Wills who had assisted in the designs of the 999 and the Model A. A brilliant designer, it was he who designed the famous Ford "signature" trademark, to be applied as a logo on all Ford machines. Perhaps as important as his design skills, his way of thinking complemented Henry's to a remarkable degree, and they were to work together successfully for more than a decade.

The second was Canadian-born James Couzens, who had previously worked as a bookkeeper and clerk in Malcomson's coal business. A tough-minded, humourless and on occasions sarcastic man, his attention was focused solely on the financial aspects of the new business, rather than the joys of technological innovation and experimentation and given Henry's somewhat erratic record in this area, his experience would be vital in ensuring the ultimate success of the new business. Fortunately, Henry himself seems to have recognized this, and the two men, for all their differences, worked well together.

In common with most early automobile companies (and indeed, those of today), the Ford Motor Company did not actually manufacture all of the various components of its cars, but rather placed orders with suppliers

---

[61] The fact that Henry entered into talks with Malcomson about a new venture when he should have been focusing all his attention on the racing obligations he had entered into with Cooper only a few months before may go some way to explain why Cooper and Henry had a disagreement that led to the dissolution of their partnership and sheds light on the more ruthless side of Henry's personality.

for the parts that were needed. Thus it was that in early 1903 Henry and Malcomson placed orders for the parts needed to build the Model A with various local machine shops, including an order for 650 engines, transmissions and axles to John and Horace Dodge, who operated one of the most successful machine shops in the area (and who acquired minority interests in the fledgling business by way of payment for the components they supplied). As the parts began to be delivered to the Mack Avenue plant, they were assembled by ten employees into Model A cars, which were then shipped to customers. Demand for the new car, which was priced at $850, was strong from the outset[62] although initially money was tight and Couzens, beset by cashflow concerns during the first few months was forced to warn Henry when he proposed to postpone shipping a consignment of cars so that he could make last minute improvements that any delay would mean bankruptcy. Nevertheless, by March 1904, the company had assembled and sold 658 cars and had begun to pay substantial dividends to its shareholders. For the first time in his life, Henry was beginning to make serious amounts of money.

One of the reasons for this success was Couzens' financial skill. Not only did he emphasize the need to ensure that cars were shipped to customers on time, but he also took steps to establish a network of sales agents throughout the country (the first such network of car dealerships to be created) which helped to generate demand for Ford cars. Before long, the Ford Motor Company was selling hundreds of cars each month, and by 1905 had been obliged to acquire new and larger premises on Piquette Avenue.

Perhaps inevitably, tensions were beginning to grow between Henry Ford and some of his business partners, principally Alex Malcomson. 1904 had seen the introduction of three new models by the Ford Motor Company – Models B, C and F – although Models C and F were effectively improved versions of the older Model A, priced at $800 and $1,000 respectively. The Model B was a genuinely new design, a four cylinder general purpose vehicle, larger and more powerful than the other Ford models and, priced at $2,000, considerably more expensive. This was fine, of course, as far as it went and this strategy was certainly making a great deal of money for all the shareholders in the company. It was however a

---

[62] The very first purchaser of a Model A was a Chicago dentist, Dr E Pfennig.

long way from Henry's dream of manufacturing and selling large numbers of reliable and reasonably priced cars to the general public, a dream which he was now convinced could be realized in the marketplace. Malcomson for his part, together with some of the other shareholders, including the Dodge brothers, wanted the company to concentrate on producing prestigious upmarket vehicles aimed principally at wealthy customers (and indeed Malcomson insisted that Henry and Wills design a luxurious six cylinder touring car known as the Model K exactly for this purpose). Relations between the two men and their respective supporters grew ever more tense, not helped by the fact that Couzens, who had originally been one of Malcomson's employees and had only become involved in the company at the instigation of Malcomson, but who now held a small interest in the company himself, openly backed Henry's position, as did several of the other investors. Eventually, it became obvious that matters could not continue in this fashion and there was a showdown between the two sets of shareholders in July 1906, which resulted in Malcomson and his supporters selling out their interests in the company, principally to Henry. Henry and his allies were now unequivocally in control of the Ford Motor Company and in the future Henry would not hesitate to make full use of the power that this gave him.

By 1907, Henry was in the process of becoming a wealthy man. His annual salary from the Ford Motor Company was $36,000 but the majority of his earnings came from a steadily increasing flow of dividend payments made possible by the soaring profits of the company. Despite this, Henry, Clara and Edsel were still living fairly frugally in rented accommodation and the time had now come for them to build a house of their own, a project they had been planning for several years but for which until now Henry had had neither the time nor the money to pursue. They commissioned the building of a grand new house on Edison Street, costing over a quarter of a million dollars and requiring the services of several servants and gardeners. Needless to say, their new house included a garage capable of housing several cars and a workshop. However, despite this new found affluence, Henry remained strangely indifferent to money, although Clara began to develop a reputation amongst her friends for being somewhat "grand". Henry's indifference to money extended to mislaying invoices for valuable orders (something that must have driven Couzens wild) and Clara once found a cheque for $75,000 stuffed into the pocket of a pair of Henry's trousers that he had totally forgotten about.

Henry was still distracted by his dream of building a cheap and reliable car, and to this end had been experimenting with making use of vanadium steel, a new type of steel that was lighter and stronger than the steels typically used in cars at that time. In 1906, Ford had introduced the Model N, an open-topped car which utilized vanadium steel, thus making the car lighter, and which Henry had hoped to sell for less than $500. In the event, production and logistical difficulties meant that the car had to be sold at $600, which was still cheaper than the price of many other comparable cars on the market and the Model N sold well. Modified versions, known as Models R and S were released over the next year.

Henry was determined that the next car in the series would be something special. In the winter of 1906, he took one of his employees whom he liked and trusted – Charles Sorensen, a Danish immigrant who had demonstrated considerable skill at translating Henry's ideas into engineering designs – and led him to the third floor of the Piquette plant. Henry ordered him to arrange for part of the floor to be partitioned off, with access only via a door equipped with a good lock. Behind that locked door, hidden away because Henry feared that rivals might try to steal details of his designs, Henry and a small group of trusted workers laboured long and hard designing the new Model T, a car destined to be one of the most famous in history. Based on the lessons learned when designing the Model N, the Model T utilized vanadium steel but also featured a number of innovations, such as a new block housing all of the engine's cylinders (hitherto, cylinders had usually been constructed separately and then bolted together) and a new "planetary" transmission system (reducing the likelihood of the teeth on the gear cogs being stripped away). There were also three foot pedals: one for forwards, one for reverse, and a brake, as well as a magneto-sparking system, a rarity in all but the most expensive cars of the time.

When advance details of the Model T were distributed to Ford dealerships across the country in early 1908, there was general incredulity at the claims made for the new car. Nevertheless, when the car was finally released for sale in October 1908 – at the price of $825 (the price would gradually be reduced over the years to come) – demand for the Model T was such that for a while, the Ford Motor Company had to refuse to accept new orders; there were already sufficient to keep the Ford factories operating at full capacity for nearly 12 months. Robust, reliable, capable of negotiating even the dirt track roads of rural America (the Model T was incredibly popular amongst farmers), the Model T entered the popular imagination and culture in a way that no car had done before (and very few have done since), despite the fact that the first models were sold without any accessories, or indeed, some necessities, such as windscreen wipers and doors. Before long, a sub-industry had sprung up selling vital or desirable add-ons to Model T customers keen to improve their Tin Lizzies. The age of popular motoring was beginning and unsurprisingly, the profits of the Ford Motor Company soared, as did its dividend payments.

There was however one dark cloud on the horizon. In 1877, a New York patent lawyer named George Baldwin Selden, who in his spare time liked to tinker with machinery, had become interested in the internal combustion engine which was then just being developed in Europe. Realising that it might one day have a role to play in self-propelled vehicles, he had obtained a patent which would (he believed) entitle him to claim royalties should anyone succeed in building such a vehicle at some time in the future. In 1899, his patent was acquired by a group of investors who then sought to enforce it against a number of automobile manufacturers who, after considering the matter and wishing to avoid expensive lawsuits, joined with the investors in 1903 to form the Association of Licensed Automobile Manufacturers with the intention of enforcing Selden's patent against all other automobile manufacturers.

Henry was aware of the existence of the ALAM; indeed, he had tried to join it when it was established, but had been rebuffed. As a consequence, and with the fervent support of Couzens, he decided to defy the ALAM, and took out announcements in Detroit newspapers declaring that the Selden patent was invalid and offering to protect his customers from patent infringement claims. The ALAM issued proceedings a few weeks later. For six years, the Ford Motor Company fought the claims of the ALAM, until in September 1909, Judge Charles Merill Hughes sitting in the Circuit Court of the Southern District of New York, ruled in favour of the ALAM. This meant that no car powered by an internal combustion engine could be sold in the United States without the consent of the ALAM and that the Ford Motor Company (and indeed all other automobile manufacturers who were not members of the ALAM) owed millions of dollars in royalties in respect of cars they had already sold.

This was a dark time in Henry's life, and he briefly thought of selling his interest in the Ford Motor Company to William Durant, a rich self-made businessman who was in the process of acquiring various automobile companies (including Cadillac) that he would combine to form General Motors. The deal fell through however and Henry decided to fight on through the courts, unlike virtually all the other manufacturers (including General Motors) who rushed to agree terms with the ALAM.

The appeal hearings dragged on through 1910, during which time the ALAM issued notices in newspapers warning the public not to buy Ford cars, whilst Henry sought to convince would-be customers that they would be indemnified should the ALAM seek to bring proceedings against any of them. Finally, on 9 January 1911, the appeal court (to popular acclaim) dismissed the ALAM's claims, effectively ruling that the basic principles of the internal combustion engine must be available to all automobile manufacturers.[63] It was a complete vindication for Henry Ford, and a devastating decision for the ALAM, which shortly thereafter was disbanded. The American motor industry owed (and owes) a debt of gratitude to Henry Ford for his defiance of the ALAM; the history of the automobile industry in America, and quite probably the world, would have been very different had Henry bowed to the ALAM's demands as did all of the other major automobile manufacturers of the time.

Whilst battling with the ALAM, Henry had also been seeking ways to expand his company. The first step was to obtain larger industrial premises for the company was rapidly outgrowing the Piquette plant. A few years before, Henry had acquired a 60 acre disused racetrack in Detroit's Highland Park suburb and instructed architect Albert Kahn to design a modern factory to be built there. Once completed, the Highland Park plant was considered a miracle of the new industrial age, and boasting more than 50,000 square feet of glass, it soon became known as the "Crystal Palace". Production of the Model T was transferred to Highland Park in 1910, and in its first year of operation, the new plant assembled more than 18,500 cars. The following year, this figure rose to over 34,000 cars, but even at this rate of production, the Ford Motor

---

[63] Whilst Selden had made some attempts to build a self-propelled carriage for himself in the late 1870s, he had never really developed his ideas. Henry Ford, on the other hand, when the matter arose in court, could easily demonstrate that his ideas sprang from a long line of earlier technological developments made by a variety of inventors both in the United States and in Europe, thus emphasizing that no one man was in fact responsible for the modern automobile, which cast considerable doubt on the validity of the Selden patent.

Company was unable to satisfy the demand for the Model T. It was vital that Henry found ways to speed up production even more.

The Ford Motor Company had experimented with a primitive form of assembly line – essentially a rope attached to chassis of a car which was then slowly pulled past a line of workers who attached various components to the car as it passed – as early as 1908; by and large however, cars were still being assembled one at a time by teams of workers working as often as not with components which were not fully standardized and which thus required time-consuming individual alterations. This simply was not good enough and after much thought, the concept of the modern industrial assembly line – with chassis and fully standardized (and thus interchangeable) components being transported to specialized workers by means of conveyor belts - was developed. Exactly who developed the concept in its modern form[64] is unclear. The reality is that probably no one person did, although typically Henry claimed the credit. However, various other employees (including Charles Sorenson, who had assisted in the original designs for the Model T) made important contributions to the concept. The development of the assembly line speeded up the car assembly process to a remarkable degree. A time-and-motion study in the summer of 1913 suggested that it took an average of twelve and a half hours to assemble a Model T using the old manufacturing process; by the following year, after the assembly lines had been installed, the assembly time had been reduced to little more than an hour and a half. Production rates soared yet again and whilst the workforce expanded and labour costs consequently rose, Henry was able to reduce the price of the Model T (by 1913, the price of a new Model T had dropped to $440) whilst realising higher and higher profits. By 1914, the Ford Motor Company was manufacturing nearly half of America's cars. It was a magnificent industrial achievement.[65]

---

[64] Mass-production has been around in one form or another since the time of Ying Zheng, the First Emperor of China (247-210 BCE), whose Terracotta Army was produced on an assembly line. The Venetians used a form of assembly line in the 16th century to create their war galleys and the British naval docks in Portsmouth built assembly lines in 1801 (still in use in the 1960s) to produce rope pulley blocks.

[65] The new assembly lines also gave rise to Henry's famous statement to the effect that the Model T was available in any colour desired so long as it was black. The reality is that the very early Model Ts were sold in a variety of colours.

By 1913, Henry Ford was rich and his future was secure. The same could not be said for the thousands of workers who laboured in his assembly plants and those of his competitors. The work was ill-paid and (an unavoidable consequence of the introduction of assembly lines) repetitive and boring; it was difficult for workers to feel pride in their jobs. Moreover, workers had little or no job security as car manufacturers (including Ford) had no hesitation in laying men off without pay whenever production had to be suspended for any reason, or during holiday periods such as Christmas. As a consequence, the Ford Motor Company (like its competitors) had serious problems motivating and retaining its workers, and the cost of training workers only to see them shortly thereafter quit their jobs for other, more desirable work represented a serious financial drain for the company. There were also concerns at management level about the dangers posed by organized labour; to date, the car workers (many of whom were immigrants from Eastern Europe, often with an imperfect command of English) had shown little interest in recruitment attempts by union organizers, but there was always the possibility that this could change.

Henry Ford and James Couzens decided that this problem had to be tackled before it grew worse. In January 1914, Henry, Couzens and a number of other senior executives gathered to debate the matter and the idea emerged that the Ford Motor Company should double its workers' pay to $5 a day (although this figure included a work-related profit sharing bonus, which could if necessary be withdrawn). Henry was at first somewhat cautious about the proposal, although there was no question that the company could afford such largesse without noticeably affecting the dividends paid to Henry and his fellow shareholders. He allowed himself to be persuaded when Couzens pointed out that the $5 wage would be great advertising (which, indeed, it proved to be). Henry did, however, insist that the new rates should only be paid to workers who

---

Once the assembly line process was introduced, it was found that the various body paints then being used took so long to dry that they were slowing production. After some experimentation, Ford identified a lacquer paint called Japan Black which dried quickly and displayed the necessary degree of durability, giving rise to Henry's famous slogan. By 1926, new types of paints had been developed, and the Model T was again available in a variety of colours.

were "clean, sober and industrious"; evidence of a growing paternalistic tendency on the part of Henry towards "his" workers.[66]

When the pay rise was announced, the results were dramatic. The country was passing through an economic downturn and unemployment rates were high. In response to Ford's announcement, thousands of men gathered outside its factory gates seeking work, so many in fact that a riot broke out and the police had to be called to quell the disturbance with hose pipes and the Ford plants had to display "no hiring" signs. Other car manufacturers vehemently denounced Henry, calling him a "traitor" (not that Henry cared) and the press had a field day, with many newspapers criticizing Henry for making an economic blunder that one day he would rue, while other newspapers praised him extravagantly.

The effect of the pay rise on the Ford workers themselves was equally dramatic. Absenteeism rates plummeted and morale soared; workers became so proud of being "Ford men" that they insisted on wearing their factory identity cards when off duty. Immediately, they were elevated to middle class status, with easy access to credit that in turn transformed them into prospective purchasers of the new consumer goods that were now flowing out of the factory gates of America's industries. And Ford workers could now afford to buy automobiles for themselves (particularly, of course, Model Ts) and they promptly did so.

Henry's paternalism towards his workers was not limited to applying conditions to the $5 a day pay rate. Fiercely opposed to the introduction of organized labour, he nevertheless sincerely believed he had a responsibility towards his workers to ensure that they lived good and wholesome lives (as determined by his somewhat puritanical standards) and to this end, he set up a Sociological Department, the purpose of which was to ensure that Ford workers were behaving themselves when not working and living their lives according to his precepts. Astonishing as it may seem today, the Department's investigators visited workers' homes, investigating matters such as whether the Ford workers were

---

[66] The $5 a day rate was initially only offered to male workers, for Henry expected female workers to get married and then to cease work and was consequently less concerned about paying them a fair wage. Having said that, female workers at the Ford Motor Company were still probably better treated than they would have been by any other car manufacturer of the day and eventually Henry relented and the $5 pay rate was also offered to them.

married, whether they followed a religion (and noting which religion), whether they drank (Henry was teetotal) or gambled, what their hobbies were, whether they kept clean and tidy houses and so on. Henry was particularly keen to know whether his workers were saving or (in his view) squandering "their" share of "his" profits, whether they maintained life insurance and whether they bought consumer goods on instalment plans (something the investigators were ordered to discourage). If the investigators identified a worker[67] whose lifestyle did not satisfy Henry's standards, they sought to encourage the miscreant to change their ways. Whether or not the Ford workers appreciated such a paternalistic approach is open to debate; nevertheless (and perhaps surprisingly) many of those workers do seem to have accepted the intrusions of Henry's investigators into their personal lives as part of the price of being employed by the Ford Motor Company and some may even have appreciated their employer taking such an interest in them.

By the summer of 1914, Henry had become a well-known and popular figure with the American public. His stand against the ALAM, the $5 a day pay rate, his desire to ensure that the average American had access to the benefits of the new automobile technology, all ensured his celebrity status, and the press often compared him favourably to other industrial tycoons of his age. This was the time when many of Henry's fellow tycoons (most notably, but not exclusively, John D Rockefeller) were under attack by politicians and press alike for building and operating industrial monopolies and in contrast to them, Henry appeared to embody many of the virtues dear to the hearts of the average Americans of the day: hard work, thrift, a self-made fortune and a firm belief that the new technologies could and should be deployed for the betterment of everyone.

Henry enjoyed being a celebrity, although he grew irritated when crowds of curious onlookers gathered outside his house on Edison Street hoping to catch a glimpse of him, preventing him from travelling freely to and from work. Eventually, such intrusions proved too much, and he decided to move house. Originally, he considered moving to Grosse Point, where many wealthy Detroit citizens had built luxurious homes, but then

---

[67] Or other family members, for the investigators had no hesitation about questioning family members who did not themselves work for the Ford Motor Company.

decided against the idea, feeling that he would have little in common with the families who had already moved there.[68]

Instead, he decided to look back to his roots. For some years, he had been buying up farms and woodland around Dearborn, partly to create wildlife sanctuaries, for he had grown interested in ornithology as a hobby and was an early supporter of conservation measures generally. He now decided to build himself a country estate on some of the land he had acquired near the Rouge River, and considered appointing the famed architect Frank Lloyd Wright to design a suitable residence. Unfortunately, Wright was not available (he had in fact eloped to Europe with the wife of one of his clients) and the house that was eventually built was a somewhat strange castle-like structure, constructed out of grey limestone at a cost of over $1 million. Henry named his new residence "Fairlane" after the Irish town where his mother's adoptive father had been born and as might be expected, it boasted many luxurious features including a heated indoor swimming pool, a bowling alley and landscaped gardens. Electricity for the new estate was generated on site by means of hydroelectric generators powered by the Rouge River. Henry, Clara and Edsel moved into Fairlane in January 1916.

Edsel Ford was by now in his 23rd year. Unsurprisingly, as the only son of Henry Ford, he had been exposed to cars from an early age, and indeed had obtained his own car at the tender age of eight.[69] Like his father, he enjoyed tinkering in workshops, but he was also fairly studious, obtaining good grades at school and by all accounts was a pleasant, fairly easy-going young man, lacking Henry's inward focus and secretive drive but nonetheless conscientious and when the occasion demanded, hardworking. At this time, he was close to Henry in a way that Henry had never been to his father, and Henry in turn was close to Edsel. As far as Henry was concerned, there was no question but that Edsel would join him at the Ford Motor Company as soon as his schooling ended and Edsel, for his part, was happy to do so. (Henry had developed a mistrust

---

[68] He may well have been right, for this was the time of the furore about the $5 a day pay rate, and many of the rich local businessmen had been loudly critical of Henry's actions in this regard.

[69] These were the days before the introduction of the minimum legal driving age, and Edsel thought nothing of driving himself to and from school. One wonders what his fellow pupils, not to mention his teachers, thought. Henry appears not to have objected at all.

of college education that would never leave him and it seems to have been taken for granted that Edsel would not attend college.) Consequently, after graduating from high school, Edsel went to work at the Ford Motor Company. By the time he was 21, he had been made company secretary. Popular with the workers and his fellow executives, it was generally assumed that one day he would replace his father at the helm of the company.

Henry and Clara had hoped that Edsel would continue to live with them once they moved to Fairlane, and indeed the swimming pool and bowling alley had primarily been built with this in mind. Inevitably however, Edsel developed ideas of his own. He had met a young woman called Eleanor Clay, the niece of a well-to-do department store owner, and the two had developed a discreet relationship. By June 1916, and not without some misgivings on the part of Edsel's parents, who worried that they were too young, the couple were engaged, and they married in November of the same year. By 1917, they had made Henry and Clara grandparents as a result of the birth of their first child, whom they (of course) christened Henry (or Henry II as he is often referred to in histories of the Ford family); Henry II was followed by three other children: Benson, born in 1919, Josephine (born in 1923) and William Clay (born in 1925).

The Peace Ship and the War

Henry Senior had other things on his mind at this time apart from the building of Fairlane, the marriage of his only son and becoming a grandparent. The outbreak of the First World War in Europe in August 1914 had been greeted by many Americans with a determination that the United States should stay out of the conflict, and this was a view that was firmly shared by Henry Ford. In particular, he feared that the willingness of Wall Street banks (and particularly the House of Morgan) to issue war loans in favour of the Allies would lead to America being dragged into the war, a fear that was exacerbated by Henry's general contempt for "millionaire parasites" who he was convinced would regard the war as a golden money-making opportunity regardless of the consequences for the country. By now of course, Henry was a famous public figure and so when in the summer of 1915 he gave an interview to a reporter from the *Detroit Free Post* declaring his opposition to the war and stating that he was willing to make one million dollars available to fund a worldwide campaign for peace, his views were widely reported, not only in Detroit, but across the country.

Henry's views attracted the attention of Rosika Schwimmer, a prominent and flamboyant Hungarian-American anti-war campaigner of Jewish descent. She, together with another pacifist called Louis Lochner obtained an interview with Henry on 17 November 1915, during which they promoted the idea that the war could be brought to an immediate end if the United States used its influence to establish a peace commission. They persuaded Henry that in order for a peace commission to succeed, it would require Henry's public support and in particular, for him to utilize his influence in Washington in order to gain official backing for the peace proposals from the United States Government. After some consideration (and having sought the opinion of Clara, who was thoroughly in favour of the idea) Henry agreed to help. After all, he had revolutionized American car production and had turned American industrial working practices on their head by introducing "his" $5 a day pay rate; why shouldn't he be able to intervene and secure world peace when all others had failed? Within days he was on a train bound for Washington and a series of interviews with highly placed Government officials, including President Wilson himself. Henry's trip inevitably attracted the attention of the press, to whom Henry expounded the concepts underlying the peace commission proposals. During the course of his press conferences, the suggestion was made that a special ship should be commissioned to carry the peace delegates to Europe, an idea that Henry seized upon and made his own. On 23 November 1915, Henry and Lochner were granted an interview by President Wilson who was cautious and equivocal about the peace commission, even after Henry told him that he intended to charter a steamer within the next few days to serve as a peace ship. Henry and Lochner left the White House without President Wilson's public endorsement and irritated, Henry turned to Lochner and dismissed the President as "a small man".

The news that Henry was chartering a peace ship, known as Oscar II, was released to the press the next day. By and large, the American press was not impressed, some openly calling the peace plan ridiculous, and heaping scorn of Henry's pronouncements that the troops would be out of the trenches "by Christmas" but Henry pushed ahead regardless.

It had been intended that Oscar II should carry peace delegates comprising America's great and good; in practice, many of the delegates were invited on short notice (Oscar II was scheduled to depart in early December, which left very little time for preparations to be made) and were either unwilling or unable to attend. When the peace ship eventually set sail, bound for Norway, many of the passengers were journalists and most of the peace delegates who did join the mission were, to all intents and purposes, non-entities.[70]

In the frantic days leading up to Oscar II's departure, Henry's life had been complicated by Clara who by now had developed second thoughts about the entire mission. She worried about the dangers of sailing Oscar II into what was, after all, a war zone[71] and tried desperately to persuade Henry not to go. Moreover, Clara had developed doubts about Rosika Schwimmer, who had taken advantage of Henry's generous underwriting of the costs of the peace ship by spending the days before the departure ensconced in a luxurious hotel apartment, and ordering herself dresses and fur coats at Henry's expense, whilst seeming to achieve little of substance. Nevertheless, Clara was unable to persuade Henry to stay behind and, amidst scenes of confusion, Oscar II duly departed from a pier in Hoboken, New Jersey on the cold morning of 4 December 1915, waved off by a desolate Clara and a crowd of some 15,000 curious onlookers.

Life on board Oscar II rapidly descended into confusion. Before the eyes of the reporters who were on board (and who were before long cabling critical stories back to their newspapers), the peace commission delegates, without the benefit of any effective leadership, rapidly broke up into little cliques who constantly fought between themselves. Rosika did not help matters by remaining secluded in her cabin for much of the journey and, when she did emerge, attempting to give herself such airs of mystery and power that she succeeded only in irritating everybody. Henry himself managed to avoid antagonizing anyone (indeed the press freely acknowledged that he was at least sincere in his desire to work for peace), but this did not prevent the reporters from rapidly concluding that the peace effort was a hopeless fiasco, which indeed it was. By the time Oscar II had crossed the Atlantic, it was widely considered to be a "ship of fools".

---

[70] Henry is reputed to have offered Thomas Edison the sum of $1 million in exchange for Edison's agreement to join the peace ship; Edison (who by this stage had grown very deaf) either did not, or affected not to hear the offer and stayed safely in the United States.

[71] These were concerns that were real enough, for German U-boats were active in the Atlantic and had sunk the Lusitania only six months before.

Henry caught a cold during the voyage and was still unwell when *Oscar II* docked at Oslo. By now disillusioned by the whole concept of the peace commission, he decided that he wanted to go home, and booked himself a place on another liner due to sail to New York within twenty four hours, leaving the peace commission to continue as best it could without him. Several of the delegates eventually held low-level talks in Sweden and elsewhere, but achieved nothing. The war continued its bloody course, and Henry arrived back in New York anticipating that he would be derided for his peace efforts. By and large though, this did not happen, with many papers adopting the line that at least he had tried to secure peace, even if his efforts had perhaps been naïve and in any event had been doomed to failure.

For himself, although he tried to insist that the peace ship had achieved all that could reasonably have been expected, Henry was nevertheless conscious of having failed, a feeling he retained for the rest of his life. He had never failed on such a scale before, or before so large an audience, and typically unable to accept that his plans had at the very least been unrealistic, he looked around for others to blame. In later years, when his anti-Semitic tendencies had grown pronounced, he would claim that his peace efforts had been thwarted by Jewish conspirators (citing in particular the role played by Rosika Schwimmer), and the failure of the peace commission may well have been one of the factors which encouraged the gradual emergence of the darker side of his personality as the years went by.[72]

In the short run, he continued to call for the end of the war and criticized Wall Street and armament manufacturers as war-mongers. America was however inching closer to entering the war herself and as defence contracts began to be awarded with increasing frequency, Henry began to tone down his rhetoric as he recognized the opportunity for the Ford Motor Company to become involved in profitable war work. When the United States entered the war in April 1917, Henry announced that the various Ford plants would switch to war production immediately, and before long they were constructing Model Ts adapted for military

---

[72] Henry estimated that he had spent almost half a million dollars on the peace ship and later in life, took some comfort from the fact that it had at least helped to popularize the name of Ford in Europe, which boded well for post-war sales. (By this time, he had already taken steps to establish a subsidiary company in England and was anxious to expand on the continent of Europe.)

purposes and particularly as ambulances that were urgently needed on the Western Front. Moreover, he secured a contract from the US Navy to build small submarine chasers called Eagle boats, which were to be built at a new plant that he was in the process of constructing on land acquired along the side of the Rouge River, a plant that when completed would dwarf even the Highland plant in scale. He also proposed building a one-man submarine, a suggestion which did not win favour with the then Assistant Secretary of the Navy, Franklin D Roosevelt, who dismissed it as coming from a man who before "he saw a chance for publicity free of charge, thought a submarine was something to eat." The one-man submarine never entered production.

There were two problems which had to be addressed before Eagle boats could be constructed at the Rouge River plant: the river had to be deepened and the marshland on which the new plant was being constructed had to be drained. To Henry's pleasure, the US Government agreed to meet the costs of these improvements (at a cost of almost $3.5 million) as two of the terms of the Eagle boat contract. Eagle boats went into production in May 1918 (the first boats ever to be constructed using mass production techniques), but once the war came to an end in November 1918, it was found that Ford had in fact only succeeded in completing seven. Part of the blame for this lay with the Navy Department, which on several occasions had changed the design specifications for the boat, thus delaying production. Some of the blame however, lies with the Ford Motor Company, who found it harder to adapt mass car production techniques to the production of warships than they had anticipated and by the time the problems had been overcome, the war was all but over. In due course, the Ford Motor Company built over 50 Eagle boats, but was never invited to construct boats for the Navy again.[73]

---

[73] 1918 also saw Henry Ford run for the US Senate on the Democratic ticket at the personal request of President Wilson, who (rightly) believed that if Henry was elected, he would support the President's plans for the League of Nations. For a man who found public speaking difficult (as Henry unquestionably did) and who in fact did very little actual campaigning, he did surprisingly well against his Republican opponent, Truman Newberry, losing (after a recount) by 212,751 votes to 217,088. Henry, never a good loser, was delighted when the announcement of a senatorial investigation into possible electoral irregularities led to Newberry resigning his seat in 1922.

Life was also complicated for Henry Ford as a result of his relationship with James Couzens. Couzens, who owned approximately 11 percent of the company and was the largest shareholder in the company after Henry, had continued over the years in his role as the Ford Motor Company's financial watchdog. Henry had originally appreciated Couzens' abilities in this area, recognizing their importance to the growth of the company. Now however, Henry had become a figure of national importance, and began to feel restricted by Couzens' cautious (and financially responsible) approach to the affairs of the company. Relations between the two men began to deteriorate, until they reached their nadir at about the time of Henry's peace campaign in 1915. Under Couzens' direction, the Ford Motor Company published a company newsletter known as the *Ford Times*. Henry now began to intervene in its editorial content, insisting on inserting articles opposing America's entry into the war and wildly criticizing efforts of Britain and France to obtain war loans from Wall Street. Couzens objected, declaring that Henry should not use a company newspaper to set out his personal views; Henry roughly overruled Couzens, effectively stating that he held 59 per cent of the company's stock and could do as he wished. In the face of such a stance by Henry, Couzens felt he had little choice but to resign as vice president and company treasurer, which he duly did in October 1915, although he retained his shareholding and his seat on the board of directors.[74]

The departure of Couzens meant that Henry Ford had lost the services of one of the few men who had been able and willing to stand up to him and tell him the truth as he saw it, even when those views contradicted Henry's own. In the long run, it was a terrible loss for the Ford Motor Company, but in the short term, Henry felt only a sense of relief, declaring that Couzens' departure was "a good thing for the company".

Couzens was not the only minority shareholder who posed problems for Henry during these years. The Dodge brothers, who had originally supplied components for Henry's factories still held the shares in the Ford Motor Company they had been granted in compensation for components ordered in the earliest days when the company could not otherwise afford to pay for them. Consequently, they too had benefited

---

[74] James Couzens went on to have a distinguished political career, serving as the Mayor of Detroit from 1919 to 1922 and thereafter in the US Senate as a Senator from Michigan (having replaced Truman Newberry).

from the dramatic growth in the annual dividend payments now being generated by the Ford Motor Company.[75] Henry increasingly resented the need to make payments to minority shareholding "parasites", but his resentment turned into full-blown anger in 1913 when the Dodge brothers proceeded to establish their own car company, using their large dividend payments from the Ford Motor Company to fund this new venture. To make matters even worse, the Dodge brothers' new company was almost immediately successful.

Dependent as they were at that time on the stream of dividend payments from the Ford Motor Company, the Dodge brothers objected strongly to Henry's sometimes cavalier treatment of the company's finances for his own purposes (in which category they included the profit-sharing schemes for Ford workers and marketing campaigns such as offering cash rebates to purchasers of the Model T) which had the immediate effect of reducing the size of the cash pool from which dividend payments could be made. Rightly or wrongly, they saw Henry's actions as a deliberate attempt to reduce the size of their dividend payments, and they brushed aside Henry's arguments that as he owned well over half of the company, if he was hurting the Dodge brothers, he was hurting himself to an even greater extent. They also failed to appreciate any merit in the argument that by reducing the price of the Model T[76], Henry increased the number of cars actually sold, thus leading to the generation of greater profits despite the fall in the price of the cars. Matters were further complicated by the fact that in 1915, Henry had set up a new company – Henry Ford and Son Limited – to build a new tractor (which was to be known as the Fordson and eventually proved to be very successful indeed). The new company was privately owned by Henry and his family (he had no wish to deal with yet more minority shareholders) and thus had no direct connection with the Ford Motor Company. Notwithstanding this, the Dodge brothers heard rumours that Henry, while designing the new tractor, was using workers and materials from the Ford Motor Company and they worried about a possible conflict of interest on Henry's part and his apparent disregard for the interests of his fellow shareholders.

---

[75] In 1914, the Dodge brothers' shareholdings entitled them to dividend payments worth well in excess of one million dollars.
[76] By 1916, the price of the Model T had fallen to $345.

Matters came to a head in August 1916 when Henry unilaterally decided that much of the company's accumulated profits (then valued at close to $60 million) would not be distributed by way of dividends, but rather reinvested in the business, most notably to fund the new Rouge River plant. The Dodge brothers suggested that Henry should buy them out together with the other minority shareholders, but Henry refused. After all, he observed, he had control of the company and that was all he needed. The Dodge brothers responded on 2 November 1916 by issuing a writ against the Ford Motor Company, requiring the company to distribute at least three quarters of the company's profits to its shareholders in the form of dividends.

The legal battle between Henry and the Dodge brothers dragged on for more than two years. However, its outcome was never really in doubt, for it was clear to most impartial observers that Henry's actions, if allowed to continue unchecked, could effectively render the shares of the minority shareholders worthless, or nearly so. In February 1919, the Michigan State Superior Court[77] ordered the Ford Motor Company to distribute more than $19 million to its shareholders and to pay proper consideration to the interests of all of its shareholders in the future.

Despite Henry's earlier refusal to buy out the minority shareholders, he now concluded that he had little choice if he wished to avoid paying dividends to the "parasites" indefinitely. Even worse, if nothing were done, he would in the future have to take seriously their opinions and criticisms of his actions, which would hamper his ability to do what he liked when he liked. To Henry Ford, this was intolerable. Consequently, the Dodge brothers and the other minority shareholders (including James Couzens) now found themselves approached by agents offering to buy their shares. The agents initially refused to name the mysterious principal for whom they were working but the minority shareholders had little difficulty in identifying Henry as the would-be purchaser. Henry's initial offers were rejected as being far too low, but ultimately a settlement was reached, at a cost to Henry of over $105 million (on which basis the Ford Motor Company as a whole would at that time have been worth more than $250 million – this may well have been an underestimate of the true

---

[77] This was an appeal hearing; a lower court had already found in favour of the Dodge brothers in 1917.

value of the company).[78] Although it was of course irritating to Henry that he was obliged to have to make any payments to the minority shareholders, he comforted himself by reflecting that now at last his family was completely in control of the Ford Motor Company and reputedly he danced a jig around the room by way of celebration. He hastened to reorganize what was now unequivocally his company, dividing the shareholdings so that he owned 55 percent, Edsel 42 percent and Clara 3 percent of the shares.[79]

The Dearborn Independent

By this time however, Henry was no longer the company's president, for he had resigned from the post on 30th December 1918, declaring that since he was now 55, he wished to pursue other interests. These now included a local newspaper, the *Dearborn Independent*, which Henry had acquired a month before and which was soon publishing editorials reflecting Henry's views. Henry arranged for the post of president of the Ford Motor Company to be filled by Edsel[80] and he and Clara departed for a long vacation in California. However, within a few months of arriving in California (and within a month of the decision of the Michigan

---

[78] To put this settlement into perspective, James Couzens acquired his shares in the Ford Motor Company in 1903. Between 1903 and 1919, he received dividend payments in excess of $10 million. In exchange for selling his shares as part of the 1919 settlement, he received over $29 million, which is not a bad return on an initial investment of a little less than $11,000.

[79] Having such total control placed Henry in a unique position compared to his fellow industrialists; no other tycoon of the day had anything like such absolute power, not even John D Rockefeller who at the pinnacle of his career controlled far less than 30 percent of the shares of Standard Oil.

[80] Who (at Henry's insistence) avoided being conscripted for military service by citing the importance of his work at Ford to the war effort. Edsel received an unfair amount of criticism for this, during and after the war. He certainly was involved in important war work, and had he really wished to avoid the fighting without giving the appearance of doing so, he could have emulated some of his rich contemporaries by joining the military and then allowing himself to be posted to safety far from the front lines. It seems clear that Edsel himself was willing to volunteer for the armed services, but did not do so because his father objected. In allowing his father to overrule his own wishes and judgement, Edsel was setting a dangerous precedent that would increasingly repeat itself in the future. It is also notable that Henry made no attempt to defend Edsel against the charges of cowardice that were later levelled at him.

State Superior Court ordering Ford to respect the views of his minority shareholders), Henry was declaring to the newspapers that he wished to establish a new and better car company. The sale of Ford cars promptly slumped as people waited to see what Henry would produce next, and the Dodge brothers complained vigorously this was just a negotiating ploy to force them to sell their shares at a low price. It probably was. Once the settlement with the minority shareholders had been reached, all talk of establishing a new Ford motor company was dropped and Edsel told the *New York Times*: "Of course there will be no need for a new company now."

The Dodge brothers' suit was not the only legal action occupying Henry's attentions at this time. In 1916, he had managed to become embroiled in a libel claim that had its origins in raids across the United States' southern border by Mexican guerrillas led by Pancho Villa. President Wilson had called out the National Guard reservists to deal with the incursions, and the *Chicago Tribune* decided to investigate the attitude of employers to the call-up of their employees. A *Tribune* reporter contacted the Ford Motor Company to be told (not by Henry) that as far as Ford employees were concerned, they would promptly lose their jobs if they reported for duty with the National Guard. In fact, this was not the official position of the company (and a number of employees were called-up and were re-instated without question on their return); nevertheless the *Tribune* promptly published an article attacking Henry as an "anarchist enemy of the nation". The story was picked up by other newspapers and Henry, on the advice of his lawyer decided to bring a libel suit.

The case went to trial in May 1919 in the town of Mount Clemens, Michigan. Henry's lawyers were able to demonstrate without difficulty that Ford employees who had been called up to the National Guard had kept their jobs, but the lawyers acting for the *Tribune* managed to widen the scope of the proceedings so as to make them an investigation of Henry's character rather than simply the actual practices of the Ford Motor Company. When Henry took the stand, the *Tribune's* lawyers sought to explore his character by challenging his grasp of general knowledge. It did not take too many questions to discover that Henry's knowledge was patchy at best. He amused the court by suggesting that there may have been a revolution in the United States in 1812, although he wasn't aware of any revolution at any other time,[81] he stated that he believed Benedict Arnold[82] to have been a writer, and was unable to explain the nature of chilli con carne. By the time his testimony finished (and it took some time, for the questioning was relentless), Henry had revealed himself to be a man who, whilst undoubtedly talented in some respects, was remarkably and surprisingly ignorant in others, particularly for a man with his advantages. The press (inevitably) reported Henry's testimony with sarcastic glee, and his humiliation was compounded by the ultimate decision of the jury: they found that the *Chicago Tribune* had indeed libelled Henry, but awarded him only six cents in damages. Notwithstanding that many ordinary Americans in fact had a degree of sympathy for the ordeal Henry had been forced to undergo on the witness stand, the humiliation he felt as a consequence of the *Tribune* case was yet another factor that would drive the slow deterioration in his character over the next few years.

The general public first became aware of a darker side to Henry's personality in the summer of 1920. Close acquaintances had heard him make anti-Semitic comments[83] in the past, as for example, when he was seeking to explain the failure of his peace ship, and over the years he had come to believe fervently in the existence of a Jewish conspiracy, and the truth of anti-Semitic pamphlets such as the *Protocols of the Learned Elders of Zion* (supposedly a description of a plan to destroy Christian civilization, but in fact a blatant forgery produced by agents of the Tsar in the years before the Russian Revolution in order to promote anti-Semitism). The *Dearborn Independent*, acting in accordance with Henry's instructions, now launched a series of articles accusing Jews of corrupting American life and values and of illicitly seeking to control the world. As time went by,

---

[81] Only a little while before, Henry's famous quote: "History is more or less bunk" was reported in a newspaper. It is not clear that he actually said – or meant – this.

[82] Benedict Arnold's name is notorious in American (and British) history as being synonomous with treason. Born in 1741, Arnold initially served with distinction in the Continental Army following the outbreak of the Revolutionary War, but feeling ill-used by the Revolutionary authorities, he defected to the British in 1780 (attempting at the same time to surrender West Point to British forces). The British (no admirers of treachery but perfectly willing to take advantage of it) rewarded him with a pension and appointed him a Brigadier General but never fully trusted him. Arnold died in London in 1801.

[83] On occasions, he displayed bigotry against Roman Catholics too.

the allegations made in the articles became more and more outrageous and poisonously grotesque. Furthermore, some of the articles were collected together and published as a book entitled *"The International Jew"*; sales of the book were poor in America, but it sold exceptionally well in Germany.

Henry Ford's anti-Semitic campaign met with opposition in some (but certainly not all) quarters, but Henry paid no attention. He temporarily suspended the campaign in 1922, probably because at this time there were suggestions that Henry should run for President, and he gave serious consideration to the idea. Ultimately however, nothing came of the "Henry for President" bandwagon, and the *Dearborn Independent* began again to attack the Jews in 1924. On this occasion, however, the *Independent* launched an attack on Aaron Sapiro, a lawyer who had helped to organize fruit growers' cooperatives in California. The cooperatives had been set up to assist small fruit growers who were suffering as a consequence of an agricultural depression, and Sapiro had helped to establish them on a business-like basis. The *Independent* alleged that this was yet another example of Jewish exploitation, this time of innocent farmers, and Sapiro promptly sued Henry for defamation.

As ever, the wheels of justice took some time to turn, and the case did not reach the courtroom until 1927. Sapiro's lawyers were keen to place Henry himself in the witness box and when they eventually managed to serve Henry with a subpoena (which he was by no means anxious to accept), he was ordered by the court to appear before it on 1 April 1927. The day before his court appearance however, he was involved in a mysterious accident, claiming that another car had forced him off the road, but the driver of the other car (if indeed there was one, and many people doubted there was) was never identified. His lawyers promptly produced affidavits to the court in which Henry's doctors swore that the injuries he sustained would prevent him from testifying in the immediate future. Matters soon became even more bizarre when Ford's lawyers accused Sapiro of attempting to improperly influence the jury, although there were reports that if anyone was trying to influence the jury, it was Henry Ford. In any event, the court had little choice but to order that the hearing be postponed for several months.

In view of the mauling he had suffered when he last appeared in a witness box, Henry was not enthusiastic about repeating the experience, and before the new trial could commence, he instructed his lawyers to reach a settlement with Sapiro. As part of that settlement, the *Independent* published a formal statement from Henry in which he apologized not only to Sapiro for the allegations made against him, but also to the Jewish people generally for the *Independent's* anti-Jewish campaigns of the previous few years. Even now though, he sought to blame someone else for the articles, and claimed that he had been unaware of the details of the anti-Semitic allegations that had been made, adding that if he had been aware, he would never have allowed them to be published. It is doubtful that many people believed a word of it.

As for the *Dearborn Independent*, Henry closed it down at the end of 1927. His publishing venture had cost him several million dollars and unquestionably damaged his standing in the eyes of many Americans. To many others though, he remained "good old Henry Ford", a plain spoken, down-to-earth, honest American mechanical tinkerer who subscribed to good old fashioned values, wanted to improve the lives of ordinary men and women and somehow was distinct from other greedier multi-millionaires.

Evangeline

In the meantime, there had also been developments in Henry's personal life. Being firmly, if somewhat stolidly, married to Clara did not preclude him taking an active interest in other women. He became more than friendly with a number of Fairlane's female servants, although he did his best to hide his activities from Clara (who was nevertheless aware of Henry's proclivities in this regard, in general terms at least, if not always in detail). His most dramatic affair however, was not with one of his domestic servants, but with an employee of the Ford Motor Company, Evangeline Cote.

Evangeline was of French-Canadian ancestry, and had been obliged to go to work at an early age as a consequence of her father's ill-health. She joined the Ford Motor Company in 1909 as a clerk at the age of 16, and was soon promoted to be Harold Wills' secretary. As a consequence, she was in a position to catch Henry's eye, and before the long the two were having an affair.

Apart from trying to ensure that Clara remained in the dark about what he was up to, Henry appears to have made little effort to keep his affair secret. Nevertheless, even he felt a little awkward about being seen on intimate terms with a female employee who was so much younger than him. Fortunately for Henry, a solution to this problem presented itself in the form of Ray Dahlinger, one of several young men who Henry employed as personal aides and upon whose loyalty he felt he could completely rely. Whether as a result of Henry's orders, or because he sincerely wished to do so, Ray married Evangeline in February 1917, and Henry provided them with a country home set in a 150 acre estate close to Fairlane. Ray was also appointed to be the manager of Henry's farming interests, and over the course of time, the couple received other substantial gifts from Henry (although he never gave them any shares in the Ford Motor Company). Presumably in return for this generosity, Henry's affair with Evangeline continued, under the eyes of the uncomplaining Ray Dahlinger.

On 9 April 1923, Evangeline gave birth to a son christened John Dahlinger. It was widely rumoured that Henry was his true father, although Evangeline never confirmed or denied the point, and it may well be that she genuinely did not know.[84] Certainly Henry took a close interest in the child as he grew up, as his affair with Evangeline settled down into a relationship more akin to close friendship, which it did following John's birth. As for Clara, whilst she had originally disliked Evangeline and Ray, over the years and possibly as she realized that no matter how close Henry was to Evangeline, her position as Mrs Henry Ford was secure and always would be, she too became, if not exactly friendly, at least reconciled to their presence in Henry's life and her own. And she always ensured there was a warm welcome for John whenever he came to visit Fairlane.

Changes

The end of the war brought changes at the Ford Motor Company. The company moved smoothly back into peacetime car production and by 1919, thanks to a healthy (if not altogether booming) economy and a pent-up demand for new cars following the end of the war, the company's sales were enormous. By the end of the year, the company had manufactured and sold over 750,000 cars, meaning that nearly one out of every two cars sold in the United States that year was a Model T.[85]

---

[84] Towards the end of his life (he died in 1984), John Dahlinger claimed that he was indeed Henry Ford's illegitimate son.

[85] Following the end of the war, the company introduced new refinements to the Model T. In particular, it now sported an electrical self-starter, which obviated

However, despite this success, all was not well in the higher echelons of the company. Edsel was now company president, but in practice he found that he wielded little real power. Henry did not hesitate to intervene in the company's affairs and overrule his son whenever he disagreed with his plans (which was often) and this did little to enhance Edsel's confidence in his own abilities. Nor did other people have any real doubt as to who was really in charge of the company, since Henry was quite prepared to contradict and subtly (on occasions, not so subtly) disparage his son in front of other Ford executives. To make matters worse, there was also considerable rivalry between several of those executives, who were forever bickering between themselves and manoeuvring for power, something that Henry did not hesitate to encourage when it suited his purposes, but which left Edsel looking even more weak and ineffective, both in his own eyes and in the eyes of others.

An additional complication was the departure of some key and well-established figures from the company in the immediate post-war years. Although these executives all left under differing circumstances, their departures shared one common factor, namely they had all expressed opinions or taken actions to which Henry had taken exception, something that he increasingly found difficult to accept. It was becoming apparent that there was no room at the Ford Motor Company for anyone who showed anything other than blind and unquestioning loyalty to Henry and his opinions and in the long run, this would help to stifle initiative and make it harder for the company to respond to the new challenges and increasing competition presented by the post-war world.

The first departure of note was that of Harold Wills. Wills had worked closely with Henry during the early days of the company (and Henry had been the best man at Wills' wedding), but of late they had grown apart, partly because Henry disliked Wills' drinking habits and somewhat casual personal life, and partly because Wills was unable or unwilling to show Henry the deference that Henry had by now come to believe was rightfully his due. Henry showed his displeasure by simply arranging that

---

the need to crank-start the car by turning a handle, a physically demanding (and occasionally, dangerous) procedure. The electric self-starter (which was triggered by a small pedal in front of the driver's seat) was especially appreciated by female drivers.

no meaningful work should be assigned to Wills and ultimately Wills resigned.[86]

Other departures included Norval Hawkins, the sales manager (who had tried to insist on the importance of orderly office procedures, which Henry chose to interpret as insubordination) and Frank Klingensmith (originally Henry's private secretary, but who had been appointed company treasurer after the departure of James Couzens) whom Henry fired for suggesting that the company should borrow some money, something to which Henry was firmly opposed. However, perhaps the most damaging departure of all was that of William ("Big Bill") Knudsen, who had originally been hired in 1913 to help to establish a series of Ford plants throughout the country. The new plants had been constructed successfully to considerable acclaim within the industry, but Knudsen had grown increasingly unhappy with the disdainful way that Henry treated him. Perhaps even more importantly, he was not afraid to think and act independently and openly questioned whether it was not time to begin think about a replacement for the Model T. Any such suggestion was anathema to Henry Ford and by itself was probably more than enough to cause Henry to conclude that Knudsen's services would no longer be required. In any event, Knudsen foresaw the writing on the wall and decided to resign rather than wait to be fired, and duly did so in 1921.

Unsurprisingly, Henry made no attempt to persuade Knudsen to stay although this was a mistake on Henry's part. After leaving Ford, Knudsen was promptly hired by General Motors where he went on to have a distinguished career (during the course of which he saw General Motors emerge as the major rival to Ford) and he was eventually appointed company president in 1937.[87]

---

[86] Wills was not a shareholder in the company, but had a private arrangement with Henry that he should be paid a percentage of Henry's dividends, and when he left, Henry paid him $1.5 million by way of settlement of this obligation. He spent much of this money designing his own car, which was technically highly regarded but a commercial failure. Wills ultimately went to work for Chrysler; he died in 1940.

[87] In 1940, at the personal request of President Roosevelt, he was appointed Commissioner for Industrial Production and posted to Washington where he helped to coordinate US war production.

To make matters worse, the US economy suffered a sharp downturn in the summer of 1920 as the country entered into a sharp recession. Car sales plummeted, and the Ford Motor Company began to experience cash flow difficulties. Henry tried to solve the problem by announcing drastic reductions in the price of Model Ts, but this alone was not enough to halt the haemorrhaging of cash from the company's reserves. More drastic measures were needed, and in December 1920, the company was forced to suspend production at the Highland Park plant for several months. Even this was insufficient however, and at Henry's direction, the company undertook a series of cost cutting measures which involved reducing the number of workers, and demanding better terms from suppliers and Ford dealerships across the country. Drastic though these steps were, they worked. By the spring of 1921, Ford's financial position had stabilized, and as the country's economy improved over the following few years, Henry and the Ford Motor Company could again look for new challenges and opportunities.

The first opportunity to present itself must have given Henry a sense of vindictive satisfaction. He had parted company with Henry M Leland on poor terms when he had been obliged to leave the Henry Ford Company (soon to be renamed Cadillac) in 1902. Under Leland's technical direction, Cadillac had developed an enviable reputation for producing luxury motor cars, and had been acquired by General Motors in 1909. Leland had worked for General Motors for several years after this, but in 1917 he had departed to set up his own business known as the Lincoln Motor Company, specializing (again) in luxury automobiles. Unfortunately, the new company was unable to survive the sharp economic downturn of 1920, and in November 1921, it was forced to file for bankruptcy and an insolvency receiver was appointed to dispose of the company's assets.

Henry, partly at the urging of Edsel who had a weakness for luxury cars, saw an opportunity to purchase an important brand at a cut-rate price. The Ford Motor Company initially bid $5 million for the assets of the Lincoln Motor Company (then valued at $16 million) but the receiver rejected the bid as being too low. Ford then increased its bid to $8 million, and as this was the only bid received, the offer was accepted in January 1922. Henry was widely praised within the Detroit motoring community for "rescuing" the Lincoln business, and the Lincoln brand has been owned by the Ford Motor Company ever since.

Henry Leland and his son Wilfred were less happy. They claimed that Henry had promised that they could continue to run the Lincoln business as they saw fit, and that for this reason they had supported Ford's bid; however, once he gained control of the business, Henry lost no time sending his own executives into the Lincoln business with an agenda to remake it in the image of Ford, and particularly, to introduce modern mass production methods. The Lelands soon found themselves at odds with Henry and the new executives who were seizing control of what had been their business, but could do little about it. Finally, on 10 June 1922, Ernest Liebold (Henry's private secretary) arrived at the Lincoln plant to deliver the coup de grâce; Wilfred was fired and his father resigned.[88]

The Ford Motor Company had entered the 1920s as America's (and indeed the world's) leading motor manufacturer in terms of sales. However, the Model T, which had contributed so much to the company's success, was by now increasingly seen as old-fashioned, something that no number of improvements could alleviate. To make matters worse, the company was facing increased competition from its rivals and particularly from Chevrolet (now part of General Motors), which claimed an increasingly large share of the popular car market as the decade progressed, and Ford's position as the market leader suffered accordingly. In 1923, Ford had a market share of over fifty percent; by 1926, that market share had slipped to a little over a third. It was clear to just about everyone that the day of the Model T was passing, and a new car would be required.[89]

Unfortunately, while most people appreciated the importance of introducing a new model as soon as possible, Henry was not one of them. As far as he was concerned, there was simply no need to replace the Model T, which in his opinion was more than adequate to meet the motoring needs of the American public indefinitely, and for a long time he resisted the very idea of a replacement car, despite the earnest

---

[88] One of the reasons why the Lincoln Motor Company had failed under the guidance of the Lelands was because its production techniques were antiquated and costly. Furthermore, the Ford Motor Company had just acquired the Lincoln business. Why wouldn't Henry want to improve its manufacturing efficiencies and thus its financial performance by introducing new production techniques that he knew would work?

[89] At this time in its history, the Ford Motor Company only produced one car model at a time.

entreaties of Edsel[90] who was well aware of the need for change. However, as sales of the Model T continued to fall, even Henry eventually had to admit the wisdom of Edsel's advice. In May 1927, the month the fifteen millionth Model T rolled off the assembly line, the Ford Motor Company announced that it would cease production of the Model T in preparation for the launch of a new model later in the year.

The new car, called the Model A (and not to be confused with the Ford Motor Company's original Model A which had been produced in 1903), went into production in October 1927, and went on sale in Ford showrooms across the country in December 1927, to widespread public acclaim. Available in a variety of versions and colours, it had what we would now consider a conventional set of driver controls, in the form of clutch, brake and throttle pedals, a four wheel brake system and a four cylinder engine capable of producing a top speed of over 60 miles an hour. Carefully priced between to be just a little cheaper than its principal rivals (the price varied from $385 to $570, depending upon the version purchased), orders flooded in for the new Model A; so many in fact, that Ford initially had difficulty in fulfilling them. This was partly because the Model A was technically more complex than the Model T, which led to difficulties in re-tooling the Ford plants which in turn meant that fewer Model As were built in the initial months following the launch than had been anticipated. Nevertheless, even allowing for these technical difficulties, the transfer of production from the Model T to the Model A took longer than it should have done, surely a consequence of Henry's purging Ford of so many of its competent senior managers, and his arrogant unwillingness to listen to the advice of those managers who did remain. In time, the production difficulties were solved, and the Ford Motor Company eventually sold nearly five million Model As, but the damage was done. By delaying the withdrawal of the Model T and the introduction of a modern replacement, Henry had allowed his rivals to establish their credibility with the car-buying public. Both General Motors

---

[90] Edsel's views were shared by Ernest Kanzler, a former lawyer who at Henry's invitation had become a manager in Ford's tractor business before being appointed vice-president at the Ford Motor Company. In January 1926, Kanzler sent a memorandum to Henry, in which he pleaded eloquently for Ford to produce a new car for the popular market. Henry, ignoring Kanzler's recommendations, began to ridicule Kanzler before his fellow executives, and then in August 1926, whilst Edsel was out of the country, fired him.

and the Chrysler Corporation (Ford's two principal rivals) were now competing fiercely for sales, and in 1931, Henry Ford had to watch General Motors claim a larger market share than the Ford Motor Company. The days of Ford's overwhelming predominance had ended.

Henry Ford's company may no longer have been America's largest car manufacturer, but Henry himself, now in his late sixties, was still one of the richest men in the country, with unlimited opportunities to indulge his fancies and hobbies. His interests ranged widely; for example, he established a museum in Dearborn in which he assembled a wide range of historical objects, largely concentrating on American historical curiosities (such as the chair in which President Lincoln was sitting when he was assassinated) and industrial artefacts, including an early Newcomen steam engine shipped to Dearborn from England. The foundation stone of the museum was laid by Thomas Edison (eventually the museum would house a vial containing his last breath) and next to the museum Henry established a "village", intended to portray American rural life at the beginning of the twentieth century. The museum and village complex is now a US National Historic Landmark, and remains open to the public.

Henry had strong views on dietary and agricultural matters. Always opposed to the use of tobacco and alcohol, he now embraced the notion that "you are what you eat", believing that the enforcement of a proper diet would not only reduce the need for hospitals but would also lead to fewer crimes being committed, thus reducing the need for jails. In his view, people should avoid eating red meat (and chicken was potentially suspect); on the other hand, he had a great fondness for vegetables and during the Depression he ordered staff to grow them in allotment gardens. Most of all, Henry was fascinated by the soyabean, and he encouraged its cultivation on his various farms. Part of his attraction to the soyabean was its potential nutritional value and he hired scientists to invent various soyabean dishes, such as soyabean pastries, cheeses and biscuits, which he then tried to persuade Ford executives to eat, much to their dismay, for by all accounts they tasted revolting. He was also interested in the possible use of soyabeans in industrial processes. Thus Ford researchers explored ways of using soyabean oil in industrial paints, and the use of soyabean fibres in textiles. Henry went so far as to have a suit made from soyabean fibres, although this was not a great success since the fabric produced had a tendency to rip at awkward moments. Soyabean-derived products were in fact used in Ford cars throughout much of the 1930s, and in the early 1940s, Ford produced an experimental car (never put into production) that was largely constructed from soyabean-derived plastic.[91]

Fordlandia

He also took a considerable interest in rubber production, rubber being a vital component for the construction of automobiles. Despite the fact that the rubber tree originated in the rain forests of South America, by the early 1920s, the majority of the world's rubber came from Asia, most notably from the British and Dutch possessions of Ceylon, Malaya, Burma and Indonesia, where the rubber tree had been introduced in the 1870s. Henry disliked being so dependent on foreign sources of rubber, and in 1928 acquired approximately 25,000 square kilometres of land near the Brazilian town of Santarem where he proposed to establish the largest rubber plantation in the world.

Transferring a number of Ford executives to his new property to oversee and run his new enterprise, he hired scores of local labourers to work the new plantation, and to house them all, a pre-fabricated town was built, comprising not only homes but also a power plant, shops, a hotel, a hospital and a golf course, as well as a rubber processing plant. Inevitably, the new town planted in the middle of what had once been a rain forest was named Fordlandia and soon became a local wonder.

Unfortunately, in his haste to establish his new venture, Henry failed to note that none of the executives he had transferred to run his new venture were botanists, or indeed had any practical experience in the operation of rubber plantations, and nor did he think to consult any botanists before proceeding with his plans. As a consequence, the operation was doomed from the start. The rubber trees in the new plantations were planted far too close together, and often in soil that was insufficiently fertile, a problem exacerbated by soil erosion thanks to the clearance of the original trees of the rain forest to make way for the new plantation. Moreover, in Asia, rubber trees had few if any natural enemies; in Brazil, they were all too vulnerable to diseases lurking in the rain forest surrounding the plantation and within months a particularly

---

[91] Today of course, there is considerable interest in the possible use of soyabean products, both as a foodstuff and as a potential raw material for industry. By encouraging experimentation into the soyabean, Henry was more of a pioneer than was generally appreciated at the time.

pernicious form of blight appeared that decimated many of the closely packed trees. Actual rubber production during the first three years of operation was so little as to be negligible.[92]

To make matters worse, Henry also sought to impose his paternalism upon the local Brazilian workers who, unlike many of their counterparts working in Ford's factories in America, were unwilling to accept instructions from their *Yanqui* bosses as to how they should conduct their personal lives. Local workers particularly resented attempts to prevent them drinking alcohol (even in their own homes) and to oblige them to eat American-style foods in their workplace cafeterias rather than the local foods they were used to. Being expected to attend "uplifting" American-style social events (such as book recitals and Henry's beloved square-dancing) during their free time also did little to enamour the Brazilian workers to Ford's paternalism, and this despite the fact that the workers were well paid by local standards. As time passed, the resentment of the workers grew until December 1930, when the workers decided they had suffered enough from Henry's high-handedness, and staged a riot which started in the workers' cafeteria but soon spilled out into the streets of Fordlandia itself. Many of the American overseers, facing the wrath of the workers, hastily abandoned the town and took refuge on boats on the nearby river. Order was only restored three days later with the arrival of Brazilian soldiers.

The next few years saw little improvement; eventually Henry bowed to the inevitable and hired botanists who assessed the plantation and told him the truth, namely that the site of Fordlandia was most ill-suited for a rubber plantation. Still grimly determined to establish a South American rubber plantation of his own, he purchased yet more land fifty miles south of Fordlandia, land that he was advised would better suit rubber trees, and established another town, which he named Belterra. This time, he imported rubber trees better able to withstand the dreaded blight, and rubber production of a sort commenced, but never of the quantity that Ford had hoped for. By this time, however, the Second World War had broken out, and the Japanese had succeeded in overrunning many of the

---

[92] Rubber production was not helped by the insistence of the American overseers that the local workers work in regular shift patterns as if they were in the middle of a car factory in Detroit, rather than work instead during the early morning and late afternoon and evening as was local practice in order to avoid the heat of the mid-day Brazilian sun.

Dutch and British rubber plantations, denying their output to the Allied war effort. In response, the Allies concentrated on expanding their production of various types of synthetic rubber; by 1944 the output of synthetic rubber from Allied factories was twice that of the world's production of natural rubber before the start of the war. With the economics of natural rubber production fragmenting before his eyes, Henry finally decided to abandon his rubber plantation, and sold it back to the Brazilian government for a quarter of a million dollars. The entire project had cost him millions.

When the Model A was introduced, Henry may well have believed it would stay in production for as long as the Model T, but this was not to be. Commercial pressures as a result of increased competition and the advent of the Great Depression following the Wall Street Crash of 1929 meant that Ford had to introduce a new model (initially known as the Model B, and subsequently as the Ford V8) in 1932. Henry was once again deeply involved in its design (the V8 was the last car design to which Henry made a significant contribution). By now his behaviour towards his staff was notably peculiar, and his temperament increasingly volatile. He also displayed paranoia, and accused staff of attempting to pass trade secrets to his rivals.

Henry's reputation as an enlightened employer was now tarnished, and was about to get worse. The hard economic circumstances of the Depression had forced the Ford Motor Company to reduce the size of its workforce, to lower the wages and increase the working hours of those workers it did employ. Unsurprisingly, the morale of Ford workers suffered accordingly and labour unrest increased. Henry, vehemently opposed to the concept of organized labour and determined that the Ford workforce would remain union-free, authorised the establishment of the Service Department, essentially a private security force, headed by an tough ex-US Navy diver and former champion boxer called Harry Bennett, whose job was to prevent theft from the Ford plants, to maintain order on the factory floors and to eradicate any signs of labour agitation.[93] Bennett, who liked to claim close links with various mobsters, took to the role with great relish, and before long, he was wielding great

---

[93] This included summarily sacking any worker who drove (or a member of whose family drove) a car manufactured by anyone other than Ford.

(and in the eyes of some, sinister) influence over Henry, to the increasing unease of Edsel.

On 7 March 1932, Communist labour activists organized a protest march of several thousand (unarmed) unemployed workers through Dearborn, intended to culminate in a demonstration to be held outside the gates of Ford's Rouge River plant, calling for labour reform and the improvement of wages and other benefits. As they entered Dearborn, a line of Dearborn police ordered the demonstrators to disperse and when they failed to do so, fired tear gas and water cannons at them. This merely succeeded in breaking the demonstrators into separate groups of men all determined to reach the gates of the Ford plant. They broke through the police lines and upon reaching the plant, they called for Bennett, who came out to speak to them, only to be immediately pelted by rocks. Struck in the head, he fell over and in the confusion, one of the march's organizers, Joseph York, fell on top of him. At this moment, the police opened fire on the demonstrators, killing four (including Joseph York) and wounding twenty more before the demonstrators dispersed.

The police and members of the Service Department tried to seize the cameras of the reporters covering the march, but to no avail; the Rouge River massacre was widely reported across the country the next day, and the reports were overwhelmingly critical of the Dearborn police, the Ford Motor Company and Henry himself. From once being regarded as the champion of the ordinary American worker, Henry was now seen by many as a representative of the ugly face of American industrialization; it was a reputation he would never fully succeed in shaking off.

The Rouge River massacre increased demands for the introduction of unions onto the shop floors of America's car manufacturers. During the first decades of the twentieth century the American Federation of Labour – the AFL – had shown little interest in expanding its activities into car factories – there were other more fruitful fields to explore in other industries, and in any event, there was little call for union protection from the car workers themselves. This changed however during the hard years of the 1930s, especially after President Roosevelt's government sanctioned new statutory rights to collective bargaining, and (fearful of industrial strife) sought to encourage compromise between workers and factory owners.[94] 1935 saw the creation of the United Auto Workers

---

[94] Henry was not an admirer of Roosevelt.

Union, more aggressive than many of the older unions affiliated with the AFL, and determined to establish a presence in the factories of Detroit's car manufacturers.

The UAW decided to concentrate first on Ford's rivals, and a wave of strikes at General Motors led to its management agreeing to recognize the UAW in February 1937. Chrysler, Ford's other great rival, followed suit a few months later, and suddenly, the Ford Motor Company was the only major car manufacturer in the United States that refused to recognize a union. Henry Ford and Harry Bennett responded by increasing the number of guards employed by the Service Department.

Union leaders wasted no time in turning their attention to Ford. On 26 May 1937, a UAW official called Walter Reuther[95] (a former Ford worker who had been sacked for labour agitation) and a number of other UAW representatives gathered at an overpass near the Rouge River plant to hand out union literature, watched by a number of thugs from Ford's Service Department and several reporters. The UAW officials were ordered to leave Ford property, and then suddenly and without warning, they were viciously attacked by the Service men, in full view of the press cameramen who recorded everything. The UAW officials were outnumbered and stood no chance; they were beaten semi-unconscious and their bodies simply dumped at the side of the road. Again the newspapers were full of reports condemning Ford's inhumanity, and this time, unlike the case of the Rouge River massacre, it was clear that it was Ford men rather than the police who had unleashed the violence. And yet Henry Ford continued to refuse to recognize the UAW, despite the entreaties of Edsel, whose health by now was seriously suffering as a result of his strained relationship with his father and his deeply felt concerns about the future of the company, in particular the pernicious influence of Harry Bennett.

Henry would maintain his opposition to the introduction of organized labour into the Ford workforce for four more years, during which time Bennett and the Service Department, with Henry's full approval, stamped down even harder on any sign of unrest. The slightest suspicion of sympathy with the union's cause was considered sufficient grounds for firing a worker. A man's length of service or ability to carry out his job counted for nothing, and the Service Department was quite prepared to

---

[95] Walter Reuther would later go on to become the President of the UAW.

emphasize its position by the use of violence. At the same time, the UAW intensified their efforts at the various Ford plants. Unsurprisingly, in such an environment, the profitability of the Ford Motor Company slumped alarmingly.

Matters reached a climax in April 1941, when a dispute at the Rouge River plant snowballed into a plant-wide sit down strike by over 50,000 workers. Federal and state officials refused to become involved, and Henry finally agreed to permit the Ford workforce to determine by secret ballot whether they wished union representation, and if so, by which union. By some accounts, Henry was still convinced that the workers would demonstrate their loyalty to him by rejecting the suggestion that they wanted union protection; if he did believe this, he was doomed to be bitterly disappointed. Over 95 percent of the workforce voted for union membership, whilst over 70 percent chose to become members of the hardline UAW. Less than 2,000 workers out of a workforce of nearly 80,000 voted for no union representation at all.

The Last Years

The 1930s also saw Henry increasingly concerned about the possible impact of a large inheritance tax bill arriving from the US Government in the event of his, or Edsel's, death. These concerns were exacerbated after President Roosevelt's administration overhauled the tax laws in the mid-1930s, so that death taxes at a rate of 70% could be levied on estates worth more than $50 million. While Henry had always expressed disdain for the sons and daughters of the wealthy who merely inherited their money rather than working for it, he was by no means enthusiastic about handing over the bulk of *his* estate to the US Government. Moreover, faced with a large tax bill upon his death, his surviving family would have no choice but to sell a large number of their shares in the Ford Motor Company, thus raising the prospect of control of the company passing to outsiders. Henry and Edsel felt they had little choice but to consult specialist tax lawyers who could help them to mitigate the problem.

As a consequence of the tax advice they received, the Ford family's shares in the Ford Motor Company were split into two – Class A shares and Class B shares. Class A shares would represent 95 percent of the old shares (and thus the bulk of the company's wealth) but have no voting rights; voting rights would be attached only to the Class B shares which would represent the remaining 5 percent of the old shares. As a consequence, the Ford family could hope that even if a large tax bill were to descend upon them, they could settle it by selling Class A shares and yet retain total control of the company. Furthermore, taking advantage of the tax laws, Henry and Edsel established a new charity, the Ford Foundation, to which they could pass their Class A shares free of tax, thus dramatically reducing their tax bill. Indeed, it has been estimated that as a result of adopting this approach, the Ford family avoided a prospective inheritance tax bill of more than $300 million when Henry died in 1947.

The outbreak of the Second World War in September 1939 saw Henry publicly supporting the America First movement, whose aim was to keep America out of the war and one of whose principal spokesmen was the famed aviator Charles Lindbergh. As he had in the days of the First World War before the United States joined the hostilities, Henry strongly objected to supporting the Western allies, and particularly the British.[96] Henry's antipathy towards the British extended to him refusing to build several thousand Rolls-Royce-designed engines which were urgently needed for British Spitfires and other warplanes, despite the entreaties of William Knudsen who by now had been appointed to coordinate US war production. Henry did however agree to manufacture B-24 Liberator bombers for the US Army Air Corps[97] and in order to be able to do so, sanctioned the building of a new aircraft factory at Willow Run, near Dearborn, which would eventually become an important part of America's war effort. And once the United States entered the war, the Ford Motor Company produced vitally needed equipment such as tanks, antiaircraft guns and troop carriers.

---

[96] While Ford's UK subsidiary was heavily involved in the British war effort, Ford's subsidiary in Germany was also involved in the German war effort; there has been much debate as to whether this was with the active approval of Henry Ford. Certainly Henry Ford appears to have had no problems with taking profits from the German subsidiary in the years before Pearl Harbour, although Ford was not the only American company to do this. It is, however, interesting to note that on 30 July, 1938, Henry's 75th birthday, he was awarded (and accepted) the Grand Cross of the German Eagle, a diplomatic honour instituted by Hitler for "deserving foreigners".

[97] This was not Ford's first foray into aviation; during the 1920s and early 1930s, a Ford subsidiary had developed and marketed small private planes, including the Ford Tri-Motor, the world's first all-metal plane, of which nearly two hundred were built before Henry shut down production during the Depression.

By now, Henry was in his late seventies, and his health was beginning to fail him. He had suffered minor strokes in 1938 and again in 1941, which affected his memory, and made his mood swings even more noticeable, but his determination to remain in control of his company remained resolute. Harry Bennett was now almost always to be found at Henry's side, willing to transform the least of Henry's wishes into reality. Bennett's power in the company, backed as it was by Henry, now extended far beyond the Service Department, in practice eclipsing that of Edsel, nominally at least, the company's president.

Despite Henry's strokes and advanced age, it was Edsel's health that was now seriously giving cause for concern. Years of stress dealing with his father and the political machinations within the Ford Motor Company had taken its toll, and in the late 1930s, he had been forced to consult doctors over mysterious stomach pains that had begun to plague him. The doctors diagnosed cancer, and in January 1942, Edsel had an operation to remove much of his stomach. By this time however, the cancer had spread elsewhere and there was little more the doctors could do. Edsel's health deteriorated rapidly. He survived until 26 May 1943; he was 49 years old when he died.

Henry's grief at the loss of his only son was compounded by guilt and an instinctive desire to blame anyone – anything – apart from himself. In the early 1900s, he had grown interested in reincarnation and, when not seeking to blame Edsel's cancer on his drinking, he tried to comfort himself that Edsel had not really died, but nevertheless, it was several months before he began to resemble his old self again.

In the meantime, there was the Ford Motor Company to run, and the first issue to decide was who to appoint as company president in Edsel's place. There was some suggestion that Harry Bennett should be appointed, but several members of the family (including Edsel's widow Eleanor and Clara, his mother) were vehemently opposed to this. Eventually, Henry decided to resolve the situation by taking the post himself. He also indulged in a purge of senior executives, removing a number who had supported Edsel over the years, including Charles Sorenson, who had been with Henry for 35 years, and who had sought to oppose Bennett's growing influence over the company.

As old faces departed, new ones arrived. Henry II, Edsel's oldest son, had been serving in the US Navy; he was now released so he could assist the war effort at the Ford Motor Company. Henry II had no doubt that his father had died as a consequence of the way he had been treated by Henry and his cronies, especially Bennett, and he was determined to "save" the company and so justify his father's life. This was easier said than done; Henry Ford, old though he was, still controlled the company and Bennett's influence over Henry was stronger than ever.[98] For the next few months, Henry II and Bennett were involved in a struggle for influence over the company; however, whilst Bennett had the advantage of having worked with Henry and for the company for many years, Henry II had the advantage of support within the family. Moreover, during the latter months of the war, Henry's support for Bennett grew less robust as his mental and physical health worsened and Clara began to assume more and more control over his daily activities. Matters eventually came to a head in September 1945, when Henry finally yielded to pressure from Eleanor and Clara and agreed to appoint Henry II as president of the Ford Motor Company, with full powers to hire and fire. The appointment was confirmed during a board meeting on 21 September 1945. By the end of the day, Harry Bennett had been forced to resign, and the Ford Motor Company had set out on a new course under a new captain.

Once Henry had passed control of the company to Henry II, his horizons constricted dramatically. He continued to decline physically – his eyesight began to fail – and on occasions, he demonstrated signs of mental confusion. At other times, though, he seemed almost his old self, and he and Clara busied themselves with their estates and farms, often in the company of Ray and Evangeline Dahlinger. In early 1947, they spent some time in Richmond Hill, Georgia, where some years before Henry had bought land, before returning to Fairlane on 6 April 1947. The next day, a flood disabled the private electric plants which still supplied the estate with electricity, and that evening, Fairlane was heated by fires and lit by candlelight. Henry decided to go to bed early with a glass of milk.

---

[98] Indeed, at one point, Henry's lawyers reputedly prepared a codicil to his will, establishing a trust to run the company for ten years after Henry's death, with a view to excluding Henry II from the company presidency. Bennett was named as secretary to the trust. When challenged over the codicil's existence, Bennett is supposed to have destroyed it, although if the codicil was valid – and there is some suggestion that by this time, Henry's mind was such that a court may well have declared it not to be valid – its mere destruction by Bennett would not have invalidated it.

He was taken ill near midnight while the power was still off; a doctor was called, but by the time he arrived Henry Ford had died. He was 83.[99]

His body was laid in state in the Henry Ford Museum, and an estimated 100,000 people came to pay their last respects; 20,000 gathered outside St Paul's Cathedral in Detroit where the funeral was held. Detroit's traffic stopped as the funeral started, many city businesses were closed, and many of its citizens wore black to mark his passing.

The world he left was very different from that into which he had been born. Cars were now ubiquitous, as were the industrial production processes he had helped to pioneer, and the automobile industry was now a vital part of America's economy, thanks to a large extent to Henry's efforts during the early days of the Ford Motor Company. He achieved much in his life of which he could be proud. But his legacy also had a darker side. His anti-Semitism, his opposition to even the slightest concession towards organized labour, his unwillingness to accept criticism or to accept that any point of view but his could be valid, his endorsement of thuggery and espionage on his own workers, his lack of gratitude to colleagues and perhaps most of all, his strange intolerance to his only son who only wished to help his father and to see his father's company succeed, all show a side of Henry that is not in the least admirable. Henry's successes certainly benefited a large number of people, all around the world; in contrast, his darker side was experienced directly by only a relatively small number of people, but at least some of those who suffered as a consequence (including members of his own family and some of his closest colleagues) did so to a considerable extent.

One thing is certain. In the early days of motoring, it was Henry, more than any other enthusiast, who pioneered the concept of a popular, affordable and straightforward car for the average man in the street and the industrial processes needed to produce it; the majority of his competitors at the time had focused solely on building luxury machines for the wealthy elite. Without Henry, the world of popular motoring, and the growth of the automobile industry in the form we know it today may have been delayed for ten years, or twenty years or possibly even longer. And that would have had profound effects (good and bad) across all aspects of society, all around the world.

---

[99] Clara, his widow, died in 1950.

Joseph P Kennedy

"I have no political ambitions for myself or my children…"
Joseph P Kennedy (1888 – 1969)

Early Days in Boston

Joseph Patrick Kennedy, a man who would in due course make a multi-million dollar fortune, be appointed American Ambassador to the Court of St James and see several of his children achieve high political office in the United States (and in the case of his son Jack, the highest political office of all), was born in Boston, Massachusetts on 6 September 1888. His father, Patrick Joseph Kennedy – whose nickname was PJ – came from a Boston Irish family; PJ's father, another Patrick, had emigrated from Ireland to the United States in 1848 during the turbulent times of the Irish potato famine. However, unlike many other Irish Catholic immigrants of the times who were fleeing the famine for their lives, PJ's father, who was the younger son of a relatively prosperous farming family in County Wexford, travelled to America in the hopes of finding a better and more prosperous life. Patrick's son PJ, and his children and grandchildren were to find such lives; sadly Patrick himself was doomed not to.

On the journey across the Atlantic, Patrick had met and courted another young Irish immigrant, Bridget Murphy, whom he married on 28 September 1849 and the couple set up home in a cheap and crowded tenement in East Boston near the harbour. Life in Boston must have come as a rude shock to Patrick and Bridget after rural Ireland; this was a time of mass immigration and horrendous living conditions for many in the city, there was blatant discrimination against the Irish, and the Boston Brahmins, the elite families who controlled all aspects of city life, did all they could to keep the Irish in their place. It was hard for an Irish Catholic to gain any form of skilled employment and like other immigrants in similar situations, the Irish in Boston turned to each other for mutual support, laying the groundwork for the awesomely effective political machine that the Kennedys would exploit so successfully in the years to come.

Many of Patrick's fellow immigrants eventually found work as labourers constructing the continent-spanning railroads that were then being built; Patrick was luckier and managed to find skilled work in a cooperage, making barrels for liquor and food businesses. He and Bridget started a family, first, three girls, Mary, Margaret and Johanna, and then a longed for son, John, born in 1854, who sadly died the following year. PJ was born on 14 January 1858, but the family's joy at his birth was short-lived; his father Patrick succumbed to cholera and died in November of that year leaving Bridget with four infant children to support.

Bridget rose to the challenge. For a while she worked as a clerk in a shop and then, when she had amassed sufficient savings, she opened a little shop of her own in Border Street, with living quarters above it. As her daughters grew old enough, they began to help their mother in the shop, as did PJ for a while, but the family, sensing that PJ was the key to the future, ensured that he went to school and attained at least some education. Within a few years however, he was working at the docks as a stevedore, (like his mother, he sensed that in saving money, he was accumulating the means to improve his situation, and that of his family) and actively looking for opportunities.

PJ found the opportunity he was seeking when he was 22, in the form of a bar in Boston's Haymarket Square. He bought it and soon proved himself to be a success as a barkeeper; he became popular with his customers even though he himself rarely drank, and acquired a reputation for being a good listener. Within a few years, his business interests had expanded to include other bars and a wholesale liquor business that he called PJ Kennedy & Co.

His political interests grew as well. PJ became interested in Democratic politics (almost unavoidable for a Boston Irishman) and by the age of 27, helped by his popularity with his drinking customers, he was elected as a representative to the Massachusetts State Legislature. He would eventually serve five terms as a representative, and later three terms as a state senator. He became a powerful figure in Boston politics, working with other local Irish Catholic politicians as they steadily gained political control of Boston from the Brahmins.

PJ combined success in politics with success in his personal life; in 1887 he married Mary Augusta Hickey, whose father was also in the liquor business. The Hickeys were also actively improving their family's circumstances; one of Mary's brothers became mayor of Brockton, another became a police captain and a third became a doctor, graduating from Harvard Medical School. Clever and shrewd, Mary proved an invaluable asset to PJ as he manoeuvred and worked in the murky waters of Boston politics.

She was also to prove herself to be an admirable mother. She and PJ had three children: Joe was the firstborn, and was followed by two girls, Loretta and Margaret. PJ wanted his son to be called Patrick Joseph III, but Mary vetoed the idea, insisting on reversing the Christian names. The reason, she advanced publicly was that she didn't want any "little PJ's" running around the house; in private, she is said to have admitted that she wanted her son to sound "less Irish".

Joe Kennedy's childhood was privileged indeed compared to those of his immediate forebears. The Kennedys were not wealthy when compared to many Boston Brahmin families; nevertheless PJ's commercial interests allowed them to live comfortably by the standards of the time (far more comfortably, in fact, than Joe Kennedy would later seek to imply) and they held a respectable position in the Boston Irish Catholic community. Despite this, neither they nor any of the other Irish Catholic families had yet really been accepted socially outside the narrow confines of Irish Boston and Mary at least was keen that Joe should have the opportunity to shine in the wider world.

The first step was to ensure that Joe received a suitable education. Initially, Joe attended the Boston Catholic Xaverian School, but when he was thirteen, he was enrolled in Boston Latin, a school whose alumni included Benjamin Franklin, John Hancock, John Quincy Adams and other famous names in American history. Academically, Joe did not achieve great success at Boston Latin and his grades were generally mediocre; in other ways, however, he was more successful, being appointed a colonel in the school's army cadet regiment (which won a city-wide drill competition) and named captain of Boston Latin's baseball team (he was widely acknowledged as an excellent baseball player). He also became captain of his class in his final year. These achievements were all the more remarkable bearing in mind that the majority of the school's pupils came from well-connected Protestant Boston families who tended to view the Irish Catholic community with disdain and even contempt. Joe did not allow this to prevent him from pursuing the goals he wished to achieve. Even as a young child, he had shown a strong competitive streak (a competitiveness which would appear again and again in his descendants) and this eagerness to compete became more pronounced at school. Boston Latin afforded Joe his first real opportunity to meet people from backgrounds other than his own and he swiftly learned that he could not only compete with such people but also beat them. He also learned to gauge success not by other people's standards, but by his own.

It was usual for Boston Irish Catholics to attend either Boston University or the Catholic College of the Holy Cross. Mary however, recalling that her brother had in his time attended Harvard, insisted that Joe should also go there. Joe was accepted and began to attend courses but once more preferred to focus his attention on social advancement rather than academic achievement. At Harvard he again encountered social snubs and slurs from some of his fellow students and their families and although he would resent the treatment he received at Harvard for the rest of his life, he did not allow this to deter him. He gained something of a reputation as an avid (and none too subtle) social climber but failed to gain entry to Harvard's more prestigious clubs such as the Porcellian or Fly (Franklin Delano Roosevelt also failed to gain entry to these clubs during his time at Harvard); eventually Joe was elected a member of the Hasty Pudding Club.

One goal that Joe desperately wanted to achieve was to be awarded a varsity letter for baseball. The standard of sports generally (and baseball in particular) at Harvard was much higher than at Boston Latin and during his college years he struggled to shine as a sportsman as he had at school; nevertheless he managed to achieve a place on the baseball team. However, he was kept on the benches during his final year and did not play in a single game, until the very last game of the season against Yale. In the ninth inning, the team captain, Charles McLaughlin, suddenly asked that Joe be put into the game (thus assuring him of a letter). Just before the end of the game, the Yale batsman was put out by Joe Kennedy and the game was won by Harvard. By all tradition, McLaughlin as team captain should have been given the ball as a trophy; but Joe refused to surrender it, arguing he had won the ball and was going to keep it. Contemporaries of Joe Kennedy never forgot this story as an example of his drive to win and his determination to keep the fruits of his winnings.

In later years, it became clear why McLaughlin had given Joe the chance to win his varsity letter. McLaughlin had wanted to open a movie theatre in Boston after graduation and in order to do so, he needed a licence from City Hall. A few days before the game, McLaughlin received a visit from some of PJ's deputies, who essentially gave McLaughlin a simple choice: "Let Joe win his letter and you get the licence. No letter, no licence."

Whilst at Harvard, Joe made his first serious foray into money-making, teaming up with a friend and operating a part-time bus business that took tourists on guided tours around famous Boston landmarks. Joe's friend was responsible for driving the bus, while Joe provided the commentary for the tourists. The business was a success, and earned Joe $5,000. Running a bus for tourists did not however feature in Joe's long term plans and after graduation he abandoned the business.

Marriage and Money

University life and running a bus tour business were not the only things occupying Joe Kennedy's attentions. For some time he had been pursuing Rose Fitzgerald, the talented and cultured daughter of Boston Mayor John F ("Honey Fitz") Fitzgerald, and reputed by some to be the best-looking girl in Boston (if not the whole of the United States). Her father, like PJ, had also flourished in the world of Boston politics and indeed had been even more successful than PJ, having been elected first to the Massachusetts State Senate and then the US House of Representatives before becoming the Mayor of Boston. He was a sometime ally and sometimes political opponent of PJ, and initially was less than enthusiastic of Joe's pursuit of Rose. Despite this parental opposition and the long trips abroad that Rose undertook from time to time in the company of her father, the relationship between Joe and Rose grew.

Honey Fitz's opinion of Joe began to change after Joe graduated from Harvard in 1912; with PJ's help, Joe was appointed a state banking examiner, a post which allowed him to learn how banks operated. One bank in particular caught Joe's eye, the Columbia Trust (in which his father held an interest), which was threatened by a takeover by the First National Bank. The possibility of such a takeover was viewed with hostility by some in the Boston Irish community, who regarded it as an attempt to exclude them from the banking world and Joe decided to become involved in the fight. With support from his father and others within the Irish community, he saved the bank from First National and arranged for himself to be appointed the bank's president, anointing himself in the press as the "youngest bank president in the country" in the process.

By the summer of 1914, Joe had overcome the last of Honey Fitz's objections, and he and Rose were engaged. They were married on 7 October 1914 by Cardinal O'Connell and after a lavish reception, departed for a two week honeymoon at White Sulphur Springs in West Virginia. On their return, Joe and Rose set up home in the Protestant Boston suburb of Brookline, away from traditional Kennedy and Fitzgerald neighbourhoods. Before long, Rose was expecting their first child and Joe was focussing on his latest goal: to become seriously wealthy and a person of consequence in the world.

For the next few years, Joe Kennedy concentrated on working as a banker. Ever eager to promote himself, he cultivated the local newspapers, promoting an image of himself as a young eager, hard-working no-nonsense businessman. The publicity paid off; in 1917, America having entered the First World War, he was offered a job (at a salary of $20,000) as a manager at Bethlehem Steel's Fore River shipyards, which were busy building warships. He accepted the post, which from Joe's perspective, had the advantage of allowing him to participate in the war effort without the necessity of joining the military and actually fighting, although this did not attract the unqualified admiration of a number of his fellow classmates from Harvard. There is no doubt that Joe more than fulfilled his duties at the shipyards. Before long, he was responsible for a workforce of more than 20,000 workers and took special pains to ensure that they were provided with appropriate facilities, such as proper and effective canteen facilities. Production at the yards soared after Joe Kennedy's arrival, with 36 destroyers being built and launched by Armistice Day. Joe worked so hard that he developed ulcers, a condition from which he was to suffer for the rest of his life.

His work at the shipyards also brought him into contact with the US Naval authorities. In particular, he met Franklin D Roosevelt, then Assistant Secretary of the Navy, a man who was to play a major role in Joe's life in the years to come. Their first meeting was not a success from Joe's point of view. Bethlehem Steel had built some warships for the Argentine navy, but the Argentine government had not paid for them and Charles Schwab, the Chairman of Bethlehem Steel, refused to authorize their release until the debt was paid. FDR felt it necessary to intervene in order to keep the goodwill of a friendly government, and Schwab sent Joe to meet with FDR.

FDR has often been described as having the appearance and mannerisms of a languid patrician to those meeting him for the first time and it is possible – indeed likely – that this caused Joe to underestimate him. In any event, when FDR asked Joe to release the warships to the Argentinians, Joe refused and continued to refuse even when FDR simply stated that if the warships were not released, he would authorize sending armed troops and naval tugboats to get them. The meeting ended and Joe subsequently described FDR to Charles Schwab as a "smiling four-flusher". FDR sent in the tugboats and troops, released the ships to the Argentinians and Joe was furious and embarrassed. This was a pattern that was to be repeated more than once in the future as FDR bested Joe again and again; in FDR, Joe had encountered a man he simply could not manipulate, intimidate, out-think or outmanoeuvre. In later years, this was to cost Joe dearly.

Once the war was over, Joe needed to find another job. He persuaded Galen Stone, a rich investment banker, to give him a job in the Boston branch of his stock broking business, so that he could learn about the stock market. His salary was half of what he had been paid by Bethlehem Steel but Joe didn't care; for him, the stock market was the place where he would begin to really make his fortune.

It did not take Joe long to grasp the essentials of the stock market and the tricks used by Wall Street operators, many of which would now be illegal. One of his earliest triumphs was a blatant example of insider dealing and involved a company called the Pond Creek Coal Company. Joe, learning that this company was to be acquired by Henry Ford, borrowed money and bought 15,000 shares of Pond Creek at $16 a share. When news of Ford's acquisition reached the market, the price of the shares soared, and Joe was able to sell his shares, repay the money he had borrowed and made a personal profit of over $200,000.

Other similar deals followed and Joe's money-making ventures became more and more sophisticated as he became increasingly confident of his financial abilities. He said to a friend: "It's easy to make money in the markets. We'd better get in before they pass a law against it." One of his favourite activities was to set up stock pools with like-minded traders. Stock pools, which are now illegal, involved traders colluding between themselves to buy and sell shares of a particular company, causing its share price to rise, creating the false impression of a boom and drawing in other, less knowledgeable investors. Once the share price reached a particular level agreed by the stock pool operators, they would quietly sell their holdings, leaving the outsiders holdings shares that would swiftly fall in value.

Immoral though such activities were and are, they were not actually illegal when Joe indulged in them and they certainly generated large profits for him. However, there were rumours that Joe did not simply make his money out of the markets and that there was a darker side to his fortune. This was the time of Prohibition, bootleggers and gangsters, and it seems likely that Joe had maintained his family's interest in the liquor business even after the passing of the Eighteenth Amendment in 1919. Dark stories circulated at the time of his dealings with gangsters and in later years, several major underworld figures would suggest that Joe Kennedy had been seriously involved in the bootlegging business, one of them describing Joe as "one of the biggest crooks whoever lived". Today, it is generally accepted that Joe had some form of financial dealings with gangsters during the Prohibition era and that part of the fortune that he made had its origins in illegal liquor.

By the mid-1920s, Joe Kennedy was a rich man. He was also a man with a large and growing family, for Rose had been producing children regularly since their return from honeymoon in 1914. First born was a boy, another Joseph Patrick, known as Joe Junior, who was born in 1915. Joe Junior was followed in 1917 by another son, John Fitzgerald, commonly known as Jack, and then a daughter, Rosemary, who was born in 1918. Three more girls followed: Kathleen ("Kick") was born in 1920, Eunice Mary in 1921, Patricia in 1924 and then another boy, Robert Francis ("Bobby") in 1925. The two youngest were Jean Ann born in 1928 and Edward Moore (Ted) born in 1932.) Their family was important to both Joe and Rose, but inevitably, at least in the early days, the bulk of the work of childcare fell on Rose's shoulders (albeit that she had the help of nannies and tutors). Rose was keen that the children should be disciplined, frugal and happy, although she discouraged excess emotionality.[100] Rose also stressed the importance of religion.

Joe, with support from Rose, emphasized the need for members of the family to stick together and support one another, a trait which developed into the "Kennedy clannishness" which was later noted by in-laws, family

---

[100] In later years, frugality was not a trait at which several of the children were to excel.

friends and journalists alike. At the same time, Joe (who arranged for substantial trust funds to be set up for each of the children as they were born) and Rose stressed the need for the children to be competitive, announcing at one time: "We don't want any losers here". The result was an incredibly cohesive, if competitive and sometimes argumentative family, and one which tended to look within itself for support, guidance and friendship rather than outside the family bounds.

One thing that had not changed despite Joe's increasing financial success was the treatment of the Kennedys by their Protestant neighbours. Rose in particular suffered many minor disparaging snubs from the ladies of Brookline, whilst Joe was blackballed when he applied to join a country club. This was the last straw for Joe. "You can go to Harvard and it doesn't mean a damn thing" he is said to have declared. "The only thing these people understand is money." Stating that Boston was no place to raise Catholic children, he moved his family from Boston to New York in 1927.

Although still active in the markets, Joe now decided to involve himself in a new money making venture. He had been interested in the movie business for some time, and shortly before the move to New York, had acquired control of a production company, Film Booking Office of America, commonly referred to as FBO. Under his direction, FBO specialized in producing simple low budget movies, which received little or no critical acclaim but played well on Main Street and (most importantly) made money. Joe now sensed the time was ripe to take a more active role in the movie business. Moving to Hollywood (he left his family behind in New York and he did not see them, other than fleetingly, for over two years), Joe entered into a series of merger negotiations with various Hollywood production and distribution companies which eventually led to the creation of Radio-Keith-Orpheum, or RKO, as it was more popularly known, a company valued at over $80 million. Joe Kennedy made a profit of over $2 million on the deal (as well as charging $150,000 for his services in respect of the mergers) and later he sold his remaining interests in FBO for several million dollars more.

Money was not the only attraction that Hollywood had to offer Joe Kennedy. Devoted to his family as he was, this did not prevent him from pursuing women vigorously all of his life (and there is little doubt that Rose was aware of her husband's activities in this regard – it would seem that she closed her eyes to them, while ensuring that at no time did they threaten the future of the family itself. They never did). Hollywood, particularly in the absence of his family, offered Joe many and varied opportunities to stray. His most dramatic entanglement was with Gloria Swanson, one of the most successful actresses of her day, whom he met in 1927. Before long, Joe Kennedy had arranged for Swanson's husband, the surprisingly passive Marquis Henri de la Coudraye, to be offered a lucrative job in Paris, which conveniently removed him from the scene, and he and Swanson were spending many of their nights together. Why he was interested in her is easy to understand; what she saw in him is harder to explain, though she had reached a stage in her career where she wanted to take control of her business affairs (which were in a shambles) and undoubtedly she was impressed with Joe's growing reputation as a shrewd and successful man of business.

Joe gave her financial advice, helped her to set up her own management company, Gloria Productions, and later agreed to produce a movie for her. The film was Queen Kelly, which was written and was to be directed by Erich von Stroheim. Unfortunately, Joe's business commitments prevented him from keeping as close an eye on the filming as he should; despite Swanson's repeated objections, von Stroheim's artistic temperament got the better of him and his interpretation of the script became ever more outlandish, lurid and (by the standards of the day) disgusting. There was simply no way that the movie as shot by von Stroheim would pass the censors and when Joe Kennedy finally saw some of the footage, he declared it to be one of the greatest failures of his life. The project was shelved. Queen Kelly ultimately cost Gloria Swanson nearly a million dollars.

Joe's affair with Swanson died away after the Queen Kelly debacle and he returned to Rose and the children in the spring of 1929, an undoubted multi-millionaire, worth perhaps $8 million to $10 million, but so stressed and suffering such pain from his ulcers that he was forced to check into a hospital for several weeks.

Wall Street and the New Deal

Once out of hospital and back in business, Joe Kennedy took a closer look at the stock market and didn't like what he saw. For years the markets had been rising, and now it seemed everyone was buying stocks without any analysis or restraint, borrowing money if necessary in order to do so. Indeed, it was popularly assumed that share prices simply couldn't fall, that they could only continue to rise, or at worst, would remain static. Joe, recognizing the lunacy of such a conclusion, quickly decided that the time had arrived to be prudent ("Only a fool holds out for top dollar" he told one friend) and disregarding advice to reinvest his Hollywood profits, he began quietly and systematically to liquidate the shares that he did own. When the stock market crashed in October 1929, it was less of a disaster for Joe than an opportunity, for as the market fell, he sold it short and made yet more money.

The 1929 Wall Street Crash may not have inflicted any direct financial damage on Joe Kennedy, unlike many of his contemporaries, but nevertheless 1929 and 1930 seem to have marked a turning point in Joe's life.[101] He was still willing to run risks for money, but he grew more conservative and cautious in his outlook; having made his money, his first priority was to preserve it for the benefit of himself and his family. Making yet more money was now less important. His principal concern now was that of revolution and social change, a concern that grew as the Great Depression bit deep into America, the unemployment lines lengthened and the shacks of the homeless spread. "In those days, I felt and said I would be willing to part with half of what I had if I could be sure of keeping, in law and order, the other half" he later noted. He foresaw that the Great Depression would herald the inevitable shifting of power from private business to Government and concluded that in order to gain the power needed to protect the family, he (and in due course his children) would have to become players in the political arena.

Joe's opportunity to make his mark in the political world came in 1932, when FDR, by now Governor of the State of New York, declared his candidacy for the Presidency of the United States. Joe hastened to join the FDR bandwagon, notwithstanding that many other Irish Catholics were supporting Al Smith, another Presidential contender. He contributed to FDR's political war chest, and threw all his influence into the battle to get FDR nominated and then elected.

Once FDR was safely in the White House, Joe Kennedy settled back to await his prize; he had after all been raised in a political culture that virtually dictated that a supporter was entitled to a suitable reward. He anticipated receiving a Cabinet post, and told friends that he was hopeful of being appointed Secretary of the Treasury. He was to be disappointed;

---

[101] His father, PJ, died of a heart attack in 1929. Pre-occupied in Hollywood, Joe chose not to attend the funeral.

the appointment went to the little known William Woodfin, an old friend of FDR. As the weeks went by, and the other major posts were filled, it became obvious that there was no place for Joe in the first rank of FDR's administration. The simple fact was that neither FDR nor his closest political advisers trusted Joe Kennedy; nevertheless, they were aware that alienating Joe after all his efforts to get FDR elected was potentially dangerous, and anyway, they were likely to need his support (financial and otherwise) in the 1936 Presidential election. Various efforts were made to find him a mid-ranking post (at one point, the post of Ambassador to Ireland was mentioned, but Joe rejected it out of hand), before FDR played a masterstroke.

A cornerstone of FDR's New Deal was the creation of the Securities and Exchange Commission, or the SEC, a regulatory body intended to encourage economic reform and recovery by the supervision of financial bodies, with a particular emphasis upon the activities of Wall Street. FDR announced that Joe Kennedy would be the first Chairman of the SEC, an appointment that did not carry Cabinet rank, but was nevertheless very much in the eyes of an American public now suffering in the depths of the fourth year of the Depression. FDR's reason for choosing Joe may partly have rested upon the concept of "find a poacher and make him a gamekeeper"; after all, who better than one of the most effective Wall Street operators to police Wall Street? The press, though, were generally horrified, at least at first, as were many on Wall Street who did not hesitate to compare Joe Kennedy to Judas, taking his thirty talents of silver from a Democratic President who seemed hell bent down the road to socialism.

Joe Kennedy, though, flung himself into his new role with relish. Naturally, he did all he could to ensure maximum press coverage of his activities; nevertheless, he took his job seriously and under his guidance, the SEC introduced sensible and workable reforms. By the time he stepped down from his post, in the late summer of 1935, it was widely acknowledged (even, perhaps somewhat grudgingly, on some corners of Wall Street) that Joe Kennedy had done a good job.

FDR was running for re-election in 1936 and Joe again threw himself into the Presidential campaign. Aware of the deep antipathy to FDR within the business community, he (with the assistance of journalist Arthur Krock) wrote a book entitled *"I'm for Roosevelt"*, aimed at bolstering support for the President's policies, arguing that such policies were vital if the business world and the nation were to survive. The book included a statement by Joe that he had no political ambitions for himself or for his children, a statement that attracted increasing amounts of wry derision in the years to come.

Notwithstanding this public disavowal, Joe's goals now included the Presidency, either for himself or, if this was not possible, for one of his sons, with Joe Junior being considered the most likely candidate. Joe's public profile at this time meant that this was by no means an impossibility, albeit that no Roman Catholic had ever been elected to Oval Office.

Once the 1936 Presidential election was over, Joe again awaited a call from the President offering him a Cabinet post, occupying himself in the meantime by acting as a business consultant to various companies. Once more he was to be disappointed, when the call did come (in 1937), he was offered not a Cabinet post, but rather the Chairmanship of the US Maritime Commission, a new agency intended to support the US merchant marine. Swallowing his disappointment, he accepted the post and once again performed creditably.

Joe's luck in obtaining a suitable political appointment changed, or seemed to change, in December 1937. The US Ambassador to Great Britain had been ill for some time and his condition had now deteriorated to such an extent that he was forced to tender his resignation. Joe quickly made it known that he wanted the job, although FDR, on hearing this, initially vetoed the idea. FDR then thought about it further and began to see advantages in the appointment. To begin with, it would be popular amongst Irish American voters and would enable FDR to pay his political debts to Joe Kennedy. Moreover, notwithstanding the disclaimer in "*I'm for Roosevelt*", FDR, always suspicious of potential rivals, had sensed Joe's political ambitions and may well have concluded that life would be much simpler with Joe Kennedy on the other side of the Atlantic. FDR was also well aware of Joe's talents and his proven ability to be his own man, and hoped that Joe's independence could prove to be an asset when representing the United States in a Europe increasingly beset by the threat of war. All in all, there was much to be said in favour of the appointment and when it was announced (to general acclaim), Joe was delighted. As a consequence of the appointment, he would be entitled to be called "Mr Ambassador" and he would cling to this title for the rest of his life.

Joe's family also occupied much of his attention following his return from Hollywood. With the birth of Teddy in 1932, it was now complete, and Kennedy family life oscillated between three houses Joe had acquired: a five acre estate in Bronxville near New York City, a winter holiday home in Palm Beach, Florida and (most famous of all), the family compound at Hyannisport, at Cape Cod in Massachusetts. During this time Rose was often away travelling, and Joe spent a lot of time with his children. He was strict with them, but also close to them and they all grew up with a strong desire to please him and to fulfill his wishes. Moreover, as the children grew up, the older children (especially Joe Junior) also began to inculcate the spirit of Kennedy competitiveness and clannishness into their younger brothers and sisters.

Two of their children in particular were giving Joe and Rose considerable cause for concern. Jack, their second son, had suffered since his earliest childhood from a series of serious yet mysterious illnesses that had variously been diagnosed as leukaemia or hepatitis. It would be years before Jack was diagnosed as suffering from Addison's disease. A treatment for Jack's condition involving cortisone pills would eventually be developed in the mid-1950s and this would enable him to control the disease with considerable success, just in time for him to make his run for the Presidency in 1960. In the 1930s, however, the cause of the malady was unknown and Jack was frequently physically weak and in considerable pain.

Jack's suffering was made worse by back problems that would become more severe as he grew older. His bad back and illnesses made it difficult for him to compete physically with Joe Junior (who perceived Jack as his principal opponent in the ongoing family rivalry, and reacted accordingly), although Jack never gave up trying to compete with his older brother. Unable to match Joe Junior's physical prowess, Jack found other ways to assert himself within the family arena, and to some extent was cast as the family clown, a role which he carried into the schoolroom (to his father's serious displeasure) and which undoubtedly affected his academic progress for a time. There was nevertheless a serious and thoughtful side to Jack's personality, which would become more apparent as the years went by.

Serious though Jack's problems were, Rosemary's were even more so. It had become apparent even when she was very small that she was in some way different from her brothers and sisters. Doctors were consulted and

Rosemary was eventually diagnosed as suffering from a form of mental disability. In a family as competitive as the Kennedys, this was a particularly heavy burden to carry. Although the family made strenuous efforts to involve Rosemary in their activities and to minimize the differences between her and the other children, it was inevitable that as she grew up, Rosemary would to some extent become aware of those differences. She grew to resent the limitations as to what she could do and aspire to achieve, as compared with her sisters and brothers and that resentment would express itself in fierce rages and sometimes violence against those near to her. Joe in particular found it difficult to accept the reality of Rosemary's condition and eventually, he would take steps in the hope of solving it.

Ambassador to the Court of St James

Joe Kennedy sailed for London in February 1938 and before long had settled himself into the American Embassy. Rose and several of the children followed some weeks later. Immediately, Joe began his old game of courting the press, seeking to build up the public image of himself,[102] and the British press at first made much of him and his family. As did London society; the doors of the wealthy and the famous were flung open for the rich and (when they wished to be) charming Kennedys, who found themselves fêted and welcomed in London in a way that would have been unimaginable in Boston, or even New York. Even Joe's bluntness and occasional lack of diplomatic decorum (he once referred to Queen Elizabeth – mother of the present Queen – as a "cute trick") was regarded with amused tolerance. Joe revelled in it all.

Determined as he was to raise his profile and that of his family, Joe also wanted to play a major role in shaping US foreign policy in Europe. Until this time, Joe had mastered every role he had undertaken; it was soon apparent however that his money-making talents and his skills for self-marketing were woefully inadequate for the challenges presented by late 1930s European politics, dominated as they were by the growing menace of the fascist dictators, fear of the spread of Bolshevism, the head in the sand idealistic naivety of the leaders of Great Britain, a politically divided France and an America where there was strong public support for the

---

[102] He is said to have commented to an aide: "We're only going [to London] to get the family into the Social Register. When that's done, we come on back and go out to Hollywood to make some movies and some money."

principles of isolationism. Joe identified himself with British Prime Minister Neville Chamberlain's appeasement policy and strongly supported the view that the western democracies would have to find some way to live with Hitler and Mussolini. In this of course, he was not alone; many people at the time supported appeasement as the only sensible way of dealing with the Nazis.[103]

Nevertheless, the policy of appeasement was failing even as Joe arrived in London to take up his appointment as US Ambassador. Less than two weeks after he arrived, Nazi troops were marching into Austria in order to secure its incorporation into the Third Reich (Joe, refusing to see the significance of this move, reported to Washington that he believed it would not have any effect on the United States or upon his post in London), while September 1938 saw what Winston Churchill called the "Tragedy of Munich", in which the British and French shamefully acquiesced to Hitler's seizure of the Sudetenland from Czechoslovakia in the desperate and ultimately vain hope that this would satisfy Hitler's territorial demands. To widespread but certainly not universal acclamation, Chamberlain returned from Munich clutching a piece of paper and announcing he had secured "peace in our time" and amongst his most fervent supporters was Joe Kennedy. In the months following Munich, Joe Kennedy spoke publicly in favour of the Munich "compromise", a fact that did not escape the notice of Herbert von Dirksen, the German ambassador to Britain.

Willing to speak out in favour of appeasement, Joe Kennedy made no attempt to protest against the Nazis' increasing persecution of the Jews or any of their other victims. (At one point, von Dirksen, following a conversation with Joe Kennedy, sent a cable to Berlin indicating that Joe Kennedy fully understood Germany's Jewish policy, and adding that in von Dirksen's opinion, Joe would get on well with Hitler). As public revulsion at the Nazis' actions and beliefs slowly grew on both sides of the Atlantic in the months following Munich, there was increasing criticism of Joe's support for appeasement, and while he could still claim considerable support, his influence in Washington slowly began to ebb away. At the same time, FDR's public stance against the Nazis was

---

[103] At this time, the Kennedys made many visits to Cliveden, the country estate of the British branch of the Astor family, who were prominent supporters of the appeasement policy.

hardening and the gap between the political positions of the two men was becoming noticeable.

At Munich in September 1938, Britain and France had offered Germany the Sudetenland on the understanding that the rest of Czechoslovakia would be allowed to remain free. On 14 March 1939, less than six months later, Hitler brazenly broke this understanding and seized the remaining territory of Czechoslovakia. In response, the British and French issued a declaration guaranteeing the safety of Poland, which was generally anticipated to be the next victim of Hitler's aggression. Joe Kennedy watched the slide towards war with despair and became increasingly strident in his urgings that America should maintain its isolationist stance.

German troops crossed the Polish borders on 1 September 1939; two days later, Joe was asked to attend No 10 Downing Street, where Chamberlain gave him a preview of the speech he would make to the nation in a few hours time declaring that a state of war existed between Britain and Germany. Kennedy returned to the US Embassy to call FDR and tell him the news, declaring that it was "the end of the world" in tones that were so stricken that FDR was forced to comfort him.

At the outbreak of the war, Joe arranged for his family to return to the United States. Then, as the months of the Phony War passed, he continued to urge that America should stay out of the fight, and he did so in terms that were increasingly interpreted as being anti-British in tone. Moreover, he made little secret of the fact that he believed that Germany would ultimately defeat Britain, and that Britain's best hope lay in seeking to reach some sort of accommodation with the Nazis while there was still time. The reservoir of goodwill that he had accumulated in London evaporated almost overnight, and increasingly he was regarded by the British as a defeatist and a coward. By this time, the US State Department's view of Joe was not much better, whilst FDR and Winston Churchill[104] had by now initiated their historic exchange of correspondence, thus enabling the President to bypass Joe entirely in his

---

[104] Who, having predicted the dangers of Nazism from the political wilderness of the backbenches of the House of Commons for years, had now rejoined the British Cabinet as First Lord of the Admiralty, and would within months become British Prime Minister. Winston Churchill and Joe Kennedy cordially despised one another.

communications with the British Government whenever he wished to do so. Joe's awareness of the growing contempt for him on both sides of the Atlantic and of FDR's private communications with Churchill, coupled with his inability to influence FDR or US foreign policy and his (genuine) concern as to whether the western democracies could succeed in a struggle with Nazi Germany, merely served to increase Joe's frustrations and antipathy towards the President. Nevertheless, conscious of the forthcoming Presidential elections in 1940, FDR was content that Joe should for the moment remain as US Ambassador and thus kept out of the domestic political arena.

May 1940 brought the fall of Belgium and the Netherlands to the Nazis, the miracle of Dunkirk[105] and the expulsion of the British expeditionary troops from the continent of Europe. On 16 June, France sought an armistice from the Nazis and Britain, now under Churchill's leadership, prepared to fight alone. Before long, British fighter planes were engaging the Luftwaffe in the skies over southern England and German bombs were dropping over London and other British towns and cities. In response, Joe rented a country residence outside London to which he frequently fled whenever the bombing raids were threatened. This attracted further public derision – "I thought my daffodils were yellow before I met Joe Kennedy" was one phrase that was heard. Also heard (it is said) was the following rhyme:

> *Joe, Joe, Kennedy, Kennedy*
> *Went to the Court of St James*
> *Where he was frequently seen*
> *With the King and the Queen*
> *At cricket and other games.*
>
> *Said Joe, Joe, Kennedy, Kennedy*
> *Before England went to war*
> *Swapping stories with ducal tories*
> *Is what God made me for.*
>
> *But when the bombs began to fall*
> *All over London town*
> *Said Joe, Joe, I must go*
> *England has let me down.*

---

[105] Operation Dynamo, as the evacuation from Dunkirk was code-named, ended on 4 June 1940. More than 338,000 British, French and other Allied troops were safely returned to England.

Joe Kennedy may have been regarded as a coward and a defeatist, and possibly even a Nazi sympathizer, but he still found time, even now in the midst of a war and his ambassadorial duties, to focus on money-making activities from time to time. In particular, his liquor import business was thriving, and he was accused by rivals of using the influence of the US Embassy to secure urgently needed shipping space on the merchant convoys travelling across the Atlantic for the importation of Scottish whisky into the United States.

By now though, angry at the way he was being treated by FDR, the British and the press, and missing his family, he was increasingly anxious to return home, and made this known to the State Department in no uncertain terms. Keen to re-enter the American political arena, he also hinted that he might support Wendell Willkie, FDR's Republican opponent in the forthcoming Presidential elections. FDR, determined to prevent this, authorised Joe's recall "for consultations" in mid-October 1940.

Joe returned to the United States on 27 October 1940, having flown from London via Lisbon and Bermuda. He was greeted by Rose, several of his children, and a request (order) from FDR to come straight to the White House before speaking to any of the dozens of reporters who were waiting to interview him.

He and Rose immediately travelled to the White House; en route, Rose counselled him to be calm when dealing with FDR, reminding him that the President had after all appointed Joe as American Ambassador to London, and that turning on FDR in a fit of pique might very well damage Joe Junior's political future, if not Joe's own. Joe listened and reluctantly agreed and when he and Rose arrived at the White House, they found themselves greeted by FDR at his most smooth and cajoling. FDR listened as Joe listed his complaints and frustrations, appeared to agree with much that Joe said, and Joe allowed himself to be persuaded into agreeing to make a speech endorsing FDR's third term as President.

Shortly after FDR was re-elected came the incident that finally and unequivocally killed Joe Kennedy's political career. He agreed to give an interview to Louis Lyons, a reporter for the *Boston Sunday Globe*. It may be that he thought that much of what he had to say was off the record, or that his frustrations with FDR and concerns for the future prompted him to speak out, to show that he still had the power to influence events; regardless of his motivations, the interview was a disaster for Joe

Kennedy. Lyons' subsequent article based on the interview was entitled *"Kennedy Says Democracy all done in Britain, Maybe Here"* and in it he quoted Kennedy's isolationist views and belief that the war had already led to the end of democratic life in Britain and could see the emergence of a British national socialist government. The article also quoted disparaging remarks by Kennedy about the British Cabinet and Eleanor Roosevelt, and described Joe's fears that entry into the war could spell the end of democracy in the United States itself.

The public outcry over the article was enormous, both in the United States and overseas. Overwhelmingly, Kennedy's views as articulated in the article were denounced (although the German newspapers approved) and Joe's attempts to disavow the article went unheeded. The situation was exacerbated when a story was leaked to the press to the effect that Kennedy had advised movie-makers in Hollywood not to make movies that the Nazis would find offensive. Joe was summoned to FDR's country estate, Hyde Park, to discuss the situation. The interview did not go well or last long, and (reportedly) within a few minutes, FDR asked Joe to leave the room, and then declared to his wife Eleanor that he never wanted to see Joe Kennedy again (although, in fact, he did).

Joe Kennedy's ambassadorship and his prospective political career were, to all intents and purposes, over, and Joe Kennedy knew it. From now on, slowly at first but with increasing intensity over time, the focus of Joe's life and ambitions (money-making and womanising apart) would swing away from himself and towards his children, for if Joe were to achieve his political ambitions, he would have to do so by proxy, via his children, whilst he remained in the shadows, out of the public's gaze. Fortunately, in Joe Junior, his eldest son, he had the ideal candidate to fulfil those ambitions.

The War Years

Joe Junior was 25 years old in 1940. He regarded himself (and to a large extent, was regarded by others) as the leader of his generation of Kennedys (he was, for example, godfather to his youngest sister and brother, Jean and Ted). He enthusiastically subscribed to the developing legend of the Kennedy clan, and did his best to instil its concepts into his younger siblings. Confident and cocky, and with his full share of Kennedy arrogance, he idolized his father and sought to imitate his ability to control others, often with considerable success. He clashed often with Jack, whom he sensed had the capability to be a rival, and yet his position of "Number One Son" was never seriously challenged. Like his father, he went to Harvard and demonstrated an interest in politics, on occasions clashing with his father at the family dinner table with such fervour that he was banished from the dining room. Fundamentally though, Joe was pleased with Joe Junior, and regarded him as the standard bearer of the next generation. Joe Junior emulated his father in other respects too; there was no doubt of his interest in, and his ability to charm, young women.

Inevitably, Joe Junior became involved in Democratic politics, and managed to become a member of the Massachusetts delegation to the 1940 Democratic Convention. Officially, he appeared as a supporter of Jim Farley, technically a presidential candidate, but one who was soon to be swept away in the FDR landslide. As that landslide unfolded, most of the other delegates rushed to support FDR, but Joe Junior remained loyal to Farley, despite FDR's representatives getting in touch with Joe in London asking him to speak with Joe Junior. (Joe, to his credit, is reported to have said that he wouldn't wish to unduly influence his son, although of course, by this stage, he was anxious to send a message to FDR that Kennedy support should not be taken for granted). Joe Junior's support for a rival to FDR was noted by FDR activists and not forgotten.

However, Joe Junior was anxious to shine in the world as soon as possible, and he saw his opportunity as the spring of 1941 saw America inching closer to war. Abandoning his studies at Harvard, he volunteered for the US Navy, joining as an officer cadet and subsequently specializing in Naval aviation, somewhat to his father's dismay. Nevertheless, on completing his training course in Florida, it was Joe Kennedy who awarded Joe Junior his wings at the graduation ceremony in May 1942.

Jack too, was beginning to stir his father's interest. Jack had begun to claw his way back to academic respectability, and like his brother and father, had gone to Harvard. His interest in history had grown, and as part of his studies, he had prepared an academic thesis on the topic of Munich. His father saw an opportunity here, and arranged for Jack's thesis to be turned into a book entitled "*Why England Slept*", boasting a foreword by Henry Luce, owner of *Time-Life* (and an influential Republican). It became a bestseller, in part thanks to Joe Kennedy's influence with the publishing industry and Joe was delighted.

Like his elder brother, Jack decided he wanted to enter the military, but his back problems initially led to him being rejected by both the Army and the Navy. During the summer of 1941, he followed an arduous exercise regimen designed to improve his fitness and eventually (after some high level string-pulling by Joe), Jack was accepted by the US Navy as an officer and posted to a desk job in Washington. He was joined in Washington by his sister Kick, who had accepted a job as a journalist for the *Washington Times-Herald.*

In the meantime, Rosemary's mental condition and behaviour had been worsening and the Kennedy family found it increasingly hard to control her as she became aware of, and fought against, the restrictions that were necessarily imposed upon her. Eventually, desperate to find some form of treatment that offered any hope, Joe began to investigate the possibility of brain surgery, and in particular, the technique of pre-frontal lobotomy. Pre-frontal lobotomy (which involves severing connections between the pre-frontal cortex and the rest of the brain, or in extreme cases, destroying the pre-frontal cortex entirely) was then still experimental, and has now largely been abandoned by the medical profession, but at that time there remained optimism that it offered possibilities that other forms of surgery could not. In particular, several medical experts believed that it could be used to modify a person's behaviour. Joe allowed himself to be convinced that it offered real hope for Rosemary and in the autumn of 1941 (without telling Rose) he authorized a lobotomy to be carried out on Rosemary. The results were a disaster. Rosemary was left virtually incapacitated and unable to speak, and lived the rest of her life under constant care in mental institutions. She died on 7 January 2005.

Rosemary's operation was swiftly followed by and overshadowed by the events of 7 December 1941, when the Japanese attacked the US Pacific Fleet at Pearl Harbour[106] which led to America's entry into the Second World War. When news of the attack reached Joe, he promptly cabled FDR with the message: "Name the battlefront. I'm yours to command." However, FDR failed to offer Kennedy any serious post in his wartime administration.

Joe instead turned his attention to the forthcoming Senatorial elections. Republican Henry Cabot Lodge Jr was standing in those elections for re-election as a Senator from Massachusetts, while FDR was keen to secure the Senate seat for the Democrats. FDR supported Congressman Joseph Casey in his bid to be nominated as the Democratic candidate, but Joe

---

[106] On that same day, Japan also attacked British possessions in the Far East.

(who had hopes that Joe Junior would run for the governorship of Massachusetts once the war was over) saw Casey as a possible future political rival for his son and therefore was anxious to eliminate him as a threat. Joe would have liked to contest the Democratic primary election himself, but could not since he was not officially a Massachusetts resident. Fortunately, he had the ideal candidate in his father-in-law, Honey Fitz, who was now 79 but anxious to fight another political campaign. Honey Fitz contested the Democratic primary, losing to Casey but inflicting so much damage in the process that Casey went on to lose badly to Senator Lodge, so badly in fact that he left politics forever. Joe was satisfied with the result; as far as he was concerned, he had removed a future political opponent from the field and in addition, had sent a shot across FDR's bows warning him that Massachusetts was Kennedy territory.

By the summer of 1942, Joe had two sons in Navy uniform although neither was near any fighting. Joe Junior was serving with a Navy squadron in Florida, whilst Jack was still serving behind a desk at the Office of Naval Intelligence in Washington. Whilst in Washington, Jack spent a lot of time socializing with his sister Kick and her friends and it was through his sister that he met Inga Arvad, a Danish-born journalist. Before long, she and Jack were lovers. Unfortunately, Inga had a colourful past, knew several senior Nazis (including Hermann Goering) socially and had interviewed Adolf Hitler personally on at least two occasions. The FBI, suspecting she was a Nazi spy, kept her under surveillance and soon found out about her affair with Jack, and passed details on to his naval superiors who were understandably concerned about the relationship. So was Joe Kennedy, who before long knew all about Jack and Inga. Although some in the Navy wanted Jack to be cashiered, he was instead transferred away from Inga, first to Charleston, South Carolina and then (thanks to his father's influence) he was assigned to sea-going duties, which required him to attend Naval classes on seamanship in Chicago. Jack's affair with Inga petered out. He worked hard in his naval classes and volunteered to serve in PT boats, small but fast motor torpedo boats used by the US Navy to attack larger surface ships. Before long, he had been posted to the South Pacific, where he was soon given command of PT109.

Joe, his personal political ambitions thwarted, and with no war-time post offered to him, settled back to pursue his financial interests. Still more interested in preserving his fortune than making yet more money, and continuing to fear that social unrest could bring financial ruin to him and his family, he elected to move his legal residence to Florida for tax reasons and began to invest extensively in real estate, initially simply in an attempt to preserve the value of his capital. Joe took especial delight in purchasing properties in highly leveraged deals, putting down small payments, funding the balances by way of low cost mortgages and then ferociously increasing rents in order to cover the cost of the borrowings. If the tenants could not afford the rent increases, they were simply evicted in favour of new tenants who could afford them. Inevitably, Joe Kennedy was accused of being a rapacious and greedy landlord, which tarnished his public image even further. Sitting comfortably in Palm Beach (for he seldom inspected the properties he was buying) he simply ignored his critics.[107] Taking advantage of depressed property prices, Joe Kennedy made extensive purchases of land in Manhattan and the Bronx, but also further afield, for example, in Florida, Texas and even Brazil. Joe's financial returns from his real estate ventures were spectacular and before long, he had made yet another fortune as a result of his property investments. Indeed, by 1945, he was in a position to buy the Chicago Merchandise Mart, described as a "city within a city" and at that time the largest office building in the world in terms of floor space. Joe paid $12.9 million for the Mart; the Kennedy family would retain ownership of it for over 50 years, before selling it in 1998 for more than $500 million.

Although Joe was not directly involved in the war, nevertheless even he was not immune from its destructive effects. This first became crystal clear on 3rd August 1943 when a Naval messenger appeared at the family compound at Hyannisport carrying a telegram for him. Briefly, the telegram announced the loss of Jack's motor torpedo boat, PT109, and stated that Jack was missing in action. Several days of anguish and confusion would pass before Joe received news that Jack had in fact survived the sinking of PT109.

The facts of the PT109 incident are easy to state. On 1st August 1943, US Naval intelligence received word of a Japanese convoy, escorted by four destroyers, passing though Blackett Strait in the Solomon Islands. A number of PT boats, including PT109, were sent to intercept the convoy

---

[107] It may have been thoughts of this period of Joe's career that prompted his daughter Eunice to observe: "My father built his financial empire with a secretary and a telephone".

but failed to locate it. PT109 was heading back to base in the early hours of the morning of 2 August when a Japanese destroyer, the Amigari, suddenly appeared out of the darkness, cutting PT109 in two before its crew had time to react. Two crewmen died in the collision, and three others were injured. Jack and the other survivors clung to the wreckage until daybreak and then swam to a nearby uninhabited island, Jack towing a wounded crewman for four hours. The survivors lacked adequate supplies of water and were exhausted; nevertheless, Jack made several unsuccessful attempts to reach nearby islands in the hope of finding help. After a few days, the survivors were contacted by local islanders and, having scratched a message requesting help onto a coconut, Jack persuaded them to deliver the message to nearby allied forces. Six days after the collision, they were finally rescued by a PT boat.

The newspapers made much of the heroics of the crew of PT109, and especially praised Jack's bravery in seeking help for his crew after the collision.[108] Inevitably, Joe Kennedy stoked the media's interest, persuading the *Reader's Digest* to cover the story, which it duly did. The *Digest's* resulting article would frequently be quoted and reprinted during Jack's political campaigns in the years to come. For the time being though, Jack was a hero in hospital, and when he recovered, he was appointed to command another PT boat, before eventually being invalided home suffering from back pain and malaria.

The attention paid to Jack in the wake of the PT109 incident galvanized Joe Junior into seeking frontline experience for himself. Feeling that his younger brother had scored something of a coup within the family (which undoubtedly he had), Joe Junior pulled strings and was posted to a US Naval squadron based in Cornwall in England, where he carried out air patrols alongside his RAF counterparts, seeking out U-boats that threatened the merchant convoys traversing the North Atlantic. Important though this work was, it did not fully satisfy Joe Junior, and he kept his eyes open for other ways to distinguish himself in the eyes of his father, his family, the world and himself.

While Jack Kennedy recovered from his war wounds, and Joe Junior flew long and arduous patrols out over the Atlantic, the Channel and the Bay

---

[108] There were some however who asked how a Japanese destroyer could have got so close to the PT boat to cut it in half without anyone noticing and sounding the alarm.

of Biscay, it was the turn of Kick (now effectively Joe's eldest daughter) to occupy the centre stage of the family's attentions. In March 1943, she had resigned from her job at the *Washington Times-Herald* and volunteered to work for the Red Cross in London. Arriving in England in mid-June, she was welcomed by the friends she had made during her previous time in London during her father's ambassadorship (for, unlike her father, she had remained popular with her English friends despite Joe's isolationist views). Apart from a genuine desire to help with the war effort, her principal reason for travelling to England had been her relationship with an English aristocrat, William Cavendish, Marquess of Hartington, known to his friends as Billy Hartington.

Kick and Lord Hartington, the eldest son of the Duke of Devonshire (and thus heir to one of the oldest and most respected Dukedoms in the country), had met and grown close during Kick's previous stay in England. It had appeared then that little could come of the relationship, for Kick was of course a Roman Catholic, and the Cavendishes were Protestant (indeed, they had been awarded their Dukedom as a result of the help they had provided William and Mary in seizing the throne from the Catholic King James II during Britain's "Glorious Revolution" of 1688). There had seemed little or no way to solve this impasse at a time when such matters were taken more seriously than they are today. Now however, in the midst of the war, it was increasingly apparent that the relationship between Kick and Billy Hartington (now a serving officer in the British Army) was sincere and growing deeper and would lead to marriage if only the religious impediments could be overcome. One of the problems was the issue of which religion Kick's and Billy's children should be raised in, should they have any; for various reasons, from the perspective of the Cavendishes, it would be difficult for the children to be raised as Catholics, and yet the Roman Catholic Church required this in the case of "mixed marriages". Attempts were made to obtain a dispensation, but none could be obtained, and in the meantime, the position of several of the Kennedys (in particular Rose and some of Kick's younger sisters) hardened, and an exchange of anguished correspondence on the topic of the marriage criss-crossed the Atlantic. Joe Junior however, was staunch in his support of Kick, and Joe Kennedy made sure that Kick knew that he would stand with her regardless of which decision she reached.

Eventually, in April 1944, Kick and Billy became engaged, agreeing to marry in a civil ceremony, thus sidestepping the religious issues (at least in their own minds) for the time being. The issue of whether their children should be raised as Catholics or Protestants could be addressed after the war if and when such children appeared. Rose was horrified and heartbroken and said so vehemently and at length, but the marriage went ahead on 6 May, one month before D-Day. To his sister's delight, Joe Junior arrived to give the bride away. The press in America made much of the marriage, placing an immense strain on Rose; nevertheless, Joe, while trying to support his wife, also showed his support for Kick when he sent his daughter a cable saying: "Remember you are still and always will be tops with me." Eventually of course, the press interest died down and Rose, if not in agreement with the marriage, at least began to appear to be somewhat more reconciled to it. Meanwhile in England, after the honeymoon, Kick (now the Marchioness of Hartington) and Billy were parted, for he was under orders to participate in the invasion of Europe that followed the D-Day landings.[109]

By now, Joe Junior's overseas posting was over and he was preparing to travel back to the United States when he heard that experienced pilots were being sought for a special mission. In June 1944, the Nazis had unleashed their latest terror weapon, the V1, against southern England, and the Allies were desperate to attack the bunkers in northern France, Belgium and Holland from which the V1s were launched. Ordinary bombing raids had little effect on the launch bunkers, buried as they were and protected by thick concrete walls, and so the Allies decided that the best way to attack them would be by means of bombers heavily loaded with high explosive. The idea was that a pilot would fly a bomber carrying explosives over the Channel, aim it at the target and then bail out by parachute; the bomber would then be guided via remote control from another plane until it hit its target.

The plan (code-named Project Aphrodite) was risky in the extreme, not only because of the dangers of bailing out of the bomber at high speeds and low altitudes, but also because there were serious concerns that the explosives on board the sacrificial plane might detonate prematurely for a variety of reasons, including air turbulence, plane vibrations and random

---

[109] Harold Macmillan, who was British Prime Minister between 1957 and 1963, married Billy's aunt, Lady Dorothy Cavendish in 1921. Thus, during the term of Jack's Presidency, the US President and British Prime Minister were related (albeit by marriage), a fact which seems seldom to have been noted by political commentators of the time.

electrical discharges. Nevertheless, when Joe Junior learned of the mission, he persuaded his superiors that he should be allowed to volunteer for it, sensing that here was an opportunity for him to match the exploits of his younger brother in the Pacific. Despite the fact that previous attempts to attack bunkers in this manner had failed, during the course of which at least one pilot had been killed and many others seriously injured, Joe Junior was placed in command of an attack which was scheduled to be launched on 12 August 1944.

Just before six p.m. on 12 August, a Navy PB4Y plane code named "Zootsuit Black" and crammed full of high explosives, with Joe Junior at the controls, took off from an airfield in Suffolk and headed for the coast and occupied Europe. Zootsuit Black was accompanied by the guidance plane, a third plane tasked with the job of keeping a photographic record of the mission and a flight of Mustangs providing fighter support. One of the officers on board the photoreconnaissance plane was Colonel Elliott Roosevelt, one of FDR's sons.

At approximately 6.20 pm, while still flying over England, the guidance plane sent out the signal which would arm the explosives in Joe Junior's plane; seconds later, Zootsuit Black exploded in a huge fireball, damaging several of accompanying planes and buildings on the ground and instantaneously killing its crew. No trace of their bodies was ever found.

The next day, 13th August 1944, was a Sunday. Joe and most of the family, including Jack, who had now been released from hospital and was slowly recovering his health, were gathered together at Hyannisport. After lunch, Joe Kennedy had gone upstairs to sleep, and the rest of the family were quietly enjoying a lazy afternoon when two priests arrived, asking to speak with Joe. Rose woke Joe, and Joe listened to the news of the loss of his eldest son. At first, Joe hoped the report was mistaken, as it had been in the case of Jack, but it was all too clear that there was no hope. Joe Junior was dead.[110]

---

[110] Joe Junior was subsequently awarded a posthumous Navy Cross, and a new destroyer was named after him. His brother Bobby would later serve for a time as a Naval crewman on board the USS Joseph P Kennedy Jr, which would also play a role in the Cuban Missile Crisis during Jack's Presidency.

Politics and Tragedies

Inevitably, all of the Kennedys, and Joe in particular, took a long time to recover from Joe Junior's loss. Popular legend has it that upon Joe Junior's demise, Joe Kennedy's political ambitions immediately centred upon Jack; however, the process was more complex than this. Gradually though, as the family emerged from its grief, and the end of the war approached, it was apparent that the standard of the next generation of the family had been passed to Jack, who (perhaps initially with some reluctance) now felt that politics should indeed be his path though life. And Joe, for his part, without Joe Junior's dazzling presence to distract him, began to appreciate Jack's qualities in ways that he had, perhaps, failed to do in the past and realized that Jack might well be capable of wining the political prizes that he had so earnestly desired for Joe Junior.

But, before the war was over, the Kennedys suffered another blow. Kick had travelled back to the United States to be with her parents following Joe Junior's death, whilst her husband, Billy Hartington, was fighting in northern Belgium with his regiment, the Coldstream Guards. On 10th September, he was leading a unit in the field when a German sniper shot him through the heart. He died instantly and Kick was a widow at the age of 24. On learning of her husband's death, Kick travelled back to England to be with the Cavendishes, and seldom visited the United States again.[111]

With the ending of the Second World War in September 1945, Joe Kennedy was able to concentrate on building Jack's political career. The first question, namely for which post Jack should run, was settled in November 1945 when Massachusetts Congressman James Curley (an old political rival of Honey Fitz) decided to stand for election as the Mayor of Boston, which required him to surrender his seat in Congress. Jack announced he was a candidate for the seat that Curley was vacating, and despite his continuing frail health, campaigned for the seat as though his

---

[111] After the war, Kick met another wealthy English aristocrat, Lord Peter Fitzwilliam, who was not only Protestant but also married. Rose strongly disapproved of the relationship between Kick and Lord Fitzwilliam, but Joe, whilst not exactly enthusiastic, indicated he was willing to meet Lord Fitzwilliam. On 13 May 1948, two days before the meeting was scheduled to take place in Paris, Kick and Lord Fitzwilliam were killed in a plane crash in the south of France. Joe identified Kick's body and consented to a request by the Cavendishes that Kick be buried at Chatsworth, their ducal seat in Derbyshire.

life depended on it. However, there was little doubt that it was Joe who masterminded and controlled Jack's campaign, providing the necessary funding (which allowed Jack to campaign without the usual worry for political candidates of how to attract sufficient financial support to enable them to run at all) and extending his immense influence on Jack's behalf. Leaving nothing to chance, Joe established his campaign headquarters in Boston's Ritz Hotel, and in a brilliant campaign, set out to sell Jack to the electorate. Focusing on Jack's wartime exploits, he arranged for copies of the *Readers' Digest* story about PT109 to be sent to every registered voter in the district, and took steps to ensure that the local media constantly stressed Jack's status as a war hero, which struck a chord with many voters who had themselves until recently been in military service. Under Joe's direction and guidance, the rest of the Kennedys pitched in to help as well. The campaign saw the first use of Kennedy family tea parties held in a deluxe hotel in Cambridge to which hundreds of female registered Democrat voters were invited "to meet the candidate and his family". The parties attracted the derision of some old time political operators, but the voters came and idolized Jack and his family, and such tea parties henceforth became a hallmark of Kennedy political campaigns. Jack met the potential problem of Jack being the son of a very rich man head on by admitting that he was perhaps the only candidate who had not "come up the hard way". Such was the attractiveness of the candidate and the Kennedys generally, and the effectiveness of the Kennedy political machine under Joe's direction, that voters simply seemed not to care about Joe's wealth or history.

Thanks to his own hard work, and Joe's financial support and political influence and judgement, Jack handsomely won the Democratic primary election on 18 June 1946, and given the political nature of the Eleventh Congressional District, it may almost have been an anticlimax when he went on to win the actual election on 4th November later that year. Indeed, for the foreseeable future, the Eleventh Congressional District would remain "Kennedy territory".

Jack was a distinctly unimpressive freshman Congressman (although his continuing health problems were a constant and painful distraction) and few observers would have predicted his future political career. From Joe's perspective, however, the Kennedys had now succeeding in placing a player on the first rung of a political ladder that could lead to the greatest prize of all. For the moment, Joe could sit back and pursue his money-making activities whilst preparing for the next round of political struggles.

Jack won re-election to Congress in 1948 and 1950 with ease, but then he decided with his father's support that his next step should be to run for the Senate in 1952. His Republican opponent was Henry Cabot Lodge Jr, one of Massachusetts' two senators and a descendant of a venerable New England family, very much of the type that had led the Kennedys to leave Boston for New York in 1926. Moreover, Lodge's grandfather, Henry Cabot Lodge Senior had defeated Honey Fitz in the Senate elections in 1916 and thus for the Kennedys, and Joe in particular, the 1952 election constituted unfinished family business.

Lodge would be difficult to beat. He had successfully defended his Senate seat against all challengers for years and was highly respected throughout the state; moreover, 1952 was also a presidential election year, and the Republicans, having selected Dwight D Eisenhower as their presidential nominee (partly as a result of the efforts of Lodge himself), were widely anticipated to win back the White House for the first time since 1933.

To overcome these perceived disadvantages, Joe financed Jack's campaign to an unprecedented degree, and ensured that the Kennedy political machine was tuned to an unparalleled state of efficiency, capable of operating throughout the state, raising Jack's profile even in areas where the Kennedys had hitherto made little impact. Once he had arranged for Jack's younger brother Bobby to be appointed as campaign manager, Joe took rather a hands-off approach to the actual management of the campaign. There is, however, no doubt that Joe took a close – and on occasions – vocal interest in the campaign's progress and exercised his influence behind the scenes; for example, he made a loan of $500,000 to the financially troubled but influential (and usually Republican-supporting) *Boston Post*. The *Post* had been expected to endorse Lodge but instead endorsed Jack. Subsequent denials of both Joe and the *Post's* owner, John Fox, that there was any connection between the loan and the endorsement were not widely believed.

The 1952 elections did indeed see a Republican landslide, with Eisenhower overwhelming the Democratic presidential nominee, Adlai Stevenson, and many Republican candidates winning other electoral contests. Against this background of Republicanism triumphant, Jack's victory over Lodge, albeit that it was a very close contest, was all the more remarkable. And Joe Kennedy had the much relished satisfaction of seeing his son rise another step up the ladder of political power.

Jack Kennedy served in the Senate for eight years, during which period he grew into a nationally recognized politician, despite the fact that he did not actually achieve a great deal as a US senator. He did, however, succeed in separating his public image from that of his father and Jack's political views, particularly as regards foreign affairs, began to diverge from those of the Ambassador. The political differences between them became particularly noticeable at the time of the 1956 Democratic Convention, which saw Adlai Stevenson again nominated as the Democratic presidential candidate. Stevenson decided to allow the Convention to select his vice-presidential nominee and Jack, vigorously supported by Bobby, allowed his name to be put forward as a potential candidate, notwithstanding Joe's strong advice to the contrary. Joe, on holiday in the south of France, had no doubts that Eisenhower would easily beat Stevenson once again, and feared that if Jack's name were on the ticket, the subsequent electoral defeat would be blamed on Jack's Catholicism rather than any failure on the part of Stevenson, possibly irredeemably damaging Jack's career. Nonetheless, Jack (and Bobby) decided to proceed, and indeed Jack did well in the first ballot against rival Democratic contenders Hubert Humphrey and Estes Kefauver. He nearly won the second ballot. Thereafter however, support began to ebb away from Jack Kennedy in favour of Kefauver, and Jack was forced to withdraw his name from the contest and urge that the Convention nominate Kefauver, which it duly did.

At first sight, Jack's failure to win the vice-presidential nomination (the only political election he ever lost) was a potential disaster; in fact (as Joe shrewdly observed) it was a blessing in disguise and ensured that he was untainted by the inevitable failure of the Democrats to win back the White House in 1956. Moreover, Jack's graceful withdrawal as a contender for the vice-presidential nomination had been watched on television across the nation and attracted much favourable comment. When Jack sat down with Joe to discuss his political future at Thanksgiving in 1956, Joe was convinced that Jack had a realistic chance of winning the 1960 presidential election and succeeded in persuading Jack that this was the case. Thereafter, the 1960 presidential election dominated the Kennedys' political lives.

Politics was not the only interest in Joe's life. Money-making remained important of course, although Joe was careful to ensure that his financial activities did not cast any shadow on Jack's political career (for example, Joe had divested himself of his liquor interests as early as 1946, when Jack first ran for Congress). Nevertheless, his wealth continued to grow, so much so that in 1957, *Fortune* magazine estimated his fortune to be in excess of $200 million, listing him as one of the richest men in the country. Much of his wealth had come from his real estate speculations, although he had generously funded a variety of trusts for the benefit of his family. As far as personal tastes were concerned, neither he nor Rose lived particularly exorbitantly, considering how wealthy they were, (although Joe worried about the extravagance of several of his children) and they did not acquire large mansions, collect expensive artwork or racehorses or any of the other usual accoutrements of the seriously wealthy. Joe's money, primarily, was used to protect the family, to fund the Kennedys' various political battles and generally to exert Kennedy influence and power, and Joe was content that this should be the case.

His family also occupied his attention. The early 1950s had seen a flurry of weddings as his children began to marry, beginning with Bobby who married Ethel Skakel in 1950. Other marriages followed, most notably Jack's marriage to Jacqueline Bouvier in 1953 and before long, Kennedy grandchildren began to appear. On the whole, Joe enjoyed good relationships with his children's spouses (particularly his daughters-in-law), although when the English actor, Peter Lawford, proposed to marry Joe's daughter Patricia, Joe is reputed to have said that the only thing he would hate more than having an actor as a son-in-law would be to have an English actor as a son-in-law. Nevertheless, the marriage went ahead.

It was, however, Jack's bid for the Presidency which primarily occupied Joe's attention. Again, Bobby was appointed campaign manager and the Kennedy family and its political machine went into overdrive, this time on a national basis, all funded by Joe. Memories of Joe's isolationism and possible anti-Semitism were not forgotten, and he took even more care than usual to ensure that he remained out of the spotlight – so much so in fact that his absence was noticed and commented upon. "Jack and Bob will run the show, whilst Ted's in charge of hiding Joe" went one piece of doggerel from this time.

Following Jack's narrow victory over Republican candidate (and then-Vice-President) Richard Nixon in the 1960 Presidential election, rumours circulated to the effect that Joe's connections with organized crime may have helped to deliver election victory to Jack, particularly in relation to the key state of Illinois, where Jack won by a wafer-thin margin of 8,858 votes. Whether or not that is the case, when President-elect Jack

Kennedy went to meet the press at the armoury at Hyannisport on the morning after the election, Joe Kennedy, at his son's insistence, went with him. It was moment for them both to cherish.

In the weeks preceding Jack's inauguration, Joe spent a great deal of time with Jack as he worked to assemble his new administration, advising his son as to the suitability of possible candidates for various posts. Joe recognized that Jack's election as President meant that he no longer simply belonged to the family and indeed admitted as much to a reporter, but some things remained the same. In particular, Joe felt strongly that about two matters, the first being that Bobby should accompany Jack to Washington as US Attorney General, arguing that Jack would need the support of at least one family member in his new Cabinet. Jack and Bobby were at first unconvinced, not least because they feared charges of nepotism if Bobby were to be so appointed, but Joe remained firm in his views and eventually persuaded Jack. Bobby took a little longer to persuade, but eventually accepted the appointment.

The second matter concerned his youngest son, Ted, 27 years old and still to some extent the "baby" of the family. Ted, who enjoyed a warm and close relationship with all the family, and especially with his father, was generally popular, although he was developing a reputation for being capable of reckless behaviour. He had chosen to study law at the University of Virginia, and in 1958, had married his first wife, Joan Bennett. Enjoying a considerable income from the trusts established by his father, Ted was under little pressure to find regular employment. Nevertheless, he had worked hard for Jack in the western states during the 1960 election campaign, and Joe was determined that Ted should run for Jack's now vacated Senate seat, arguing that Jack and Bobby had achieved what they wanted and that it was now "Ted's turn". Neither Jack nor Bobby thought that this was a particularly good idea, but again Joe was adamant, and again Joe got his way. There was, however, the small matter that Ted was still to young to serve as a US senator; this problem was disposed of by arranging for a friend of Jack's to serve in the seat until Ted was old enough to run for the US Senate, which he duly did, being sworn into office in January 1963.

Before this happened, however, fate struck down Joe Kennedy in a particularly cruel and physical way. On 19th December 1961, not quite one year into his son's Presidency, Joe suffered a serious heart attack whilst playing golf in Palm Beach. The attack left him almost completely paralyzed and unable to speak, although his mind was still active. Immediately, he ceased to be a power, dominant or otherwise, within the family. Confined to a wheelchair, under the constant care of a nurse, he could only sit and watch helplessly over the years to come as first Jack and then Bobby were assassinated.

Then, on the night of 18 July 1969 came the tragedy of Chappaquiddick when a car driven by Ted crashed off a small bridge into a deep pond on an island off Cape Cod. Ted managed to escape from the submerged car; his passenger, a young woman called Mary Jo Kopechne did not and died. The resulting scandal seriously damaged Ted's political career for the rest of his life, was a factor in his being unable to win the Democratic nomination for the Presidency in 1980 and certainly played a part in shattering the glittering Kennedy image that Joe and the rest of the family had worked so hard to create over so many years.

Joe himself did not long survive Chappaquiddick. His physical condition worsened rapidly over the summer and autumn of 1969, and on 18 November, he died aged 81. He was survived by Rose and five of his nine children, all of whom were with him when he died, and was buried in the Kennedy family plot in Brookline. Rose died in 1995, aged 104.

Joe's legacy was complex and controversial. Unquestionably, he financially enriched his family beyond the dreams of earlier generations, and the fortune he built will be enjoyed by Kennedys for many years to come. He was also primarily responsible for creating the myth and the reality of the Kennedy political dynasty, which has seen few equals in America, before or since. Kennedy political power remains a force to be reckoned with, particularly in Massachusetts, and it may be that one day that power again will manifest itself across the United States in one of the great American offices of state.[112]

However, Joe Kennedy's name is also associated with selfishness, appeasement, and financial and political trickery. Whether and to what extent all of these charges are justifiable is open to some debate; nevertheless, it remains the case that in pursuing the path he did, Joe Kennedy did hurt others, both within and without his family, and

---

[112] Certainly it is generally accepted that Senator Ted Kennedy served with distinction during his many terms in the US Senate, and other members of the family have at various times filled (and continue to fill) important political and diplomatic posts.

sometimes severely. Having said that, Joe's primary concern was always to protect and enhance the prestige of his family, and he brought the full weight of his fortune and his varied talents to bear in seeking to achieve this goal. It is also important to remember that in many ways, his goals became the goals of his children – all the Kennedys wanted and enjoyed the power and prestige of being Kennedys, and all relished the glory of winning the various political offices that fell within their grasp. Moreover, there is little or no evidence that Joe had to force his children to pursue the goals that they did. They *wanted* to succeed, not least in order to please their father. And under his guidance, for a few short years, they dominated American consciousness to a remarkable extent.

There is one last point to be made. Having built his fortune, Joe struggled for the rest of his life in order to see his children occupy positions of political power, finally achieving his ultimate goal in early 1963 with all three surviving sons in high political office. Yet what is noteworthy is how swiftly this moment passed, and how short a time Joe was granted to enjoy the fruits of his political labours.

Illustrations

1. John Jacob Astor

2. Astoria, 1813

3. "The Commodore"

4. Cornelius Vanderbilt and Jim Fisk

5.   Andrew Carnegie

6.   Bobbin boys at work

7.   John D Rockefeller

8.   Political cartoon from 1904, depicting Standard Oil as an octopus with tentacles penetrating into all aspects of American life.

9.   Henry Ford

10.   1903 Ford Model A

11.   1910 Ford Model T

12. Joseph P Kennedy – Bank President, 1914

13. Joseph P Kennedy – Ambassador to the Court of St. James

14. Joe Kennedy and family at Hyannisport, 1948

Select Bibliography

Ron Chernow – *Titan: The Life of John D Rockefeller Sr.*: Warner Books, 1998

Peter Collier & David Horowitz - *The Rockefellers: An American Dynasty*: Jonathan Cape, London, 1976

Peter Collier & David Horowitz - *The Kennedys: An American Drama*: Simon & Schuster, 1984

Peter Collier & David Horowitz - The *Fords: An American Epic*: Collins, 1988

Virginia Cowles - *The Astors*: Weidenfeld & Nicolson, London, 1979

John H Davis – *The Kennedys: Dynasty and Disaster 1848 – 1984*: McGraw-Hill, 1984

John Steele Gordon – *The Scarlet Woman of Wall Street*: Weidenfeld & Nicolson, New York, 1988

John Steele Gordon - *The Great Game: A History of Wall Street*: Orion Business Books, 1999

Robert Lacey – *Ford: The Men and the Machine*: Heinemann, London, 1986

David Nasaw – *Andrew Carnegie*: The Penguin Press, 2006

Edward J Renehan Jr. – *Dark Genius of Wall Street: The Misunderstood Life of Jay Gould, King of the Robber Barons*: Basic Books, 2005

Edward J Renehan Jr. – *Commodore: The Life of Cornelius Vanderbilt*: Basic Books, 2007

David Sinclair - *Dynasty: The Astors and Their Times*: J M Dent & Sons Ltd, London and Melbourne, 1983

Arthur Vanderbilt II – *Fortune's Children: The Fall of the House of Vanderbilt*: Michael Joseph, 1990

Index